Greenwich
Village
AND
HOW
IT
GOT
THAT
WAY

Greenwich Village
AND HOW IT GOT THAT WAY

by Terry Miller

CROWN PUBLISHERS, INC.   NEW YORK

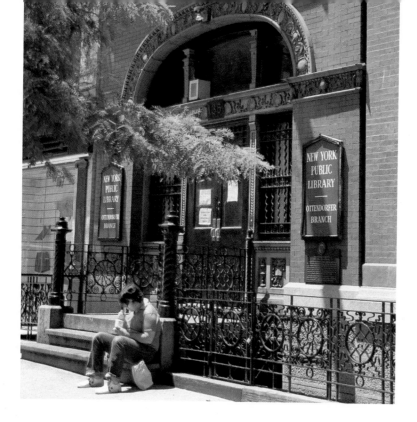

Published by Crown Publishers, Inc., 201 East 50th Street, New York, New York 10022

CROWN is a trademark of Crown Publishers, Inc.

Manufactured in the United States of America

Book design and maps by June Marie Bennett

Library of Congress Cataloging-in-Publication Data

Miller, Terry.
  Greenwich Village and how it got that way / by Terry Miller.
  1. Greenwich Village (New York, N.Y.)—History. 2. Greenwich Village
(New York, N.Y.)—Description—Tours. 3. New York (N.Y.)—History.
4. New York (N.Y.)—Description—Tours.
I. Title.
F128.68.G8M55 1990
974.7'1—dc20   89-38610
                                                          CIP

ISBN 0-517-57322-9

10 9 8 7 6 5 4 3 2 1

First Edition

CONTENTS

INTRODUCTION   1

1 CHRISTOPHER STREET
AND SHERIDAN
SQUARE   12

2 WASHINGTON
SQUARE   50

3 BROADWAY:
"A PROMISCUOUS
CHANNEL"   76

4 THE
NORTH
VILLAGE   112

5 THE
WEST
VILLAGE   150

6 THE
SOUTH
VILLAGE   194

7 THE
EAST
VILLAGE   236

AFTERWORD   281

ACKNOWLEDGMENTS   285

SELECTED BIBLIOGRAPHY   289

INDEX   294

INTRODUCTION

Jefferson Market Courthouse
at dawn.

This portion of New York appears to many persons the most delectable . . . the look of having had something of a social history.
— *Henry James, 1881*

The district where the new ideas of America are born.
— *Quentin Crisp, 1988*

St. Luke's Place

To the Indians on the island of Manatus, it was Sapokanican, their little settlement beside the great river. Early Dutch settlers of New Amsterdam knew it as Noortwyck. After the British took over, it was the village of Greenwich, a sleepy cluster of farms and estates two miles north of the uproar of the growing city of New York.

All that changed in the summer of 1822. As it had done before, yellow fever struck the city and the residents dealt with that terrifying epidemic the only way they knew: they fled. Overnight, the few hundred residents of Greenwich awoke to find their yards and farms overrun with sixty thousand New Yorkers.

Greenwich Village was thought to be immune to such epidemics because of its naturally healthful climate—though it was merely free of the unsanitary conditions breeding the disease in the

West Eleventh Street

The West Village in 1825, looking south from Hammond (West Eleventh) Street.

The West Village today, looking south from Jane Street.

city. The coming of winter weather quelled the disease, as it had during earlier epidemics, and once again most New Yorkers returned to the city. But some chose to remain permanently in this healthful country setting, and over the next decade Greenwich Village took on much of its present appearance. It's still going strong after more than 150 years, a country village within a city, a tight-knit community that embraces its nonconformists and fiercely opposes outside intervention. It conjures up associations so ingrained into our consciousness—bohemians, artists, beatniks—that it has won a listing in the Oxford English Dictionary. Its impact is widespread, as tangible as the buildings in which Villagers have lived and worked over the years. We know Greenwich Village—or do we?

Certainly we know its popular image: elegant row houses on quirky tree-lined streets, wearing the shifting colors of fall and spring. Like a crazy quilt, properties often follow the irregular lines of farms, streams, or Indian paths—forming a visible link to a time when this village in the country was more open country than village.

Unlike lower Manhattan, where skyscrapers have turned New Amsterdam's streets into twisting canyons hidden from the sun, Greenwich Village for the most part has been kept free of high-rise towers. And yet within a few blocks of each other still stand two

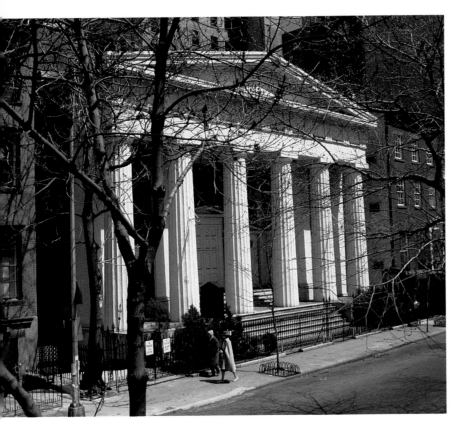

The former Village Presbyterian Church, dating from 1902, now an apartment building.

Charles Lane

A Carmine Street stable, now a residence.

nineteenth-century Village buildings, each of which presaged the skyscraper era.

Greenwich Village seems to revel in the unexpected, to take the unusual in stride. Villagers strolling along West Thirteenth Street accept without question that row houses there should part to admit a midblock Parthenon, a former church now recycled into a residence.

They are not amazed when suburban houses sprout on secluded Charles Lane, a cobblestoned alley that two centuries ago marked the north wall of a state prison.

Greenwich Village hangs on to the artifacts of its past, signs of which are everywhere. In fact, the Village and its residents pioneered a process best described as self-reinvention. Among today's city planners and architects this technique is known as *adaptive reuse,* though Villagers have for years thought it agreeable to fashion a residence out of an unused stable—or to invent a persona with integrity out of a conformist or unused life.

Yet much of the Village is hidden from view, inaccessible even to lifelong residents. The area is rich in skylit artists' garrets, though most of them are private residences that are not open to inspection. Each has a unique charm, an individuality that one studio can only suggest.

A back house hidden off West Tenth Street, east of Hudson Street.

The Village also has numerous back houses, former carriage houses recessed deep inside the blocks in which they stand. They can be reached by way of an alley or enclosed passageway—but only by residents and their guests.

The Jefferson Market Courthouse, a landmark and an emblem of adaptive reuse, has a clock tower that is visible across the Village. Unfortunately, the works of its four enormous clocks, so critical to the public campaign for landmarking laws, must remain for reasons of safety closed off from public visits.

Nor have many Villagers been able to inspect the great bell that hangs in the clock tower. Local legend has it that the bell—cast in 1863 for a fire tower that once stood on this site—cannot be rung today for fear of structurally damaging the tower in which it is confined. Consequently, about the only Villagers who have heard its profound peal are those who were around when I rang it. It's loud—but the tower survived.

Even Washington Square Arch, best-known symbol of Greenwich Village, has a secret: it's hollow. Inside the structure, above the archway itself, there is a dim chamber lit only by tiny skylights overhead. It can be reached by way of a winding staircase that rises in utter darkness within the arch's west pier. In 1917 six stealthy "revolutionaries" briefly visited here on their way to the arch roof,

The Thirteenth Street studio of the late Village artist, Elmer Stoner.

Inside Jefferson Market clock tower, showing the clockworks and 1863 fire bell.

Inside Washington Square Arch, looking east.

Bleecker Street Playground

Folksingers in Washington Square in the 1980s.

MacDougal Street today, looking north.

intent on proclaiming the Village a free and independent republic. But their proclamation only made official what Villagers have always known.

For decades, free spirits have gathered in Washington Square. Even the simple act of serenading the crowd here can have political implications, as the city found in 1961 when it tried—and failed—to ban folksingers from the park.

Running south of the square is MacDougal Street, the hub of the beatnik world of the 1950s and long a bastion of an unpredictable counterculture. Local preservationists cringed when TV crews came here for on-the-street interviews on the eve of the 1969 Historic District vote. "You mean somebody would want to change this place?" one young iconoclast replied on the broadcast.

Sixth Avenue sketch artist
Jonathan McCrary.

"Nobody'd come here if it wasn't for these buildings," he declared. One doubting preservationist, hearing her cause unexpectedly championed, later said she was ashamed she hadn't trusted the kids.

But Village street life isn't restricted to the counterculture. You will also see families relaxing in a local playground, a visitor from California having a portrait made of her best friend, or a seasonal gathering at a sidewalk café like the one outside the historic White Horse Tavern.

And street life is nothing new for the Village. The passing parade in Little Italy is little changed in many respects, though the Sixth Avenue El no longer thunders outside the second-floor tenement windows. One of several overlapping communities within Greenwich Village, Little Italy still values family bonding, a quality portrayed in the 1988 film, *Moonstruck,* parts of which were shot on location in the Village.

Many films are shot on Village streets these days. Yet Villagers watching such shoots might be surprised to learn that talkies were perfected and introduced to the world right here in the Village. So was the first practical television, an ungainly affair that took up half a room when the members of the press watched its 1927 debut.

Some treasures of the past are long gone, yet even these have their effect on the Village of today. An elegant manor house stood in the heart of the West Village from 1726 until 1865; it was famous as the centerpiece of Sir Peter Warren's vast estate. The property was whittled away until, at the time of the mansion's demolition, all that remained was the property bounded by Charles, Bleecker, West Fourth, and Perry streets. But the house was replaced by a block of row houses that still exhibit a remarkable uniformity of style.

The White Horse Tavern on
Hudson Street.

Growing up under the El in Little Italy.

The first simultaneous relay of picture and sound over distance—in other words, the first public demonstration of television.

**Peter Warren's manor house,
which vanished in 1865.**

Greenwich Village today is, in large measure, the product of such idiosyncracies—each with its own story. Some tales have long since been lost, and only the whimsy remains. What story, for example, lies behind the elegant lions that have guarded the entrance to 6 Washington Square North since 1831?

On a more modest scale, what prompted the appearance of a stone squirrel in front of an aging row house on Christopher Street?

If such whimsies abound in the Village, they are not all relics of the past. Not too long ago, someone went to some trouble to install a neon palm tree in their West Fourth Street window, and it's been glowing nightly for years.

Strolling through their neighborhood, Villagers pass such sights daily, along with many sites of national and worldwide significance. Sometimes even they are unaware of what major event occurred somewhere between their dry cleaners and the supermarket. The present and the past converge here as unexpectly as the streets do. As a consequence, the best tour through Greenwich Village is a tour through time as well as space.

Time is visible here, like the strata of rock layers in a quarry.

Villagers don't destroy their past; each generation adapts this place into a community that suits its needs and taste. So the Village is the sum total of those who have lived here. Its buildings can be pointed out to anyone walking by—but Greenwich Village itself can only be seen through a walking tour of the imagination.

This book offers just such a tour, one that would be enhanced by a real walk but does not require it. Only a mental walking tour allows us to "see" events of the past as well as the present, to "meet" Villagers from both then and now, to sense the romance that can be found here.

It's really the best way to appreciate Greenwich Village—and how it got that way.

W. 14TH ST.   E. 14TH ST.

1 Christopher Street
and Sheridan Square

2 Washington Square

3 Broadway

4 The North Village

5 The West Village

6 The South Village

7 The East Village

1 CHRISTOPHER STREET AND SHERIDAN SQUARE

Village Cigars, on Sheridan Square at Christopher Street since 1922.

For over three centuries, Christopher Street has led from the east bank of the Hudson River into the heart of Greenwich Village—serving more purposes than to channel the traffic. Christopher Street has been a borderline between Dutch *bouweries*, between British colonial estates, and between early American farms. Its seven short blocks can still offer three nineteenth-century churches, each of which is just across the street from a twentieth-century gay bar. Here you'll find Off Broadway's most popular theaters and a sidewalk mosaic that once was the city's smallest real-estate plot. Prisons once stood at either end of Christopher Street, one being re-

placed by a brewery and the other by
a garden. Its side streets reveled
in the bizarre "goofy" clubs
of the 1920s, jazz clubs
in the fifties, and piano bars
in the seventies. The street's name
became the title of the opening number of *Wonderful Town*, the 1953 Broadway musical set in
the Village. And since 1976, it has also been the
name of a popular gay literary magazine.

Christopher is one of seven streets that con-

1 Federal Archive Building (site of Greenwich Market)
2 Site of State Prison
3 6 Weehawken St.
4 St. Luke's-in-the-Field
5 Site of P.S. 3
6 Grove Court
7 17 Grove St.
8 Twin Peaks
9 The Whittemore Mansion
10 The Patterson Grocery
11 Site of the Pirate's Den
12 Circle Repertory Company (formerly the Nut Club)
13 Site of Greenwich Village Inn (later Circle in the Square)
14 One Sheridan Square (formerly Cafe Society)
15 Site of Greenwich Village Theatre
16 Village Cigars & Hess Estate Street Mosaic
17 Marie's Crisis
18 184 W. 4th St. (formerly the shop of Sonia Bright)
19 The Stonewall
20 Northern Dispensary
21 137 Waverly Pl. (former home of Edgar Allan Poe)
22 14 Gay St. (formerly home to Ruth and Eileen McKenney)
23 Jefferson Market Courthouse

verge to form the disorder known as Sheridan Square. Into this confusing intersection have come several generations of Villagers—and the tourists who gawk at them. For seventy years, sightseers have bused through Sheridan Square, scanning the sidewalks for bohemians, beatniks, hippies, gays—anyone whose appearance can confirm what visitors seem to sense: Things Are Different Here.

But in a way, the gawkers and those gawked at have seen one another before. Few Villagers are natives. Most are refugees from the same hometowns and farms to which the sightseers will return. Both the Villager and the tourist are on vacation from conventional life, but the tourist's vacation will soon end. Villagers stay on, intent on inventing and living out an unconventional life that's right for them. You can do that here.

As a lyric in *Wonderful Town* put it, Christopher Street is a typical spot in Greenwich Village. As such, it's a good place to begin our tour of the Village—and we'll start where the street itself began, on the waterfront.

THE WATERFRONT

The waterfront, looking north along West Street from Christopher Street, during the June 1988 Waterfront Festival. When not raising funds to fight waterfront development, Villagers relax on the few piers remaining.

Prior to the landfill projects of the 1850s, people could still spot the sandy cove where Christopher Street began. The cove was the most prominent feature of a cape jutting into the Hudson River. The cove proved an excellent beachhead for local Indians bringing to shore the lobsters and oysters that thrived in these waters. They may also have brought ashore the striped bass whose descendants later became key to scuttling the billion dollar Westway landfill scheme of the 1970s. Long before Europeans arrived here, Indians trekking inland from this cove established a path that was known in the mid-1700s as the Skinner Road and renamed Christopher Street in 1799.

Long after the Indians were dispersed, the cove and the path remained associated with food. In the 1790s, Jersey farmers ferried their produce here to supply residents of this growing country community, and a small makeshift market grew up on the south side of Christopher. By 1812, the city had formalized it as Greenwich Market by building stalls—and only six years later had to enlarge it to meet demand. By then the crush of carts and wagons arriving and departing caused traffic jams that no street of standard width could accommodate. So with the 1818 expansion, the market was moved just far enough south to allow for a widening of the approaches. To this day, the two blocks of Christopher Street nearest the river are twice as wide as standard city streets—a long-vanished market the cause.

THE ARCHIVE

One block inland on Christopher Street, a massive structure known as the Archive—the largest building in the West Village—has stood since 1899 on the site of the old Greenwich Market. Each of its ten floors covers more than an acre, requiring its brick walls at street level to be three feet thick. Built as a warehouse for U.S. Customs, it was long used to store files and documents—hence its name, the Federal Archive Building. Under the terms of a 1949 law designed to recycle vacant historic structures, it was declared surplus in 1976 and began a twelve-year odyssey toward conversion into 479 rental apartments. After several delays and some $115 million in costs, the Archive Apartments opened in June 1988 with units ranging from studios priced at $1,400 a month to a penthouse on the newly built eleventh floor costing $3,400 a month.

This cove on the Hudson River marked the west end of an Indian path that later became the Skinner Road, known since 1799 as Christopher Street. Beyond the cove is the south wall of the 1797 state prison.

WHERE "UP THE RIVER" WAS

Across Christopher Street from the growing Greenwich Market, New York chose a riverside tract as the site of a new state prison. Erected in 1797, the building stretched about 200 feet fronting on Washington Street.

One contemporary account described the new facility as located "at the extremity of the city . . . where prisoners, unseen from the world, can expiate their transgressions in contrition and repentance." Criminals down in the city put it more bluntly and devised a phrase to describe being sent here. Their phrase, "up the river," has been absorbed into our language.

Villagers took pride in this facility at first; its chapel, bathing rooms, and workshops made it a most progressive institution for its day. But by the mid-1820s, the blocks surrounding the prison were solidly residential. Villagers began to insist that the prison be removed. Their demands were met in 1829 when the state replaced the facility with a new prison fifty miles farther "up the river"—the famous Sing Sing in Ossining, New York. This wasn't the first time Villagers had forced a government retreat, nor would it be the last.

POST-PRISON DEVELOPMENTS

Tucked half a block above Christopher Street, an inboard wooden staircase leads to the second floor of 6 Weehawken Street. Initially home to a boat builder, its ground floor—opening on West Street—has been by turns a clam house, a saloon, and for some years now a quiet waterfront gay bar, Sneakers.

A large electric sign for years promoted Beadleston & Woerz, the brewery that rose in 1857 on the site of the old state prison. Sections of the prison's foundation were incorporated into the construction of the later building, which survived into the late 1930s. New construction at that time created the warehouse now used by Bookazine, a major book distributor for the New York area. Even this building follows the prison's property lines and may rest on foundation segments that are nearly two hundred years old.

After Greenwich Market moved inland in 1832, a small waterfront alley behind the shuttered prison gave way to form tiny Weehawken Market. The two markets jointly served the area until 1844, when competition from the larger, inland Jefferson Market (a renamed Greenwich Market) caused the tiny waterfront market to close. Its site was sold by the city to developers, the result being the shortest street in New York, Weehawken Street. Six wood-frame houses were erected there in 1849, but only one of the brown-shingled oddities remains.

A 1920 view of West Street north of Tenth. Most of the waterfront bars and hotels in front of the brewery still stand, though they have no landmark protection.

St. Luke's Chapel on Hudson Street south of Christopher. The massive Archive Building has been the backdrop for this chapel since 1899. A 1986 apartment tower, the Memphis Downtown, can be seen beyond the tree to the right.

GOIN' TO THE CHAPEL

The state prison seems consigned to a remote Village of the past until you recall that its contemporary neighbor a block away still stands.

Villagers who demanded the removal of the prison worshiped and were wed at St. Luke's-in-the-Field. Some were even buried in its courtyard cemetery, which, like the chapel complex itself, no longer survives intact. Yet, even in its incomplete state, St. Luke's-in-the-Field is clearly a pioneer of urban planning.

In October 1820, Greenwich parishioners of Trinity Church petitioned for their own house of worship, one closer than Wall Street. Trinity agreed, and gave them the northernmost portion of a vast tract it held by Royal Decree since 1705—a plot bordering Greenwich Market. While the new church was under construction, the upper room of a nearby fire watchtower provided the congregation with temporary quarters.

To build their chapel they hired James N. Wells, then less an architect than a gifted carpenter. It was Wells who placed the church at the center of the large plot, facing the dirt road that became Hudson Street. Then the innovation: he surrounded it with congenial row houses, which broke rank only to give access to the chapel. Instead of dividing the enclosed land into separate backyards, Wells unified the block by leaving it an enclosed common.

St. Luke's has been cited by the Landmarks Preservation Commission as the most significant ensemble in the West Village. Unfortunately, several of the enclosing row houses are gone, replaced by a church gym and school, which fortunately maintain a low profile. Among the survivors is 487 Hudson, the boyhood home of writer Bret Harte and today the St. Luke's Parish House.

Grove Street runs east for barely a hundred feet before twisting its direction about forty-five degrees, indicating a property line of 350 years ago. At the break, between 8 and 10 Grove Street, a passageway leads to Grove Court, recessed deep inside the block.

Enough of the ensemble survived to suggest the complete plan, though a 1981 fire struck a nearly lethal blow to the chapel itself. Its interior was completely gutted, and for a time it was feared that the walls had been fatally weakened. Villagers of all stripes rallied in support of a church that had long aided Village charities, supported the homeless, and assisted recovering alcoholics. Schoolchildren donated their allowances, and local gay bars held fund-raisers. As a result of these and other efforts, the church received an unsolicited $160,000 just one month after the fire. A reconstruction program was undertaken that allowed a rebuilt St. Luke's to reopen in 1985.

The first warden of St. Luke's was Clement Clarke Moore, a classical and Oriental scholar who dabbled in poetry. The year St. Luke's opened, Moore wrote a Christmas poem to delight his own children. Without Moore's knowledge, a friend later sent it to the Troy *Sentinel,* which published it in 1823, bringing unexpected fame to Moore as the author of "A Visit from St. Nicholas," better known to most children as " 'Twas the Night before Christmas."

GROVE STREET: A BORDERLINE CASE

It's the very image of a Greenwich Village street: tree-lined, narrow, with a midblock forty-five-degree twist for no apparent reason. But as is often true in Greenwich Village, there's a reason for the odd twist in Grove Street. You just have to know where to look.

Grove runs alongside Christopher Street, but that doesn't mean they're parallel. They converge at their eastern ends, though to the west near Hudson Street they're a full block apart. That's where Grove Street bends—a shift that the six streets south to Downing Street copy. Connect these seven street bends with an imaginary line and you've re-created a property line dating from 1633. To the west along the river was the farm of Dutch settler Jan Van Rotterdam; to the east, the vast country estate of Wouter Van Twiller, the second director general of the New Amsterdam colony. Over the years, paths on these separate properties served their various owners' needs, and some of those paths became today's roads.

One such path, a segment of today's Grove Street, was dubbed Cozine Street in 1809. By 1811 it seems to have jumped the ancient

Dutch boundary and extended itself under a new name, Columbia Street. Two years later, it was renamed Burrows Street, honoring a lieutenant killed in the War of 1812. But a decade of confusion with neighboring Barrow Street led to a final name switch to Grove Street in 1829.

At that time St. Luke's builder James Wells was at work on the five elegant row houses that still stand on the first block of Grove Street. Wells designed 2 through 10 Grove to complement his church just across Hudson Street, but the houses have been modified since then. Facing them across Grove Street was Public School No. 3, founded in 1818 and moved to its own structure here in 1821. The city's third school to provide free nonsectarian instruction, it was the model of progressive education. For that reason it was proudly shown to General Lafayette during his visit to New York in 1824. The original school burned in 1905 and was replaced by the present structure, but a tablet on the new building recalls Lafayette's schoolhouse tour.

**TURNING
A NEW
LEAF**

Well into the 1800s, no respectable family would live in a house not fronting on a street. Such houses were considered suitable only for tradesmen and laborers. But even tradesmen ate dinner, a point not lost on Samuel Cocks, co-owner of Cocks & Bowron, a grocery operating out of 18 Grove Street—a building that is still standing, though it has been much altered.

In 1848, Cocks noticed the passage between 10 and 12 Grove Street, which led to a parcel inside the block created by the street's odd bend. Why not turn this unused parcel into a court of back

Grove Court in 1913, barely a decade after O. Henry found in it the inspiration for his story, "The Last Leaf." A gate now keeps unwanted visitors from the court, and residents no longer dry their laundry alfresco.

Grove Court today.

houses for tradesmen and bring more customers into his grocery? The result was Grove Court, finished in 1854 and now among the most exclusive of Village addresses. Cocks would be amused to learn that such enclaves are now prized *because* they're off the streets, providing privacy. Today's residents might not know that Grove Court's original tenants won the row of six houses its nickname "Mixed Ale Alley."

Grove Court has turned a new leaf, not unlike a writer it once inspired. O. Henry used it as the setting for his 1902 tale, "The Last Leaf," writing of an ailing young woman who is restored to health by a failed painter who gives his life for hers. You may recall it as one segment of *O. Henry's Full House,* a 1952 movie filmed on Hollywood sets, not here.

Redemption through sacrifice was a theme close to O. Henry's heart. William Sydney Porter arrived in New York the year he wrote that story, direct from a stretch in a federal prison for embezzlement (little wonder he wrote under a pen name). A winter's chill in 1910 ended O. Henry's life at the age of forty-eight, much as a chill ended the life of the misunderstood artist in "The Last Leaf."

WINDOW DRESSING

When the construction of wooden houses in Manhattan was banned in 1866, the clapboard house at 17 Grove Street was already forty-four years old. Though its third floor was an 1870 addition, the house is still standing and is the largest intact wood frame house in the Village.

The 1822 Hyde House at 17 Grove, prior to its 1988 restoration, with its neighbor, the whimsical Twin Peaks.

This rare view of Bedford Street in 1913 shows the unremarkable 102 Bedford before its reconstruction into the fanciful Twin Peaks. At the corner is 17 Grove Street, looking much as it does today. William Hyde's workplace, at 100 Bedford, stands between the two houses.

Twin Peaks today.

Built in the year when the yellow fever epidemic began the population shift into the Village, it was home to William Hyde, a window sash maker who did considerable work for his new neighbors. As a result, he built a workshop behind his home in 1833, a one-story affair to which a second floor was added about twenty years later. Looking like an oversized dollhouse, his former workshop is now a single-family residence, 100 Bedford Street.

Also oversized is its current value. Hyde's property was valued at $100 when he bought it and raised to $700 with the completion of his house. The 1833 workshop added another $500 to the value. In December 1987 both properties were sold at a combined price of $1.1 million. An unspecified additional amount is being sunk into the properties by their new owner, who began a renovation in September 1988 to restore 17 Grove Street to its original nineteenth-century appearance.

SHILLY-SHALLY CHALET

Known informally by Villagers as Twin Peaks, 102 Bedford Street looks like an eccentric Swiss chalet. Wedged behind the Hyde workshop, this building's true origins are as curious as its appearance.

Clifford Reed Daily fancied himself an architect, though being tubercular, slightly hunchbacked, and temperamental, he couldn't hold even an ordinary job. By contrast, money came easily to Otto Kahn, a millionaire banker of the 1920s who took pleasure in funding artists, poets, and other struggling creative types.

The apartment house at 45 Grove Street was the last of the great Village manor houses and is the only one still standing.

The two men met by chance in 1925, and Daily proposed that Kahn fund his dream project: a new Village landmark that would inspire artists. Intrigued, Kahn agreed and bought for Daily's use a two-and-a-half-story Federal row house dating from 1830.

For two years Daily lived out his dream as few creative artists have. Tons of bricks were brought for his inspection, each truckload yielding only a handful whose shape and hue met with the architect's approval. After slowly rising to five stories, 102 Bedford was capped with the double gables that inspired its popular name. But the carefully chosen bricks vanished under a layer of stucco and half-timbers, which completed the mock-chalet look.

Artists may have found it inspiring, but Kahn came to find it infuriating. Just as construction ended, he cut off Daily's funds and took title to the building. He offered Daily $5,000 a year to clear out, an offer Daily accepted late in 1927. But before leaving for Pennsylvania, Daily vowed he'd reclaim his dream house before turning forty-five the following year. He claimed to have plunged two bottles of champagne into wet cement in the basement and said he would break them out and drink them when Twin Peaks was his once more.

Daily died six months later, without seeing Twin Peaks again. If he was telling the truth, those champagne bottles are still buried in cement somewhere in the basement.

THE WHITTEMORE MANSION

Samuel Whittemore made his fortune making steam-powered machines used by textile manufacturers to comb out, or card, cotton fibers. Whittemore's carding-machine factory stood at 175 West Tenth Street, a plot now lost to the Seventh Avenue extension. It was impressive enough to be featured in A. T. Goodrich's 1828 *Picture of New York* guidebook, and it was the source of the name of Factory Street, running from Christopher to Bank Street; since 1858 it has been known as an extension of Waverly Place.

Whittemore invested his profits in Village real estate, building for speculators many Federal row houses around the neighborhood. In 1830 he built 45 Grove Street for himself. An impressive 45 feet wide and 54 feet deep, the building had landscaped grounds, a garden, and private stables as well as a cistern and a greenhouse. But soon after Whittemore's 1835 death, his estate was cut up for development. Over the next two decades, row houses filled in the land around the mansion and occupied the last vestiges of the estate. The present 94 Christopher was built in 1854 on the site of the Whittemore stable. The greenhouse at the intersection of Bleecker was replaced that same year by the building that now houses the Village Army-Navy shop.

Raised from two stories to five in 1871, the former mansion became an apartment house with a retail shop at street level; the tall display windows were added at that time. It became a makeshift hospital during the Spanish-American War and was briefly the official residence of the city's mayor—a fact that accounts for the tall cast-iron *torchères* on the stoop, a tradition dating from Dutch times. More recently, the Whittemore mansion served as the movie version of Eugene O'Neill's residence in Warren Beatty's 1981 film, *Reds,* which was based on the life of journalist John Reed.

In fact, O'Neill never lived here—but poet Hart Crane did, and if any spirit haunts the old Whittemore mansion, it's his. After renting a second-floor room here in 1923, Crane began work on his never-finished epic of America, *The Bridge.* He worked on other poems here as well, though most brought him nothing but rejection slips from small magazines. This did nothing to soften Crane's moody nature, and friends visiting him here often arrived just in time to see his typewriter sail out the second-floor window.

The son of the Ohio candy manufacturer who invented Life Savers, Crane refused to take money from his father. His days were marked by literary rebuffs and chronic indebtedness, his nights by alcoholic binges and furtive homosexual encounters on the nearby docks, which fed the guilt on which Crane unhappily thrived. One such encounter left him unconscious on a sidewalk, where he was found by fellow Villager and friend E. E. Cummings, who hailed a cab, bundled Crane into it, and paid to have him driven home. Only after Crane's 1932 suicide at the age of thirty-three did the works created in this house begin to win him fame.

The former Patterson Grocery as it looks today, still operating at the corner of Bleecker and Christopher streets.

OF GROCERIES AND GRIDS

In 1808 the city saw the need for a plan by which New York would expand northward. Chief Engineer John Randel, Jr., was charged with the task of surveying the entire island, requiring him to set up an office in what was then the country. Accordingly, he took an upper floor of the wood frame house at what is now 329 Bleecker Street, a combination residence and grocery store built in 1802 or shortly thereafter for William Patterson.

The plan Randel devised was for evenly spaced numbered streets running from river to river, beginning with First Street. But in the Village such streets would cut on a forty-five-degree angle through plots and properties then being established as farmers sold out to developers—a process encouraged by the Common Council since December 1808. Why, they wondered, should their prospects

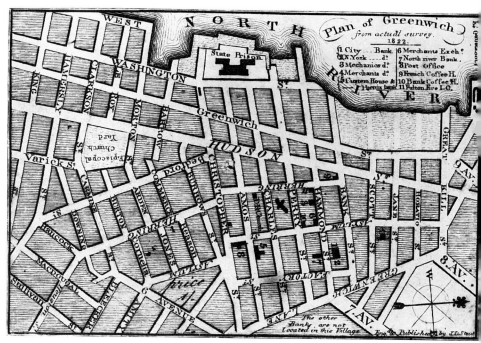

The zigzagging of Herring Street (now Bleecker Street) can be seen on this map of the West Village from 1822, four years after the local street pattern was saved. The state prison is clearly marked at the top, as is Fort Gansevoort in the upper right corner. The legend notes several banks, of which two are recessed off Bank Street. And at the map's center between Charles and Perry streets is a mark that denotes Sir Peter Warren's mansion, already 96 years old when this map was drawn.

The title page of the pamphlet that helped to save the eccentric Village street grid. Published anonymously in 1818, its author was in fact Clement Clarke Moore, the Village church warden who was soon to write a less vitriolic work, "A Visit from St. Nicholas."

be curtailed for the Council's arbitrary street grid?

The city's Common Council adopted the grid plan on March 3, 1817, and was deluged with Villagers' protests. The dispute dragged on for over a year, during which time an anonymous 62-page pamphlet laid out the case against the city: "A more needless and ill-judged attack upon private property, under colour of law and public utility, was perhaps never attempted by a public body than the regulation of the ground in and around the village of Greenwich, ordered by the corporation in 1817." The council backed down, and on October 5, 1818, the plan to regulate the village of Greenwich was limited to those portions east of the present Sixth Avenue.

Through their protests, the Village eluded the street grid that today extends north across the rest of Manhattan. But by a curious twist, one West Village building—the old Patterson grocery—was victimized by early municipal planning.

When built, it extended some 20 feet farther west into what today is Bleecker Street. That street—initially called George Street and, after 1818, Herring Street—crossed Christopher in a Z-shaped intersection called Greenwich Square. Two-way traffic here was forced to detour onto Christopher Street before going its way, creating a terrible bottleneck. When Bleecker Street was given its present name in 1828, it was decided to widen the one block north of Christopher to eliminate this zigzagging. Only the old Patterson grocery stood in the way, but it wasn't demolished—not entirely. A third of the building was sheared away, and a new brick wall became the western face of this wood frame building. In that modified form it stands to this day, its street-level shop still in use as a grocery.

"FATAL" POPCORN

Generations of Villagers have ducked into the former Patterson Grocery for a Coke or a pack of cigarettes. One look at its well-worn floorboards makes that clear. Though few who have shopped these tightly crammed shelves left behind any token of their presence, actress Glenn Close left more than that. In October 1986, on her way to the home of a Village friend to watch a Mets ball game on television, she stopped here to pick up a bag of popcorn. In her rush, she left behind her own heavily notated script of the movie she was then filming—*Fatal Attraction*. Later she realized she had misplaced the script, but she had no idea where she had left it. Hercules Dimitratos, manager of Fancy Grocery since the early 1970s, tracked down Miss Close through Paramount Pictures and returned the valued script, enabling the shooting of the film to resume.

SHERIDAN SQUARE

These convoluted intersections form Sheridan Square, where another battle over the future of the Village was fought nearly a century after the street grid plan was defeated. The outcome ended the glorious isolation long enjoyed by the West Village and turned the secluded precincts of Sheridan Square into the Times Square of Off Broadway. But Villagers turned this defeat to their advantage by winning restrictions on development as part of the first zoning ordinance enacted in any American city.

THE
UNKINDEST
"CUT"

In 1914, Seventh Avenue was extended south through Greenwich Village, slashing through the blocks below Eleventh Street. Three-quarters of a century later, Villagers still refer to this as "the Cut"—an ugly term, but it was an ugly business.

The IRT Subway wanted to run a line south from Times Square. Since the privately owned subway corporation preferred low-cost cut-and-cover construction beneath an existing street, the city condemned hundreds of structures to make this possible. Village homes and apartment buildings, factories, and churches were demolished, their families and businesses evicted, on the nine blocks between Seventh Avenue and Varick Street.

The extension of Seventh Avenue today, looking south from Sheridan Square. At the left is the former Corn Exchange Bank, now a branch of Chemical Bank, and at the center is the former home of the Nut Club, today a theater operated by the Circle Repertory. Next to it is a five-story tenement house that lost a large section of its corner at the time of the Cut.

By the summer of 1917, an open trench some 40 feet deep bisected half a mile of the West Village. Then America entered World War I, and work on the subway was suspended. Surveying their scarred neighborhood, Villagers took to joking that they needed any particular unnecessary item "as much as we need the Seventh Avenue subway." And that summer, as the adults struggled to get from one end of a block to the other, their children turned the dirt floor of the Cut into the world's most expensive softball field.

Today the Cut seems a less offending part of the landscape. Many younger residents are surprised to learn that Seventh Avenue South wasn't always there, though the scars left by the Cut persist after seven decades. Along Seventh Avenue South you can still spot buildings that weren't destroyed, but were merely shaved back. Some lost only a square foot or two per floor, while others gave up much more. Look for odd-angled corners where a building abuts Seventh Avenue South; the patch jobs of different color bricks running up to the roof mark the survivors.

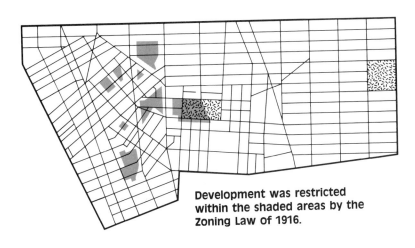

Development was restricted within the shaded areas by the Zoning Law of 1916.

Work eventually resumed, and four months before the war ended, on July 1, 1918, the Seventh Avenue subway first rolled under Sheridan Square. Shortly thereafter, the street above it was opened, and the Village was abruptly clogged with people and traffic. For the first time, through-traffic had a route along the west side of the island, one made even more appealing a decade later when the Holland Tunnel provided the first vehicular link with New Jersey. Before the Great Depression slowed things down, the irregular plots along Seventh Avenue South created by the Cut were filled with garages, auto supply shops, repair shops, and a dozen vest-pocket gas stations.

A modest rise in property values was one result of the Cut, which ended the incursion of manufacturing in the area. More important, in a move anticipating the landmarking of half a century later, Village renters, local settlement workers, and (significantly) resident owners banded together to petition the city's new Zoning Commission for protection. The result was the creation of eight separate districts within Greenwich Village that were restricted to residential use.

The corner of the 1826 house at 9 Commerce Street was shaved away for the construction of the Seventh Avenue Subway and Seventh Avenue South. The patchwork on its brick facade is clearly visible. At right, a copy shop presently rents the one-story taxpayer fronting Seventh Avenue South, which fills the empty lot behind two row houses on Barrow Street.

THE
MOUSETRAP

General Sheridan, by Joseph Pollia. Behind it is one of two stables from the 1840s that were combined in the 1930s to form a neighborhood restaurant, the Stonewall Inn. As the Stonewall, a popular gay bar of the 1960s, it was to become the setting of the 1969 riot that sparked the modern gay rights movement.

Don't let that statue of Philip Sheridan fool you. Sheridan Square was named for this Civil War general, but this 1936 statue of him isn't standing in it. Villagers mischievously placed it around the corner in Christopher Park, perhaps as a wry comment on a man best known for the phrase, "The only good Indian is a dead Indian."

Technically, Sheridan Square is only the triangular plot bound by Washington Place, West Fourth Street, and Barrow Street. But Villagers apply the name to a tangle of triangles and their surrounding streets. Sheridan Square is a maze offering the intrigue of corners to be turned; it rewards the curious with people worth meeting, places worth discovering. And like a maze, it is confusing—little wonder that guidebooks of the 1920s adopted Charles Hemstreet's name for Sheridan Square: the Mousetrap.

For seven decades since the subway opened Sheridan Square to outsiders, it's been Times Square with a sense of humor, its homes and stables having been replaced by clubs, restaurants, and theaters. Today the tempo remains upbeat here, though most of the night spots that once existed in the square are long gone. Among them were the "goofy" clubs that were at one time something of a Sheridan Square specialty. Once Prohibition began, these clubs tended to emphasize the illicit nature of the liquor they freely served, but they began as a vicarious evocation of bohemianism. Before their heyday had passed, they invented the artificial ambience that lies at the heart of modern theme parks.

The first "goofy" club opened in 1910 just off the square at the corner of Charles and West Fourth streets. The Toby Club was decorated with artificial cobwebs, huge fake spiders, and mounted skulls and crossbones made from real skeletons. Candles in wine bottles stood on a center table that was actually a coffin.

The Toby Club may have inspired former cabinetmaker Don Dickerman to go one better. In 1917, he opened one of the most famous Village clubs—the Pirate's Den—on the site where a staid 1928 apartment tower at 10 Sheridan Square now stands.

Patrons entered the Pirate's Den by way of a small oaken door opened by a doorman in full pirate garb, flintlock pistol tucked under his belt, cutlass at his side, and wearing an eye patch, a mustache, a cocked black hat, and a sneer. A narrow corridor lit with candles in ship lanterns led to the club itself. Each floor of the former stable was outfitted like the *Jolly Roger,* with tackle and coiled rope hanging from the balconies and captain's walk, and racks of pistols and cutlasses mounted on the walls. Black cannons bolted to the floor stood beside the tables, which were lit with flickering candles. To complete the fantastic setting, a fully costumed "bloodthirsty" crew (of waiters) created a bedlam of sword fights and pistol duels when not taking orders. Caged parrots

The Pirate's Den at 10 Sheridan Square, the most elaborate of the Village "goofy" clubs of the 1920s.

shrieked and leashed monkeys screamed as the old freight elevator brought the dance orchestra to each floor in turn.

The Pirate's Den and other "goofy" clubs thrived during the 1920s. Waiters at one club dressed in prison stripes and served patrons their liquor in private "cells." At another, waiters dressed as farm boys, dusted their hair with hay, put on horse blinders, and served patrons in stalls. At the Wigwam, waiters were "Indians" and hardly dressed at all. While they served drinks, a nubile Indian princess performed a sacred moon-worship dance to the tom-tom rhythms from a Victrola in the corner.

The former home of one of these popular Sheridan Square clubs survives. The Nut Club, built in 1919 on an irregular plot left by the Cut, presented comic Jackie Gleason in the 1930s in one of his first bookings. In the 1950s it became the Sheridan Square Playhouse, offering productions featuring George Segal, Robert Duvall, Jon Voight, Martin Sheen, and Colleen Dewhurst. Still standing at 99 Seventh Avenue South, it has been for nearly two decades home to the noted Circle Repertory Company. Its resident playwright, Lanford Wilson, won the Pulitzer Prize in 1980 for *Talley's Folly,* one of his many plays to premiere here.

CLOSE CALL FOR "LAST CALL"

In the final hours of June 30, 1919, from the ritzy Brevoort Hotel to seedy neighborhood taverns, Villagers drank as a last "last call" approached. Prohibition took effect that midnight and remained in effect without challenge—for exactly one day. Not surprisingly, it was a Villager who first demonstrated the unenforceability of Prohibition.

The Greenwich Village Inn had only recently opened at 5 Sheridan Square, on the street level of a theatrical boardinghouse in

Village Voices

As an adult, Palmer Williams became a CBS television producer, but he still remembers his Barrow Street childhood of sixty years ago, and the night he discovered that radio broadcasts were for real. "I was rather suspicious of radio at first," he recalled. "My father bought one in the late 1920s while we were living at 8 Barrow Street, around the corner from the Greenwich Village Inn. The radio was a crystal set that sputtered with static and could only be listened to with earphones. But I remember sitting in our living room one night when the announcer said, 'And now, direct from the Greenwich Village Inn, So-and-so and his band playing "Happy Days Are Here Again." ' I ripped off the earphones, ran and threw open the back window, and dammit, there it was: 'Happy Days Are Here Again' from across our backyard! That's when I realized it was all true. Radio wasn't faked!"

The Threepenny Opera was installed in 1954 at 121 Christopher Street, at which time the former Hudson Cinema was renamed the Theatre De Lys (after William De Lys, its founder and, briefly, its first manager). Long the most popular of Off-Broadway houses, it has been known since 1981 as the Lucille Lortel, named for the woman who has managed the theater since 1955.

which Willard Wright wrote his famous Philo Vance mysteries under a pen name, S. S. Van Dine. Barney Gallant, a one-time flatmate of Eugene O'Neill, had been hired to manage the inn. On July 2, 1919, a plainclothesman ordered a glass of sherry, which Gallant had his waiter serve, leading to Gallant's arrest. Sent to jail for thirty days, Gallant was visited by smart-set friends partying in numbers that made prison routine at the Tombs impossible to maintain. Multiple arrests, clearly, would bring the criminal justice system to its knees. Gallant was released and returned to the inn a hero.

The Greenwich Village Inn soon expanded into the basement of neighboring 6 Sheridan Square. When the Corn Exchange Bank opened next door in 1919, Villagers joked that it was there for Barney Gallant's convenience. But as the inn and similar speakeasies prospered, Prohibition existed in name only. A payoff system for "protection" was established, and the police harassed clubs that did *not* serve illegal drinks. By 1922, Police Commissioner Grover Whalen estimated that thirty thousand speakeasies operated in New York, twice the number of the establishments that had served liquor before Prohibition. Over the years, several were run by Barney, while the Greenwich Village Inn itself continued under various managements until the close of the 1940s. The adjacent Corn Exchange Bank, absorbed by Chemical Bank in 1954, has survived from Barney's day and still operates from its mock-Georgian branch on Sheridan Square.

REINVENTING OFF BROADWAY

The heyday of the Village "little theaters" of the 1920s had been pretty much forgotten by 1950, when the Loft Players started looking for a cheap place to give performances. What this fledgling troupe found was the shuttered Greenwich Village Inn, which they leased and turned into a theater. Their February 1951 debut with a revival of *Dark of the Moon* created little stir, but the same can't be said of their production of Tennessee Williams's *Summer and Smoke* a year later. Critics cheered a play they had once dismissed and welcomed its brilliant young star, actress Geraldine Page. The production's director, Jose Quintero, was also hailed as a major discovery, as was the company itself, rechristened Circle in the Square.

From this grew Off Broadway as it's known today, with many successful theaters clustered around Sheridan Square. Most famous of these was the Theatre De Lys at 121 Christopher Street. An old neighborhood cinema, it shifted to legitimate theater in 1952, and two years later proved the profitability of Off Broadway with the famous revival of *The Threepenny Opera,* a production that ran there through 1961. Meanwhile, Circle in the Square created another sensation with Quintero's 1956 revival of Eugene O'Neill's blistering drama, *The Iceman Cometh.* For this production, the theater was transformed into the shabby bar for losers in which the action occurs, and audiences nightly stumbled out into the square feeling less that they'd seen a lacerating drama than lived through one.

Circle in the Square was forced to leave its original home in 1960. A very dull apartment building replaced the row houses that had stood on the square for over a century, and whisked that historic basement space into oblivion. The Circle in the Square Company continued to offer productions—for twelve years in its theater at 159 Bleecker Street, and since 1972 in Midtown. It still controls the theater on Bleecker Street, which it leases out to producers of Off-Broadway productions.

SHERIDAN SQUARE'S THEATRICAL DEBUT

Across the square, a low-rise commercial structure (known as a "taxpayer") stands between Christopher and West Fourth streets. Built in 1931, it occupies the site of the Greenwich Village Theatre. The theater, which opened in November 1917, was built by Marguerite Abbott Barker more as a neighborhood playhouse than for professional productions. However, its earliest shows brought uptown audiences into the Village, some for the first time. One notable play was *Hobohemia,* a tart satire of Village life written by then-unknown Sinclair Lewis.

Of greater impact was *The Greenwich Village Follies,* devised

A Broadway-style house seating only 387, the Greenwich Village Theatre had an impact out of all proportion to its modest size and brief life span of thirteen years.

and staged by John Murray Anderson. As revues on Broadway tried to outshine one another in lavishness and expense, Anderson turned his meager budget to advantage and introduced the intimate revue to New York. The show, which opened in July 1919, featured popular Village troubadour-writer Bobby Edwards singing "Why Be An Industrial Slave When You Can Be Crazy?" Another Villager, Tony Sarg, devised a ballet for marionettes a full decade before he won fame for designing the first giant balloons for the Macy's Thanksgiving Day Parade. And in a topical reference to Barney Gallant's recent defiance of Prohibition, Bessie McCoy Davis sang "I'm the Hostess of a Bum Cabaret." The revue's high style and intelligence kept a "Sold Out" sign at the box office for the full six-week run, after which *The Greenwich Village Follies* established another precedent by moving to Broadway for an extended run. A second edition of this revue, under Anderson's direction, opened at the Greenwich Village Theatre in 1920, and it, too, moved uptown. Subsequent editions opened directly on Broadway, and the series continued for the rest of the 1920s. By then the look of the musical revue had been forever changed by the impact of *The Greenwich Village Follies*.

Meanwhile, back in Sheridan Square, the Greenwich Village Theatre took on a new life in 1924. Over on MacDougal Street, success had overwhelmed the Provincetown Players and their star attraction, playwright Eugene O'Neill. Several of his dramas had followed *The Greenwich Village Follies* uptown to Broadway, and the Players decided to lease the Greenwich Village Theatre to augment their renovated stable on MacDougal. As a result, the Greenwich Village Theatre saw the premieres of two key works by O'Neill, *Desire Under the Elms* and *The Great God Brown*. In time the company found the split focus to be a drain and decided to let the theater on Sheridan Square go. With that decision, the Provincetown Players lost all hope of keeping O'Neill for themselves. Broadway producers won the rights to his new plays, and the innovative Provincetown Players began a struggle for their very existence. The 1929 stock market crash brought a swift end to the Provincetown Players and, by 1930, to the Greenwich Village Theatre as well.

The taxpayer that now stands on this site has housed a succession of restaurants and banks at street level, while its second floor offers a home to a local gym for women and to the Village Independent Democrats. But this building has a secret known to few Villagers: its foundation was built to support a sixteen-story apartment tower for which the developers couldn't win financing at the time. They built only two floors, intending to complete the structure when things got better. In time the plan was forgotten, and the upper floors were still unbuilt in 1969 when Sheridan Square was placed within the newly designated Village Historic District. Now the tower will never be built.

The west side of Seventh Avenue South today, and the intersection of Christopher and West Fourth streets, where the Greenwich Village Theatre stood until 1931. Visible at the left, a few doors down Christopher Street behind Village Cigars, is St. John's Church, dating from 1822 and the third oldest church in the Village.

THE MANY LIVES OF ONE SHERIDAN SQUARE

It's a squat four-story building dating from 1834, one of several houses in the area built for profit by Samuel Whittemore. Its fame is derived from its basement, which opens into the basement of an adjoining 1902 loft building. This cellar has led several lives as a cabaret and as a theater since 1938, each life with its share of historic events.

Through most of the 1930s this basement was Four Trees, a restaurant styled like the "goofy" clubs into a fantastic setting—in this case a dungeon. It was transformed into a smart supper club in December 1938 by Barney Josephson. Determined to end the racial barriers in every club from Midtown to Harlem, Josephson believed that talent was the only factor that mattered for his musicians, and permitted a racially mixed audience to attend. Among the jazz greats he presented were Hazel Scott, Sarah Vaughan, Josh White, Mildred Bailey, Art Tatum, Mary Lou Williams, Teddy Wilson, and Big Joe Turner. The club's slogan said it all: "The wrong place for the right people." And its name is now legend—Cafe Society.

VILLAGE PEOPLE: BARNEY JOSEPHSON

I learned about prejudice when I was a kid in Trenton," Barney Josephson recalled with a wise smile. "It made no sense, whether directed at me for being Jewish or at this classmate of mine who was black. I made a point of befriending him, and it was through him that I first learned about jazz. Though I went into the family shoe business, I had this idea that one day I'd open a club that would bring audiences and good music together and to hell with these racial barriers.

"In 1938 I decided to give it a try. I picked Greenwich Village purposely. I figured I'd have better luck finding an audience ready to accept what I wanted to do. Also, rents were low and I only had $6,000 in borrowed money. I decided an interracial club would have

Barney Josephson, at a 1979 recording session for Alberta Hunter. Having coaxed her out of retirement, Josephson launched the legendary singer on her second career in engagements at the Cookery, making her the last of his great "discoveries."

to look stylish to be accepted but couldn't really afford much. A friend led me to a few Village painters, which gave me an idea. I took them to lunch at the Jumble Shop over on MacDougal Street, and told them what I wanted to do. I couldn't pay them, but I offered them the cost of their materials and a $250 open tab at the club, and they'd be able to paint whatever they wanted. That's how I got my artwork.

"One of them sent me to meet John Hammond, the record producer, and that's how I got my opening night artists. He was excited by my plan, so I opened with an unknown singer—Billie Holliday.

"About two years later he told me about a singer with Charlie Barnet's Orchestra by the name of Lena Horne. By this time, Cafe Society was pretty well established, and when I offered her a booking she accepted. I arranged things carefully to show her to advantage—one small spotlight, on her, the rest of the club lights dimmed—and the waiters were to stop serving, since that wasn't dignified. So out came Lena, looking fantastic, singing fantastic, but singing with her eyes closed. She'd only open them when she'd look up at the ceiling, never at the audience. I saw it was a problem for her, something she wasn't aware of, but how to fix it without losing her trust? After all, I was white *and* the boss.

"So I asked her into my office the next day. I said, 'You know, Lena, *we* whites'—I was always careful to include myself—'we whites have done such dreadful things to your people, given so many of you an inferiority complex, that it's said among some white people that a Negro doesn't dare look whitey straight in the eye. Now, here you are, so beautiful, with such a voice, and with such eyes, and you close them when you sing except when you're looking up at the ceiling. You look up there, you take their attention away from you. And I understand. We've done that to you. But no woman can walk in here who can rival your beauty, nor can any rival your talent. And when you're up there on my stage, I want you to think about that and know you're as good as anyone out in the audience, and look 'em all right in their goddam eyes!' "

Josephson stopped, his wise smile returning. "It worked."

Village Voices

"I opened Cafe Society as an unknown; I left two years later as a star."

Billie Holiday,
in her 1956 autobiography,
Lady Sings the Blues

A NEW LIFE

Cafe Society closed in 1950, and Barney Josephson moved over to University Place, where he ran a restaurant named the Cookery (later BBQ) until his death in 1988 at the age of eighty-six. And as he found a new career there, the old Cafe Society began a new life as a theater.

As One Sheridan Square Theatre, the former jazz club saw theatrical success with Brendan Behan's *The Hostage,* a Kurt Weill

Charles Ludlam, at left, with Everett Quinton, in two of their multiple characterizations in the original production of *The Mystery of Irma Vep*.

The entrance of the former Cafe Society at One Sheridan Square, now the Charles Ludlam Theatre and home to the Ridiculous Theatrical Company.

cabaret entertainment by Martha Schlamme, and Ben Bagley's 1965 revue, *The Decline and Fall of the Entire World As Seen Through the Eyes of Cole Porter,* which starred Kaye Ballard and Harold Lang.

At the close of the 1960s, the basement briefly reverted to club status as the Haven, a gay dance club that circumvented the jurisdiction of the State Liquor Authority by operating as a "juice bar." But in the wake of a police raid at the nearby Stonewall bar a year earlier, considerable friction remained between the growing gay community and the police. The Haven was raided by the police in August 1970, and its staff was arrested on charges that were dropped the next day. Claiming they were searching for drugs, cops smashed the club's bar, sound system, lighting equipment, and refrigerators to the tune of $75,000 damage. That was the end of the Haven.

After reverting once again to use as a theater, One Sheridan Square became by the close of the 1970s a permanent home for Charles Ludlam's Ridiculous Theatrical Company. After over a decade of presenting his plays in various Village locations, Ludlam and his cohorts here won their widest audience with productions of such Ludlam gems as *Camille, The Mystery of Irma Vep,* and *The Artificial Jungle*.

Ludlam's scripts were published in 1989, but they would have to have been printed entirely in italics to suggest the riotous style of his productions, directed by and often starring himself. His actors were always aware of the audience and quick to punch up a quote from films or literature with a sly wink, a knowing smile. While pop art turned trivial objects into icons, Ludlam harvested pop culture and served it scrambled, spiced with flashes of Mae West, Charles Laughton, Greta Garbo, Tallulah Bankhead, and Sonja Henie.

Two decades of cult success were just blossoming into broad

Close, But No Cigar

A mosaic embedded in the sidewalk on Seventh Avenue at Christopher Street is all that's left of the Voorhis, a popular five-story residence that was demolished for the subway cut. The city tried to convince its owner, the estate of Philadelphian David Hess, that this plot—which was outside the limit of cut condemnation—was useless and should voluntarily be surrendered to become part of the sidewalk. The estate hotly refused, and instead created this mosaic on the smallest property in New York, barely 500 square *inches*. In August 1938, it was bought by the owners of Village Cigars, a popular local landmark since 1922, and joined legally to their property at a cost of $1,000.

appeal when Charles Ludlam died of AIDS in May 1987. Grieving fans and friends turned the entrance of One Sheridan Square into a suitably ridiculous street shrine to their forty-four-year-old star. For over a week, Ludlam's spirit was renewed daily by a hodgepodge of lit candles, flowers in coffee cans, crayon sketches on paper plates, photocopies of his theater reviews, handwritten tributes ("Charles dead?? Ridiculous!"), and—inexplicably—a pineapple. The whole affair was liberally strewn with streamers, tinsel, and spray glitter.

But the best shrine was to be the theater itself. Succeeding Ludlam as artistic director, Everett Quinton found new success for the Ridiculous, beginning in January 1989 with his free adaptation of *A Tale of Two Cities*. Under his guidance, theater continues to flourish in this historic basement, now named the Charles Ludlam Theatre by the company. And outside, the city of New York extended its own recognition in December 1987 by renaming the block of Barrow Street fronting One Sheridan Square as Charles Ludlam Corner.

PIANO BAR HOPPING

Marie's Crisis, the piano bar at 59 Grove Street, is in an old row house dating from 1839. The name of the bar pays homage to its historic site, for in a wood frame house that once stood here Thomas Paine died in 1809. His December 1776 pamphlet, "The Crisis," boosted the sagging morale of the Revolutionary Army, much as his "Common Sense" had built support for a break from Britain. The bar's name also salutes Village restaurateur Romany Marie, who opened the first of her tearooms in 1917 on Washington Square South.

No tour of Sheridan Square is complete without a visit to the piano bars of Grove Street. Step into Marie's Crisis and test yourself against the best. See if you can keep up with the rapid-fire lyrics of "The Lady Is a Tramp" or if you really know the fifth verse of "It's De-Lovely."

Two doors away is 55 Grove Street, long the home of the Duplex, another piano bar which doubled as a nightclub. Barbra Streisand, Joan Rivers, and Woody Allen are among the many entertainers who appeared here early in their careers. In December 1989, the Duplex moved across the square to its new home at 61 Christopher Street. Tomorrow's stars may be appearing there tonight.

TEA THINGS

Tiny Tim, all dressed in white,
  Makes those uptown suckers bite.
Makes nice candy, never stale,
  Mixes it in a garbage pail.

Tiny Tim, Tiny Tim,
  All of us are sick of him.
He makes candy out of junk,
  People buy it when they're
    drunk.

—Bobby Edwards

Tearooms were restaurants in miniature, popularized just before Prohibition began and swept from the scene when speakeasies sprouted everywhere in 1923. In their brief heyday, tearooms offered modest menus, modest prices, and the modest atmosphere of beaded curtains, which uptowners saw as evidence that they were slumming. Quick to move when a cheaper storefront became available, they seldom stayed in one spot as long as six months. Some tearooms grew into larger restaurants, such as the Jumble Shop, which survived on MacDougal Street well into the 1960s. Others bowed to police harassment and added the illegal drinks that made "protection" payments necessary. Now gone, their spirit lives in the numerous Village restaurants serving twenty-five or fewer patrons, such as Chez Brigitte on Greenwich Avenue, which announces that it "seats 250—11 at a time."

The former stable still standing at 181 West Fourth became La Bohème early in 1917, the first tearoom to affect a bohemian atmosphere. Over the next few years, others appeared with such eccentric names as the Garret, the Attic, the Vermillion Hound, the Three Thieves, Ye Polliwog, and TNT.

Sheridan Square and its tearooms became famous for its unorthodox regulars, a magnet that seemed to attract loose screws. Among the screwiest attracting notice around the square was Tiny Tim—in fact, his gaunt features, pale complexion, and jet-black hair made him unforgettable. Few knew his real name (Timothy Felter), fewer passed him on the sidewalk without being offered "Soul Candy" from his cardboard tray. After failing to sell his poems to trendy Village literary magazines, Tiny Tim printed them by hand on scraps of paper and used the paper as wrapping for his Mystery Sweets. It was classic marketing, with the sugar coating and the bitter pill reversed. What the candy consisted of, no one ever learned.

When at first the candies didn't sell, Tiny Tim upped the price from a nickel to a dime apiece. Sales picked up, revealing to the poet a basic economic principle: if all else fails, raise the price. With this insight, Tiny Tim began charging a quarter. Business soared.

Another tearoom fixture was Doris the Dope, so named for her

A saddle and harness shop at 6½ Sheridan Square became the Crumperie, a 1917 tearoom run by Miss M. Alletta Crump. When the Corn Exchange Bank acquired the site in 1919, the Crumperie was barely two years old.

SONIA SHOP, Greenwich Village, N. Y.

Sonia, the Cigarette Girl, in a caricature she circulated among customers and friends.

cocaine habit. She claimed to be the discarded mistress of Oscar Wilde's boyfriend, Lord Alfred Douglas; she carried an infant son as "proof." Doris made her living by coughing, startling uptowners with well-timed guttural hacking as she panhandled them for the change on which she might live out her final days. Frugality permitted her to take a few days off from "work" on occasion for a weekend of luxury at the Brevoort Hotel. Her consumptive pose became harder for her to maintain after incredulous policemen found Doris in the nearby Washington Square fountain taking a midnight skinny dip.

Sheridan Square's most fabled figure was Sonia the Cigarette Girl. Her hand-rolled smokes were available at 184 West Fourth Street, where she ran a tiny shop a few steps from the square. Sonia thought nothing of strolling into tearooms and approaching patrons to make a sale. With Village atmosphere becoming a marketable commodity in the early 1920s, proprietors welcomed the sight of Sonia's unruly curls, brilliant red lipstick, fantastic-colored batik smocks, and sandals. When Sonia flashed her great Slavic eyes and spoke of her family, now lost in the new Soviet Russia, of her valiant struggle with poverty, patrons bought her cigarettes whether they smoked or not.

Late in 1922, Sonia vanished from her haunts. Few thought it odd, since eccentrics were exempt from conventional patterns. On May 19, 1923, Villagers were shocked by obituaries stating their cigarette girl was dead of heart failure. After a well-attended memorial, she passed into legend before anyone learned who she really was, or that most of what she'd said about herself was invented.

If pressed, she admitted her last name was Bright. But Sonia Bright was actually Ella Breistein, and she came not from Russia but from East Tenth Street where her Jewish father still lived. After leaving home at sixteen, Ella never again saw either him or five of her six siblings. Even her professed poverty was a pose: two checkbooks were found under her hospital pillow for accounts held through her sister at the Corn Exchange Bank.

Even before her death, Sonia achieved a celebrity only Andy Warhol could have explained. Like others, Ella Breistein came to Greenwich Village to re-create herself, discarding the identity she was raised with in favor of one of her imagining. Even the post office accepted the rules she made, delivering letters marked "Sonia, Greenwich Village," which was the only address she gave out. One such letter, written by her in September 1920, was found in researching this book and is published here for the first time. In it Sonia revealed which persona was her true self:

> . . . outward symbols of freedom, or appearances such as bobbed hair, smoking, drinking . . . isn't really freedom. Real freedom is the ability to create with one's hands and brain, to work in useful fields. . . . To Bob one's hair is by no means an act of freedom. I know many girls who come into my shop with bobbed hair, who look and act stupid, have no idea about art, music, or books. They cut their hair because it's stylish! . . . I bobbed my hair and adopted unconventional dress as a conscious protest against conventions followed by the ignorant mobs, against the idea of hair as Woman's Crowning Glory, etc. It is possible to achieve, to study, to have an interest in the beautiful things in life, and to have beautiful long hair. Bobbed hair is not a symbol of achievement nor even of intelligence. It is the aim of every woman today to look and act childish—that is the reason for the terrible short skirts and profuse hair bobbing. . . .
>
> I am most sincerely,
> Sonia

Sheridan Square, displaying street signs that commemorate the 1969 Stonewall Riot, which began the modern movement for gay rights.

THE STONEWALL

With Repeal in 1933, cops on the take would have lost all their extra income had it not been for gay bars. Aided by a State Liquor Authority ban on serving homosexuals, the basis of graft shifted from what was being served—to who. The occasional police raid kept the system in running order and provided the boys in blue the fun of putting on a good show. No one imagined this shakedown system would ever go out of fashion, but in 1969 it did.

The Stonewall Inn at 51 Christopher Street opened in 1930, in street-level space formed by joining two former stables built ninety years earlier. It was popular at first as the scene of weddings and banquets, but by the late 1960s a different clientele held sway. The crowd was male and ranged from college men (yesterday's preppies) to far more flamboyant types. Rumors circulated about management ties to organized crime and about a call-boy service being run from the second floor, but nobody much cared. The Stonewall was a second home to those who were considered too outrageous to gain entry to the straitlaced jazz bar two doors away.

Maybe it was the full moon, but what started as a routine police raid on June 28, 1969, ended in a full-scale riot. Conservative patrons remained docile as they were turned out by the cops, but their flamboyant bar mates were roughed up and fought back. Seeing their friends being dragged kicking and screaming into paddy wagons, the crowd in the street reacted, hurling epithets, then loose coins, then beer bottles and garbage cans. The police barricaded themselves inside and called for assistance. Within minutes, the Tactical Patrol Force was on the scene—in full riot gear.

For hours, the TPF charged the taunting crowd, which scattered through the irregular streets around Christopher Park and then regrouped. The police were dumbfounded—who ever heard of faggots fighting back? But the defiance was as real as the guns the police had drawn, guns they would have used had the reassembled crowd broken through the Stonewall's barricaded door before the TPF arrived on the scene.

The riot ended in the early morning with few injuries and only one casualty: the assumption that homosexuals would forever accept prejudice and discrimination without resistance. Annual parades are now held at the end of June in most American cities, commemorating the Stonewall Riot and the movement for gay rights that began on that night. And the former Stonewall Inn still stands, today housing a men's apparel shop.

AN ETERNAL TRIANGLE

Standing on a three-sided plot, the Northern Dispensary seems to have been here forever. Founded in 1827, it offered health care for Villagers who were too poor to afford visiting physicians. Its first home was a rented space at Bleecker and Commerce streets. This permanent home was built for $4,700 in 1831 and initially had only two stories. The top floor was added in 1854, and as this 1885 photo shows, it was designed to match the style of the lower floors. With the exterior paint now stripped away, the slight difference in brick color can be seen between the second- and third-floor windows.

The Northern Dispensary in 1885, with both faces seen here fronting Waverly Place. When Factory Street (to the right, with the cart) became an extension of Waverly (at left), the Northern Dispensary won the dubious distinction of having two walls on one street—and one side on two (the unseen side is common both to Christopher Street and Grove).

The clinic began to offer dental care in 1841 and in recent years limited its services to dentistry. However, the clinic violated the spirit of its charter in 1986 when it refused to provide dental care to AIDS patients, among them Village writer George Whitmore. The city's Human Rights Commission fined the dispensary $47,000, which proved too great a burden for the debt-ridden clinic to bear. In May 1989, the 158-year-old institution, the oldest clinic in New York, closed its doors forever—and the Northern Dispensary building was converted into a nursing home for AIDS patients.

WAVERLY WRITERS

Embracing the former Dispensary, Waverly Place has numerous connections to literature, both of the past and the present. For one thing, there's the name of the street. In 1833, residents of what was then Sixth Street chose to honor Sir Walter Scott. To do so, they renamed their street for Scott's 1814 novel, *Waverley*, though in the process the name was misspelled. Waverly Place retains its spelling error to this day.

Given this literary connection, it's fitting that Waverly Place is now the home of the Writers' Room. Filling every corner of the fifth-floor loft at 153 Waverly, the Writers' Room provides workspace for New York authors unable to work at home or those who prefer working in a professional office setting. "It never dawned on me before coming here that a place like this was needed," recalled

44

The squat white house at the center is 14 Gay Street, which gave birth to *My Sister Eileen*.

A few doors east of the Writers' Room is 137 Waverly Place, home in 1837 to Edgar Allan Poe. It was while living here that Poe was stricken with a head cold, for which he was treated at the nearby Northern Dispensary. Though without consequence, this incident appears in every Village book, making it the most famous head cold in American literary history. Just to the left of Poe's former residence is 139 Waverly Place, home in 1917 to Edna St. Vincent Millay.

LITTLE HARLEM

Renata Rizzo-Harvi, a former journalist who is now executive director of the Writers' Room. "We now have some 120 writers, some of whom are quite well established. For example, Judith Rossner, author of *August,* is at work across the hall on her latest novel. James Lapine worked on the script of the musical *Into the Woods* in the cubbyhole office next to mine. And Nancy Mitford, biographer of Zelda Fitzgerald and one of our founders, has used space here to work on her life of Edna St. Vincent Millay.

"Though we started in Midtown in 1978, our writers are much happier since we moved to the Village in 1985. The Village adds a luster to the Room, something that resonates and encourages our sense of community. Now we're seeing writers sharing information about projects, editors, and agents, and we're beginning to offer readings open to members of their works in progress. And as we integrate the Room with such established Village literary landmarks as the Cornelia Street Café and the Lion's Head, I see the Village once again becoming a literary environment."

Village manufacturer Samuel Whittemore built the charming Federal houses on the first block of Christopher Street in 1827 to provide housing for the area's middle class. But middle-class Villagers were reluctant to live in similar houses built that same year around the corner on Gay Street.

Initially, Gay Street wasn't a public thoroughfare, just an alley

My Sister Eileen in its first dramatic form, the 1940 Broadway play starring Shirley Booth, Jo Ann Sayers, and "six Brazilian Admirals."

entrance to stables. Its 1827 houses faced these stables, their early residents being blacks in service to wealthy families of Washington Square North. Even after the last of its stables were replaced in the 1840s by the present row houses there, the alley retained the scent of undesirability. The rich left the square and Gay Street became an impoverished and dangerous ghetto that lasted longer than its counterparts in the South Village.

After shedding its ghetto status in the 1920s, Gay Street gained national recognition as the mythic touchstone of Greenwich Village. It happened because two sisters from Ohio rented the basement of 14 Gay Street and lived there while they sought fame and fortune in New York. The younger one hoped to become an actress while her older sister wrote stories in their apartment and submitted them to publishers. Ruth McKenney's *My Sister Eileen* tales became a fixture of the prestigious *New Yorker* magazine and were published as a book in 1938. They forever fixed an impression of life in Greenwich Village as an impromptu whirl among loony but likable oddballs.

McKenney's deft humor stirred the mix into a myth of great durability. *My Sister Eileen* became a Broadway comedy starring Shirley Booth, which opened the day after Christmas 1940 and ran two years. Rosalind Russell played Ruth in the film version, and again a decade later in a Broadway musical version, *Wonderful Town,* with a score by former Villagers Betty Comden, Adolph

Green, and Leonard Bernstein. CBS televised *Wonderful Town* in 1958, with Russell and several others from the original cast, while Hollywood made a second film of the tale in 1955.

Tragically, Eileen McKenney never knew the full extent of her legend. Four days before her comic adventures first appeared on Broadway, she was killed in an auto accident in California that also claimed the life of her new husband, novelist Nathanael West.

VILLAGE LANDMARKS: "OLD JEFF"

The Jefferson Market Courthouse was saved from demolition in the 1960s by protests, petitions, and community pressure—the very tactics that first brought civic structures to this land 130 years earlier.

Having closed the state prison in 1829, Villagers turned their energies to Greenwich Market, still at the foot of Christopher Street but far from the inland population. The city succumbed to Villagers' petitions in 1832, and for a new market bought this irregular gore of land on Sixth Avenue where the old and new street grids clashed. Named in memory of the recently deceased former President, Jefferson Market opened January 5, 1833.

Public assembly rooms were added to the new market and were used as a police court as early as 1845. Its central location made this site ideal for another civic structure, a fire watchtower. Unlike the present tower on the courthouse, the old market spire lacked a clock, but it had a more important feature: a bronze bell six feet tall hung halfway up the wooden tower. On an observation deck farther up, bell ringers kept watch with a spyglass for smoke. Levers permitted them to ring the bell below, as it was far too loud to strike by hand. The number of bell strikes indicated the fire's location to the local fire brigade.

The municipal fire department instituted in 1865 made Old Jeff's fire bell obsolete. Enter the self-serving "Boss" William Tweed, who could spot a potentially profitable boondoggle at a glance. Under Tweed, a new municipal complex for the site was conceived in 1870. Plans were drawn, and sections of foundation were laid. The city might have been bilked of millions here had

The 1876 Jefferson Market Courthouse, which presides over Sixth Avenue at Tenth Street, was declared by architects of the time to be one of the ten most beautiful buildings in the nation. Its conversion into a library in the 1960s marked a critical victory for preservationists.

Tweed not been forced from power in 1871. Construction resumed in 1874, but only after the complex was redesigned and the bricks for the original foundation were removed, at city expense.

The new courthouse and adjoining jail were designed in Venetian Gothic style by Calvert Vaux, one of the designers of Central Park, and Frederick Withers. Capping the complex was a new tower with four magnificent clock faces. Here in 1896 writer Stephen Crane challenged a corrupt police department over the arbitrary arrest of a woman for solicitation. Here in 1906 Harry Thaw was arraigned and tried for murdering architect Stanford White at Madison Square Garden. And here on September 1, 1907, was held the world's first session of night court.

The Vaux-Withers jail was demolished in 1927 and replaced two years later by a large Art Deco structure, the House of Detention for Women. Court sessions at the Jefferson Market Courthouse were discontinued in 1945, and the great clock was allowed to stop. After a decade of decay, an apartment tower was slated to replace the graceful local landmark.

Efforts to save Jefferson Market Courthouse began at a 1959 Christmas party around the corner, in Margot Gayle's kitchen at 44 West Ninth Street. Restarting the clock was the preservationists' initial goal, a beachhead that, once claimed, would serve as a beacon of their victory. By 1960 they had achieved that victory: the clock was electrified and restarted, and for the first time in years it was no longer twenty after three. The city bowed to the neighborhood campaign in August 1961, announcing that the former courthouse would be converted into an expanded Village branch of the New York Public Library. Architect Giorgio Cavaglieri preserved as many details as possible, including the stained-glass windows, which had survived the decades of neglect intact. By the time "Old

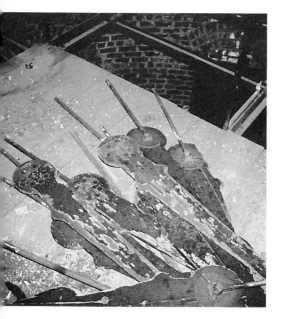

On a landing halfway up the tower of Jefferson Market Library, the original wooden hands of the clocks lie forgotten. Replaced during the restoration, they were absorbing so much water when it rained that the added weight caused the clock to run slow.

Graffiti from the Spanish-American War, inside the bell atop the tower of Jefferson Market Library.

Jefferson Country Market stalls opened on Sixth Avenue in 1833, its second floor Assembly Rooms meeting local civic needs. From this came the plan to use the site for a combined courthouse and jail, while the wooden fire watchtower inspired the present clock tower.

Jeff" reopened as a library in November 1967, Villagers had moved from this victory to an even greater battle, the landmarking of the entire West Village.

"Old Jeff's" clock tower is annually trimmed with Christmas lights to commemorate the party on Ninth Street that led to the survival of the building. Encased within this tower is the bronze fire bell from the wooden tower of a century ago. It's visible in silhouette behind the wooden slats in an 1866 photograph. Legend insists the bell can't be rung because the tower couldn't withstand the vibrations. In fact, nearby neighbors would probably crack before the tower would. The bell has been rung officially twice since it was installed in the present tower; when the victorious Admiral Dewey returned from Manila in 1899 and again when the victorious Villagers restarted their beloved tower clock. But I discovered another connection between the bell and the Spanish-American War. Hand-painted inside the bell is this faded inscription: "J. D. ROSE Aug. 10, 1898 To Hell With Spain."

2 WASHINGTON SQUARE

Gymnasts entertaining in that most democratic of parks, Washington Square.

If Sheridan Square is the heart of Greenwich Village, Washington Square is its soul. Even before a majestic marble arch rose here in the 1890s, a dignity of spirit existed in Washington Square. Like a human soul, it has intrigued generations of artists and writers, daring them to capture the elusive mystery of these 9½ acres in line and shadow, in photo and phrase. Yet the spirit of Washington Square

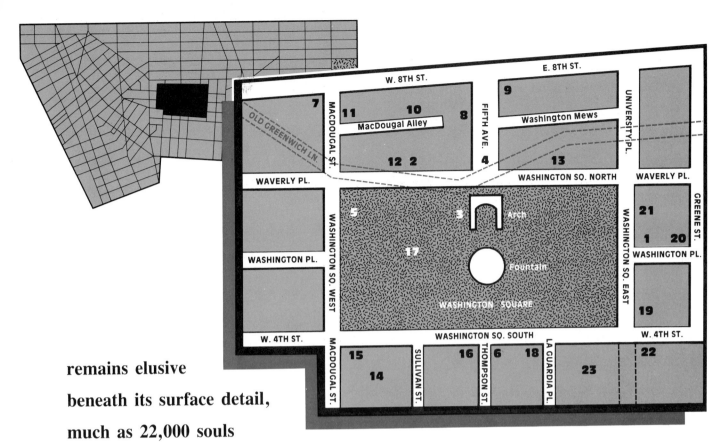

W. 8TH ST.

E. 8TH ST.

7

OLD GREENWICH LN.

MACDOUGAL ST.

11 **10** **8**

MacDougal Alley

9

Washington Mews

UNIVERSITY PL.

12 **2**

FIFTH AVE.

4

13

WAVERLY PL.

WASHINGTON SQ. NORTH

WAVERLY PL.

5

WASHINGTON SQ. WEST

3

Arch

21

GREENE ST.

WASHINGTON SQ. EAST

1 **20**

WASHINGTON PL.

WASHINGTON PL.

17

Fountain

WASHINGTON SQUARE

19

W. 4TH ST.

WASHINGTON SQ. SOUTH

W. 4TH ST.

15

MACDOUGAL ST.

14

SULLIVAN ST.

16

THOMPSON ST.

6 **18**

LA GUARDIA PL.

23

22

remains elusive beneath its surface detail, much as 22,000 souls remain buried beneath Washington Square Park.

Although the stately row houses that once surrounded the square have been replaced by bland apartment towers and by university buildings of architectural arrogance, that spirit persists. Incursions by skateboarders and acrobats, protesters and folksingers, walkers of dogs and pushers of drugs have also failed to dampen it. This once-patrician park is now open to all comers—by some alchemy, the spirit of the square transforms diversity into a vital harmony.

Washington Square has never been placid, however, nor has it been free of controversy. City planner Robert Moses mapped a road through the square in the early 1950s, but Village protests

1 Site of Henry James's birth

2 Site of 19 Washington Sq. North

3 Washington Square Arch

4 Site of original wood arch

5 "The Hanging Tree"

6 Site of 58 Washington Sq. South (Megie shack; later Bruno's Garret)

7 Site of Wouter Van Twiller homestead

8 2 Fifth Avenue (Minetta Brook Fountain)

9 1 Fifth Avenue

10 Former Whitney Studio

11 Former Jumble Shop

12 20 Washington Sq. North

13 1–13 Washington Sq. North

14 NYU Law School (site of the "Strunsky Block")

15 Site of 42 Washington Sq. South (John Reed residence)

16 Judson Memorial Church

17 Holley Monument

18 NYU Loeb Student Center (site of "House of Genius")

19 80 Washington Sq. East (formerly The Benedick)

20 NYU Brown Building (site of Triangle Shirtwaist Fire)

21 NYU University Building

22 NYU Founders' Monument

23 NYU Bobst Library

put a stop to that. In the early 1960s, the parks commissioner tried to ban folksingers from the square, to no avail. And groups of all stripes have gathered off the square to picket the apartment that Mayor Edward Koch maintained through his term of office—no doubt to the annoyance of his neighbors.

A NOVEL PUBLICIST

The person most closely associated with Washington Square never resided directly on it. Henry James was born in 1843 just east of the square on Washington Place, on a site now lost to the NYU University Building. Whisked abroad by his family when he was six months old, the young James was brought back to New York in 1847, to 58 West Fourteenth Street. Over the next few years he found himself drawn to Washington Square, particularly to the home of his grandmother, which James and his family had briefly visited when he was two. Elizabeth Walsh had since died, making it impossible for James to reenter 19 Washington Square North, though he returned to it in his mind in 1880. In that year, actress Fanny Kemble told James an anecdote, which the young writer fashioned into *Washington Square*, the 1881 tale of a test of wills between a doctor and his daughter. Through his fictional Catherine Sloper, James gave readers their first sense of the spirit of Washington Square.

VILLAGE LANDMARKS: THE ARCH

Henry James's novel was less than a decade old when, on April 30, 1890, an area five feet square was cleared and ground was broken for the east pier of Washington Square Arch. Workers had only a month to set the foundation in preparation for the scheduled ceremony for the laying of the cornerstone, but all work stopped after only ten days, halted by a grisly surprise.

Ten feet below the surface, skeletal remains were found. An-

The arch is a permanent successor to White's temporary wooden arch, built spanning Fifth Avenue half a block north of the square for the Washington Inauguration Centennial, April 30, 1889. Festooned with papier-mâché wreaths and garlands, lit with hundreds of newly invented incandescent lights, the $2,700 wooden arch was the hit of the festivities, prompting the City Committee on Art to initiate its marble replacement in a meeting two days later. By April 1892 the last block was in place, though formal dedication did not occur until May 4, 1895.

Designed by Stanford White, Washington Square Arch rises 77 feet above the foot of Fifth Avenue. Built of white marble, its east pier pedestal features *Washington in War*, carved in 1916 by Hermon A. MacNeil. Two years later, *Washington in Peace* appeared on the west pier, the work of A. Stirling Calder. White's design was patterned on his 1889 design for the original wooden arch, seen below.

other foot or two deeper, and every spade of dirt brought up bones. Residents of Washington Square North gathered to see this strange sight, evidently proof that their exclusive neighborhood had once been a potter's field. But one resident disputed this conclusion. His research suggested that a paupers' burial ground was under only the south side of the square and that the north side was the site of a formal German graveyard. The excavation soon yielded headstones dated 1803, proving him correct.

A class distinction north and south of Washington Square had predated the 1828 forming of the square itself. With tenements rising on the blocks south of the square in the 1880s, such distinctions grew more pronounced, leading some members of the City Committee on Art to question the wisdom of raising funds for a memorial arch for Washington Square. But at the cornerstone dedication on May 30, 1890, before six thousand invited guests, Henry Marquand eloquently put such questions to rest. "It is true," Committee Chairman Marquand said, "that the neighborhood may all be tenement houses in a few years. But have the occupants of tenements no sense of beauty? No patriotism? No right to good architecture?" With these words, he baptized in democracy the Washington Memorial Arch. For a century, it has made good on his words.

THE HANGING TREE

In the northwest corner of the park, amid buttonwoods, ginkgo trees, and catalpas, stands a giant elm believed by many to be the oldest tree in Manhattan. Known as the hanging tree, it was used for executions until 1819. Daniel Megie, who doubled as the resident hangman and grave digger, lived in a wooden shack where New York University's Catholic Center now stands at 58 Washington Square South. Megie's shack might well have dated from 1797, the year in which a cholera epidemic led to the use of marshland here for a burial ground. The hanging tree and several yellow fever outbreaks kept Megie busy until 1826, when the area was closed to further burials and the marsh filled in.

With suitable fanfare, the Washington Military Parade Grounds were thrown open to the public on July 4, 1828. Two oxen and two hundred hams were roasted and served, and the first of many military parades was held. Minetta Brook, which had fed the marsh, had been channeled underground, and the spacious common, elegantly landscaped, retained little sign of its funereal function. On occasion, however, the less illustrious past surfaced, as the weight of horse-drawn cannons proved too much for the rotting coffins underground. With a dull splintering sound, cannon wheels periodically sank into the earth. Considerable effort was required to pull them free. Years later, resident Edward Tailer, Jr., recalled having watched an excavation under the sidewalk near Megie's shack. Within the vaults, he said, were corpses still bearing traces of the yellow sheets in which epidemic casualties were buried.

Minetta Brook still flows under Washington Square, out of sight. Megie's shack was torn down in 1947. In fact, all traces of those years of death are gone, except the hanging tree—still living in Washington Square.

THE FIRST VILLAGE CELEBRITY

The fertile basin formed by Minetta Brook proved ideal for cultivating tobacco, as the Indians of Sapokanican discovered. And it was this rich land that attracted to the present Village its first celebrity resident, briefly the most famous man in New Amsterdam.

Wouter Van Twiller was appointed by the Dutch West India Company in 1633 as the director general of the colony, succeeding Peter Minuit. He took the entire Minetta basin as his personal country farm, or *bouwerie,* and kept the tobacco profits instead of crediting them to the colony. In time his deeds caught up with him, and in 1638 he was recalled. Believing his removal to be temporary—it wasn't—he took inventory of his holdings and created the oldest surviving document of Village real estate.

In it Van Twiller noted the dirt paths that marked the borders of his farm, all of which followed ancient Indian paths. One of his 1638 references was to the nameless border path still in use as Christopher Street. The northern boundary of Van Twiller's

The Lower Depths

The east slope of Van Twiller's hill was afforded protection by the swift currents of the Manetta, an Indian term meaning "devil water." Though routed underground in the 1820s, Minetta Brook has remained true to its name over the years, having bedeviled the foundations of structures in the area over the years.

One such building is Two Fifth Avenue, a twenty-story apartment tower constructed in 1951. Its outer entrance lobby features a transparent tube that purports to feature water squirting up from Minetta Brook, directly under this site. As the water on display seems suitably murky, the claim is accepted on faith—perhaps to stave off suggestions as to other possible sources of that water.

The doormen here are used to polite visitors. Step inside and see what you think.

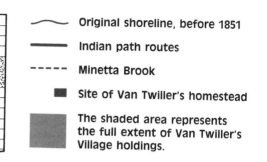

Original shoreline, before 1851

Indian path routes

Minetta Brook

Site of Van Twiller's homestead

The shaded area represents
the full extent of Van Twiller's
Village holdings.

bouwerie was another former Indian path, which he grandly dubbed the Strand. Two sections of it survive as modern Village streets— Greenwich Avenue west of Sixth Avenue and the short blocks of Astor Place. The curved section that once joined them was removed in 1828, part of the compromise struck ten years earlier to keep most Village streets to their original pattern.

The Indians had used this path to reach Sapokanican from the main trail up the center of Manhattan. Starting at the present Fourth Avenue and Ninth Street, it ran south to within a few feet of the arch site before heading to the northwest, cutting south of a blunt hill that once stood just north of the marsh (Washington Square). On that hill in 1633, Wouter Van Twiller had his homestead built. It was still there 160 years later, as indicated by its presence on a 1795 map. Though this provides us with the exact location of the house—the present intersection of Eighth and MacDougal streets—no surviving reference tells us when the house was demolished or the year the hill was leveled. But since MacDougal Street was laid out there in 1825, the Van Twiller hill would have been removed by then.

The 1890 excavation for Washington Square Arch may have provided the answer: workers found that some eight feet of landfill had been used to raise the former marsh to the square's present grade. As the area was closed to burials in 1826, the landfill may have consisted of the soil of the nearby hill on which Wouter Van Twiller's 1633 mansion stood.

ALL VISITORS ASHORE

The aquatic references continue at One Fifth Avenue. On the street level of this 1926 apartment tower is a swank restaurant bar that uses its address as its name: One Fifth. Its Art Deco appointments were salvaged from a Cunard ocean liner, the *Caronia*, and installed in the late 1970s. Seen here is the elegant carved-wood bar and, proudly displayed, a portrait of the *Caronia*. Both were shipboard features, though several stylish cityscape murals here were created expressly for the restaurant.

Pulitzer Prize–winning poet Sara Teasdale spent her final year as one of the first tenants of this building, which replaced four handsome row houses. In the 1860s, one of them housed Miss Lucy Green's School for Girls; among the daughters of New York's elite to be "finished" here was Jennie Jerome, later the wife of Lord Randolph Churchill and the mother of Winston. The distinguished instructors included writer-to-be Bayard Taylor and Elihu Root, later Theodore Roosevelt's secretary of state and winner of the 1912 Nobel Peace Prize.

One Fifth, a seagoing setting that specializes in steaks.

LIFE IN AN ALLEY

Tucked away half a block north of Washington Square are two former alleys that have become exclusive Village streets.

Washington Mews initially provided access to the stables and to the rear garden entrances of the row houses on Washington Square east of Fifth Avenue. Not until the 1930s were the rear gardens along the south side of the mews replaced by miniature houses designed to complement the former stables—then already a century old—facing them across the alley. Washington Mews and its structures are on property that has been owned since 1801 by the Sailors' Snug Harbor, which still derives income from leases here. Much of the mews is presently held by New York University on lease through the year 2002.

West of Fifth Avenue is MacDougal Alley, which can be entered only from MacDougal Street. Its maintenance as a street was begun in 1833 by John and George Rodgers, the brothers who built the first significant structure on the square, the still-standing 20 Washington Square North. In 1838 additional stables were added along the alley's north side, built to serve the new row houses rising on Eighth Street at that time.

Street numbers of the structures in MacDougal Alley initially corresponded to the numbers of the houses to which they belonged. As these stables became artists' studios in the first years of this century, their street numbers shifted piecemeal to an independent sequence—though some never shifted. As a result, 21 MacDougal Alley is on the even-numbered south side, and other alley houses retain an unofficial second number.

In July 1907, Gertrude Vanderbilt Whitney opened a studio in MacDougal Alley at number 19, now number 17½. Her work here led to her establishing the Whitney Museum of American Art. Another famous alley address is number 12 (formerly 23) Mac-Dougal Alley, the studio of painter Ernest Lawson in the years before World War I, and later of painter Guy Pène du Bois and sculptor Jo Davidson. Also notable is 1 MacDougal Alley, at the north side of the alley's entrance gates. Built as a stable in 1854, its lower floor was converted in the late 1910s into the Jumble Shop, an early tearoom that remained popular well into the beatnik era. In the 1960s the old stable became the home of Shakespeare's, an eatery that continued in operation until 1985, when the first floor became—incredibly—an organic fast food restaurant. Above it is the former studio residence of poet Edwin Arlington Robinson, whose *Tristram,* written in part here, won the 1928 Pulitzer Prize for poetry.

MacDougal Alley, one of the most picturesque enclaves in New York.

John Sloan commemorated the arch conspirators in his etching of that name, caricaturing himself in the figure at the right.

THE REPUBLIC OF WASHINGTON SQUARE

Some people thought Gertrude Drick strange, though certainly other Villagers were far stranger. After all, *she* didn't walk a pet leopard on a leash as Christine Ell did. She didn't keep a pet alligator in her bathtub, as a dancer friend of Floyd Dell did. Gertrude Drick was just your ordinary bohemian, up from Texas to study art with painter John Sloan. She did refer to herself as Woe, even had business cards printed with that name. When asked why she was Woe, Gertrude explained, "Because Woe is me," and giggled.

The rest of America spent January 1917 pondering whether the United States should get into the European war, but Gertrude Drick was figuring how to get into Washington Square Arch. Finding the small door in its west pier unlocked on one occasion, Gertrude entered and discovered the stairs that led to the monument's roof. Its inspiring view may have given Gertrude her great idea: since uptowners misunderstood everything that was important, why not declare Greenwich Village's independence?

Under cover of darkness, six rebels gathered to make their way to the arch. John Sloan brought artist Marcel Duchamp; Charles Ellis, Forrest Mann, and Betty Turner, all Village theater folk, completed the rebellious sextet. In darkness they mounted the 110 winding steps and emerged on the roof, where they strung Chinese lanterns and balloons, passed around food, and uncorked wine. One farsighted rebel brought six hot-water bottles to sit on to ward off the night chill. Woe then read her Declaration (consisting of the word "Whereas" repeated over and over, and nothing else). The celebrants fired cap guns into the darkness and declared Greenwich Village to be the Free and Independent Republic of Washington Square. They then toasted themselves until they were suitably drunk, at which point they removed their lanterns and withdrew into the night. Their balloons remained to flutter by the dawn's early light and mystify Villagers on their way to work.

WASHINGTON SQUARE NORTH

Painter Edward Hopper, in the studio he maintained at 3 Washington Square North, and in which he died in 1966. This 1947 portrait is the work of another Villager, photographer Berenice Abbott.

Within weeks of the 1828 opening of the Washington Square parade grounds, construction began on a free-standing mansion near its northwest corner, the present 20 Washington Square North. Neighbors soon joined it around the square's perimeter, though of that first generation of elegant structures, only those on the north side survive—and even they aren't exactly what they seem. The houses on the square west of Fifth Avenue are a wing of the 1951 apartment tower around the corner at 2 Fifth Avenue. Only community pressure kept the tower from rising directly on the square, as proposed, though this low-rise wing still claimed the Rhinelander mansion and four stately row houses, including the one owned by Henry James's grandmother. Just across Fifth Avenue, the houses at 7–13 Washington Square North seem to have survived intact, but these 1831 facades are now little more than false fronts concealing modern apartments that replaced the original interiors in 1939.

These alterations on Washington Square North were not the first. In 1880, number 20 Washington Square North was altered into apartments, according to a sensitive plan by Henry J. Hardenbergh, later known as the architect of the Dakota apartments and the beloved Plaza Hotel. East of Fifth Avenue, studios were placed in a renovated 3 Washington Square in 1884, to be taken up by artists and writers. Writer Edmund Wilson moved here in 1921 while he was managing editor of the *New Republic*. Among the artists who resided here over the years are Rockwell Kent, Ernest Lawson, Walter Pach, and Guy Pène du Bois.

Several years before joining the Drick Rebellion, painter John Sloan started his own revolution at 3 Washington Square North, one that reshaped the American art world. In the spring of 1907, Sloan was invited to dine here at the studio of his friend, painter William Glackens. Sloan arrived in a fury, having just learned that his urban realist paintings would be excluded from an upcoming exhibit by the all-powerful National Academy of Design. Sloan proposed to Glackens an incredible idea: why not mount works by several Academy rejects in a show sponsored by the artists themselves? Joining Sloan and Glackens in directly challenging the Academy's power were Robert Henri, George Luks, Ernest Lawson, Everett Shinn, Maurice Prendergast, and Arthur B. Davies—all Villagers at one time or another, except Davies.

In February 1908, nearly a year after Sloan met with Glackens, their rebellious art show was a reality. Critics dismissed the works on view as fit only for the ashcan, leading the painters to waggishly label themselves the Ashcan School of art. The artists were so frequently mentioned as a group that they became known as "the Eight," a label that remained attached to them long after the revolt born at 3 Washington Square was forgotten.

Washington Square North, east of Fifth Avenue. The row of thirteen homes seems little changed after 150 years, though numbers 7 through 13, seen here, have undergone more changes than meet the eye.

VILLAGE PEOPLE: "PAPA" STRUNSKY

It's an enduring Village legend: the crazy-but-lovable landlord who let impoverished tenants live rent free if he liked them. In the case of Albert Strunsky, the legend is true.

"Strunsky was a character," recalls one of his former tenants, Dr. Henriette Stoner, "but he was the most wonderful man in the world. If you couldn't pay the rent, he'd settle for a radio, for a painting if you were an artist and he liked your work. But there was more to him than just that.

"One winter Papa Strunsky had two artists in one of the heated apartments on Washington Square, and they couldn't pay. He had his handyman, Marshall, move their things to an unheated place back on Third Street while they were out, and they came back to find their apartment empty. They went looking for Strunsky to complain, and Marshall sent them around to Third Street. They walked in, and there was Strunsky on his knees, putting wood in their fireplace and lighting it. 'You couldn't pay in the heated room,' he said, 'but since you got no place to go, you might as well stay here.' "

Born in Russia, Strunsky established himself in the Village of the 1910s by delivering wines to local restaurants. He later invested in a block of apartments on the square at MacDougal Street and south around onto Third Street. His little kingdom is gone now, plowed under in 1950 and replaced the following year by the NYU Law School and Vanderbilt Hall. But a Strunskyism survives in the title tune of the 1931 film musical, *Delicious*. Lyricist Ira Gershwin had married Strunsky's daughter Lenore in 1926, and when he needed a charm song five years later for leading lady Janet Gaynor,

That's Emily in the front row, just above the head of her reclining brother-in-law, George Gershwin. To the right of Emily, just beyond friend-of-the-family composer Phil Charig, is her sister Leonore and husband, lyricist Ira Gershwin. Another famed lyricist, Howard Dietz, is in the front row, fourth from the left, and playwright S. N. Behrman is at the back, just in front of the closed door. To the right of Behrman, directly under the lamp, is Emily's handsome brother, English Strunsky. And presiding over the entire gathering in the upper right, beaming like a proud papa, is "Papa" Strunsky himself.

Missing from this June 1926 gathering is "Papa" Strunsky's illustrious sister Anna, who inspired and collaborated with writer Jack London before marrying another writer, noted socialist William English Walling. Also missing is his other sister, Rose Strunsky, whose support of philosophic anarchism often labeled her as a radical, a label which Emily Strunsky Paley casually waves away. "All my family was radical," she quips. "I expected them to be."

Gershwin recalled with delight the mangled English pronunciations of his father-in-law. As a tribute to Strunsky, the Gershwins wrote their title tune as "Delishious."

Another Strunsky outpost was Three Steps Down, a family restaurant at 19 West Eighth Street operated by Albert Strunsky's wife, Mascha. Although the couple had separated, Strunsky was present at the head of the table almost nightly, leading many Villagers to believe the restaurant was run by him—particularly as it was run almost as casually as Strunsky's real estate ventures. "And there, too, customers were always 'mein daughter' and 'mein son,' " Dr. Stoner recalls, "which is how he became 'Papa' Strunsky." Though he was generous right up to the time of his death in December 1941, his beneficence eventually caught up with him in August 1939. Yet even then, as Dr. Stoner tells it, "he was still getting checks in the mail for rent or meals he provided to those who, at the time, couldn't pay."

Strunsky's brother was a doctor who was occasionally drawn into this personal approach to business. Henriette Stoner recalls that "this young woman back on MacDougal Street had missed her rent, so Strunsky sent Marshall around to see her. She was sick with terrible stomach pains, so Strunsky calls in his brother. It turns out the woman needed an emergency appendectomy, and Strunsky paid for the ambulance, for the operation, for the hospital, everything. That's the kind of man he was. And when she was fully recovered and he found out she still wouldn't pay the rent, what do you think? He threw her out!"

To his tenants he was "Papa" Strunsky, but to daughter Emily Strunsky Paley he was just Papa. Now in her young nineties, she still vividly recalls "one indigent tenant that Papa bought a taxicab for, and he wasn't a rich man. I remember this beautiful desk one tenant left behind, in lieu of the last month's rent, I think. I had it moved to Papa's basement office, but the next time I came by it was gone. 'Where's the desk?' I asked, and Papa said, 'Oh, a tenant needed a desk so I gave it away.' And I remember going through the books once and seeing how many tenants had gone months without paying the rent. I wrote them each a very nice note, but when Papa found out what I'd done, he went to each of them and said, "Pay no attention. Pay no attention.' "

JOHN REED'S DAY IN BOHEMIA

Within a block of my house was all the adventure in the world; within a mile every foreign country." So wrote John Reed of 42 Washington Square South in *The Day in Bohemia*. He had moved there in 1911, an exuberant youth a year out of Harvard, eager to write poetry and have fun.

In 1912, number 42 Washington Square acquired another tenant, journalist Lincoln Steffens, whose 1904 book, *The Shame of the Cities*, had exposed municipal corruption and was among the most popular works of the rising Literature of Exposure. An old friend of Reed's father, Steffens encouraged the youth to trust his poetic sense. Reed followed his mentor's advice that summer while in Portland for his father's funeral; there Reed described in verse the vagaries of Village life as he knew it.

The Day in Bohemia, or Life Among the Artists appeared as a slim volume in 1913 and became a local success. Villagers were amused to find themselves or their friends mentioned by name in the poetry, and they were drawn together as a community by the exploits, pranks, and thoughts set down by one of them. John Reed was suddenly the Golden Boy of Greenwich Village, achieving a status that would have made any young poet proud. But soon Reed was caught up in new interests, in causes that brought to him a life he could never have imagined. He was to play a role in many aspects of life around the Village, and in the Russian Revolution as well. He became internationally loved and hated, and by 1920 he was dead. What began as a day in Bohemia was to end seven years later in a hero's funeral at the wall of the Kremlin.

MAKING
A CASE
FOR
ACTIVISM

Judson Memorial Church, a landmark on Washington Square South for a century. Beyond the tower is Judson Hall, built as a hotel intended to fund church activities and, along with the tower, now owned by New York University.

Judging from the messages posted in the glass case mounted beside the doors of Judson Memorial Church, this is no ordinary house of worship. The Judson congregation has long supported the posting of activist statements. For decades worshipers have entered past sharp statements condemning the Vietnam War, the arms race, nuclear weapons, abuse of the environment, and government inaction on AIDS. And for nearly a century, the Judson has aligned its activism with that of the artistic community of Greenwich Village to create its own unique blend of the worldly and the spiritual.

Edwin Judson was determined to encourage the poor immigrants of nearby Little Italy to a better life. In 1890 he decided to construct for his purpose a new church on Washington Square South, one funded by rich New Yorkers—seemingly so remote but in some cases as close as Washington Square North. The Judson's fanciful Renaissance design was by the prestigious architectural firm of McKim, Mead & White, and the stained glass was executed by John La Farge. And to honor his father, America's first missionary to Burma, Edwin Judson placed in the cornerstone a copy of his father's Burmese translation of the Bible.

Not content with traditional church activities, the Judson began hosting concerts and exhibitions in 1948. When Dr. Howard Moody took the pulpit in 1956, the Judson assumed an avant-garde posture with exhibits by Claes Oldenburg, Jim Dine, Bob Whitman, and Tom Wesselman. Two years later, it offered New York's first "Happening," a performance exhibit by Allan Kaprow that ushered in the Judson Poets' Theatre. Supported by a congregation that voted to give the group complete artistic freedom, the theater became a part of the bumptious, irreverent new theater of Off–Off Broadway for which no issue was too daring.

The Reverend Al Carmines joined Judson in 1958, soon after the Kaprow Happening and was soon using his talents to write and stage musical plays and operas in the church. Over the next fifteen years, his loyal audiences were treated to works of stunning virtuosity, several of which enjoyed commercial Off-Broadway runs. Among them were his giddy pop opera, *Promenade* (1965), written in collaboration with iconoclastic playwright Maria Irene Fornes, and *Peace* (1968), wickedly adapted from Aristophanes by Tim Reynolds just in time for the sham of the Paris peace talks.

Poor health forced Carmines to curtail his activities in the mid-1970s. For the past decade he has appeared occasionally in cabaret and as accompanist for David Summers, an acclaimed singer and Judson regular who died of AIDS in 1986. Meanwhile, Judson Memorial Church approaches its second century with its missionary zeal intact.

The glass case mounted on the front of Judson Memorial Church, here seen protesting government inaction in fighting AIDS.

WE THE PEOPLE

61,011 Died of AIDS since 1981

WASHINGTON SQUARE NOTABLES

Actress Miriam Hopkins lived on the top floor of 108 Waverly Place before heading off to Hollywood. The same building was once the home of Richard Harding Davis, a correspondent during the Spanish-American War and later the author of popular novels.

Washington Square was home to various members of "the Eight" over the years. Both William Glackens and Ernest Lawson lived in a red brick house at 64 Washington Square South, now lost to NYU's Loeb Student Center. For a time Glackens also lived at 50 Washington Square South, which in 1914 was home to Maurice Prendergast and his cabinetmaker brother, Charles (jointly known around the Village at the time as "the Prendies.") Everett Shinn lived just off the square at 112 Waverly Place, where he converted a back shed into a miniature theater seating fifty-five and, in 1911–12, offered burlesques of old melodramas, including *Hazel Weston, or, More Sinned Against Than Usual.*

In 1845, number 116 Waverly Place was home to Anne Charlotte Lynch, a teacher and poet who gathered the city's new writers before her parlor fireplace to form America's first literary salon. Among them were William Cullen Bryant, for forty years the high-principled editor of the New York *Evening Post;* Margaret Fuller, the critic and feminist; satirist and poet Fitz-Greene Halleck; Bayard Taylor, journalist for the New York *Tribune;* Herman Melville; and Edgar Allan Poe who, it is said, introduced "The Raven" to the world in a reading here.

The top floor of 80 Washington Place is a 1919 addition built by its owner at that time, composer-conductor John Philip Sousa. No such alterations were made next door at 82 Washington Place by onetime residents Willa Cather and Richard Wright. But just around the corner at 132 West Fourth Street, you can still see vestiges of a penthouse that John Barrymore renovated in 1917. After renting the top floor of this row house, the noted actor ordered thirty-five tons of topsoil for a private rooftop garden. The building walls soon began to buckle, forcing the swift removal of the dirt and an even swifter disappearance by Barrymore.

But there are those who will insist that the most famous resident of Washington Square wasn't a person. For years Americans followed the exploits of Fala, Franklin Roosevelt's dog during his White House years. After the President's death in 1945, Eleanor Roosevelt moved into the retirement apartment her husband had selected at 29 Washington Square East. Naturally, Fala became a familiar sight in the square, winning new celebrity for the nation's top dog.

HAPPILY EVER AFTER, OVER AND OVER

Facing Barrymore's transitory garden across Fourth Street is the 1860 Washington Square Church. In addition to such traditional fare as local weddings, it has hosted a number of theatrical productions over the years. But in over a century, it has probably seen nothing so strange as the marriage of Valentina Lynne Vitale to Anthony Angelo Nunzio, Jr.—as of this writing, over five hundred times.

Tony n' Tina's Wedding first appeared in January 1988, the wickedly satiric brainchild of actors Nancy Cassaro and Mark Nassar who had attended one Italian family wedding too many. The result was this mock ceremony, performed five times a week, with the paying audience as the "guests" of either the bride's family or the groom's. Upon arriving at the church, theatergoers are asked which side of the aisle they belong on, only to be frisked for firearms by someone from the "other family."

After the ceremony, everyone moves on to the dinner reception, where the performance continues. Initially, this meant a trek up to Carmelita's on East Fourteenth Street, but a few months into the run closer accommodations were provided by Vinnie's restaurant, 147 Waverly Place. Otherwise the tacky affair remained unchanged, from the Ritz Crackers and Cheez-Whiz hors d'oeuvres to the baked ziti entrée, the recipe for which was published during the run by the *New York Times*.

One local drama critic tried to maintain critical detachment by keeping to himself at the reception, watching the performance and eating his ziti. Midway through a mouthful, he was joined by the bride's father, who proceeded to unburden his soul by telling the reviewer all his problems. He finally moved on, only to be replaced by the priest, who did the same. The critic capitulated—his review was, of course, a rave.

VILLAGE PEOPLE: GUIDO BRUNO

Walking through Greenwich Village, you're sure to spot people you'd classify as eccentric, though you might be hard pressed to separate the real eccentrics from the phonies. But throughout Village history, the two have often been linked in one individual, Guido Bruno being a case in point.

You could have seen him in the summer of 1914 on Thompson Street just south of Washington Square. According to Village legend, it would have been hard to miss him in his unfashionable checkered suit ill-fit to his tall frame, his eye avoiding yours if you asked where he was from. Nor could you have forgotten his bizarre reply: "I, Bruno, have given birth to myself." In fact, he had.

At first there was no reason to link him with the sixteen-page chapbooks of doggerel that were flooding the Village, with such titles as *Bruno's Bohemia, Bruno's Weekly,* and *Bruno's Review of Life, Love, and Literature* until, in the spring of 1915, the connection became clear. Each fifteen cent pamphlet boasted that it was "Printed in Bruno's Garret," which that spring was identified as the second floor of the old hangman's shack on Washington Square. Huge letters spelling out "Bruno's Garret" fluttered beneath his window, their target the busloads of uptowners who were regularly deposited in the square, eager to explore "Greenwich Thrillage." And Guido Bruno meant to exploit them with pseudo-art and would-be poetry. Or so the legend would have us believe.

According to legend, Bruno offered concerts that consisted of his walking onstage and playing phonograph records. Art exhibits in his garret are said to have been displays of bookplates or of postcards straight from the drugstore. The reason for his artistic pose is said to have been his hope that it would help him seduce gullible girls. Legend paints him as a fraud, but it never reveals who Bruno really was.

According to his nephew, author Arnold I. Kisch, his real name was Curt Josef Kisch. Born in 1884 in Mladá Boleslav just north of Prague, in what is now Czechoslovakia, he was a more authentic Bohemian than most. He interrupted his medical studies to publish a Zionist pamphlet, which led his family to send him to America in 1907, presumably to be straightened out. But after an

Guido Bruno in about 1915, a portrait that shows him dressed "out of character."

erratic career as a publisher in Detroit and Chicago, he appeared in the Village in 1913 as Guido Bruno, using a pen name he had adopted a year earlier. Though quietly living in Yonkers with his wife and child, he set up operations on Thompson Street just below the square, on the second floor of a hovel, over the Rossi brothers' ice cream parlor. There he began printing the pamphlets that won him notoriety, boldly interspersing his own verse with works by Poe and Wilde.

After moving to the old hangman's shack at 58 Washington Square South the following spring, Bruno expanded his operations across three rooms over a street-level cigar store. One became his storeroom, piled to the ceiling with books he had printed. Beyond his printing press in the middle room, the back room was reserved for exhibitions, the first of which brought on a clash with local censors, an unhappy reminder of a similar clash that had forced his exit from Chicago. This time, after the Society for the Suppression of Vice objected to erotic nude paintings by Clara Tice, Bruno responded wittily with a mock trial. Tice was charged with the Murder of Art, and Bruno sold tickets to the proceedings.

Hindsight shows Bruno's roster of writers to be less trivial than legend would have us believe. Bruno was the first to publish verses by Hart Crane, and he introduced Aubrey Beardsley to American audiences. He also discovered writer Djuna Barnes in 1915. By artfully sailing over the censors' heads, her *Repulsive Women*

Two views of Bruno's Garret, the shack at 58 Washington Square South that dated from 1797 and was once home to the local hangman, Daniel Megie. Bruno's successor, Grace Godwin, can be seen in the window in this 1917 shot, right. Above is another view, in 1915, when Bruno was still in residence. His self-promoting sign, which annoyed Village residents, proclaimed Bruno's Garret: "To get it written, to get it spoken, to get it done, at any cost, at any hazard, it is for that only we are here."

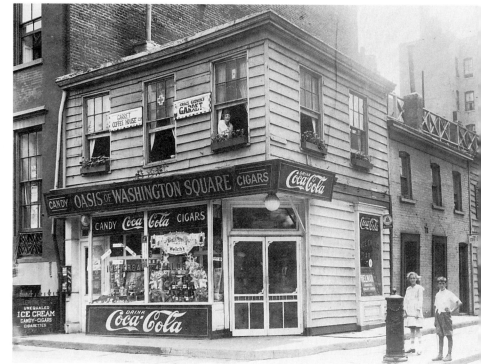

Guido Bruno in his Thimble Theatre at 10 Fifth Avenue. The peacock curtain is the work of artist Clara Tice, whose art Bruno championed.

managed to avoid another censorship tangle despite a depiction of lesbian love.

Bruno's most celebrated venture was his Thimble Theatre, which opened in July 1915 in 10 Fifth Avenue, an 1848 town house that is still standing at the northeast corner of Eighth Street. At the time, its street level housed the Diamond Disc Shop in which Charles Edison had been trying without success to sell the phonograph records his famous father had invented. A dilettante bohemian, the younger Edison was attracted to Bruno's fluttering sign, and with him planned a promotional stunt that involved playing a hand-cranked phonograph in Washington Square. Strollers unaccustomed to music without musicians were startled out of their wits by the opera overtures blaring from the bushes. After emerging from hiding, Bruno and Edison moved their unamplified player to the square's Holley Monument, where a pedestal became their sounding board. Listeners soon were drawn to 10 Fifth Avenue to hear the concerts Edison continued to present there on the second floor.

But Bruno had bigger plans for the space. By October 1915 he had installed wooden benches to seat one hundred and a stage equipped with curtains decorated by Clara Tice with butterflies and peacocks in attitudes more chaste than her earlier designs for Bruno. On February 28, 1916, the Bruno Players earned theatrical immortality with the first regular performances in America of Strindberg's brutal drama, *Miss Julie*. Its successful run was augmented in April with the addition of another Strindberg piece, *The Stranger*.

February 1916 was Bruno's zenith, but it was also the beginning of the end. Two weeks before the *Miss Julie* premiere, fire spread from a neighboring building into Bruno's Garret, causing such severe damage that he was forced to curtail his operations there. Lost were unpublished manuscripts penned by Shaw, Lincoln, Poe, Wilde, and the first great bohemian, Henri Murger. By year's end both the garret and the Thimble Theatre were history.

Bruno tried in vain to continue. He opened a book shop at 105 Fourth Avenue, but another censorship battle forced him to close. In 1922, he tried another shop at 30 East Fourteenth Street; the depression forced its closure a decade later. The masterful self-promoter died forgotten on the final day of 1942, but his eccentric spirit is to be found in *Nightwood* (1935), the novel for which Djuna Barnes is best known. In it, she created a wild Balkan character whom she named Felix Volkbein, with a son named Guido. Not a bad fate for a "charlatan."

THE "HOUSE OF GENIUS"

Village Voices

I have a rendezvous with Death
At some disputed barricade,
When spring comes back with
*   rustling shade*
And apple blossoms fill the air—
I have a rendezvous with Death
When spring comes back blue
*   days and fair.*

> —*Alan Seeger*

I never saw a purple cow,
I never hope to see one;
But I can tell you, anyhow,
I'd rather see than be one.

> —*Gelett Burgess*

The NYU Loeb Student Center, which rose on Washington Square in 1959, features Reuben Nakian's *Fledgling Students,* said to be the first abstract sculpture to be affixed to the exterior of a New York building. Far more notable, however, was the boardinghouse it replaced, the legendary "House of Genius."

Marie Branchard took over 61 Washington Square South in the 1890s, having previously run a boardinghouse in Syracuse, NY, where one of her tenants was Stephen Crane. The young writer was again her boarder here in the Village, where he is said to have worked on *The Red Badge of Courage.* As the century waned, Mme. Branchard turned this former single-family residence into a de facto arts colony.

In one room lived satirist Gelett Burgess, author of the 1895 nonsense verse that begins "I Never Saw a Purple Cow." Burgess also coined the word "blurb," which he defined as "to self-promote; to make a noise like a publisher." Another boarder, Frank Norris, here began work on his trilogy of novels which championed a new literary realism (though only *The Octopus* and *The Pit* were completed). On the second floor lived poet Alan Seeger, who filled the hallways with his mandolin playing when he wasn't writing. One of his poems, "I Have a Rendezvous with Death," turned out to have been tragically prophetic when he was killed on a battlefield in France in 1916. And on the top floor lived writer Rose O'Neill, who invented the Kewpie doll here in 1909.

Legend later added Eugene O'Neill, John Dos Passos, and Theodore Dreiser to the House of Genius roster, though they were at best just visitors. And Willa Cather's first New York apartment was not here, as is often thought, but next door at number 60. The House of Genius survived Mme. Branchard by eleven years and then fell beneath the wrecker's ball in 1948.

The "House of Genius," just prior to its 1948 demolition. Its legend survives, however, to honor the creative spirit of the Village that is linked—not always accurately—with this boardinghouse at 61 Washington Square.

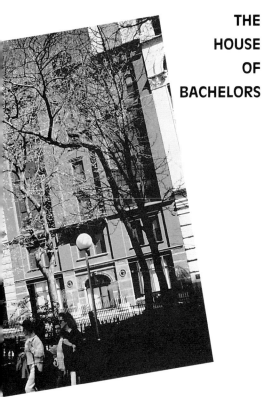

The former House of Bachelors, built as the Benedick, now NYU's Leonard Stern Hall.

THE HOUSE OF BACHELORS

Unlike the House of Genius, the building that was once known as the House of Bachelors survives at nearby 80 Washington Square East. Built in 1879 for unwed gentlemen of means, the Benedick derives its name from the confirmed bachelor of Shakespeare's *Much Ado About Nothing*. So strict were its residency requirements that even its owner was compelled to leave when he fell from grace and wed.

By maintaining respectable standards, the Benedick played a role in New York society for years. The keeper of those standards was Emma Senn, under whose rule all parties on the premises ended by 11 P.M., the hour at which all women guests were to leave. Throughout her tenure as housemistress, Emma Senn was the only woman to sleep beneath the roof of the Benedick. Perhaps as compensation for the lack of female companionship, residents were given a very free hand to outfit their rooms as they pleased.

One resident painted his suite black; another installed his own pipe organ. For reasons now lost to history, another spent the princely sum of $4,000 to line his bathroom with green marble tiles. Suites developed distinct personalities and often passed to subsequent residents with their revered furnishings intact. Little wonder that in 1925, after learning that the building had been purchased by NYU for use as a dormitory, one longtime resident was reduced to tears.

**THE
TRIANGLE
FIRE**

Late in the afternoon of March 25, 1911, pedestrians on Washington Place were horrified to see the burning bodies of young women plunge to the sidewalk before them. Something terrible was happening on the top three floors of the Asch Building at the corner of Greene Street.

When fire struck the Triangle Shirtwaist Company, seven hundred women—none over twenty-three, some ten years younger—were claiming their belongings from a cloakroom and waiting for the single passenger elevator. Highly flammable fabric was piled everywhere and may have been set afire by a stray cigarette. Regardless of the cause of the fire, many women would have escaped had the doors to the stairwell not been locked by a management that denied workers even a breath of air.

The eighth-floor workers did manage to get out, and women on the tenth floor broke the skylight and climbed to the roof. Ninth-floor workers were trapped, however. Their only escape was by way of the painfully slow elevator operated by a youth named Joseph Zito. He made five terrible trips to the flaming ninth floor; on the last, a woman enveloped in flame threw herself onto the roof of the descending cab, to the horror of those within it. She was still alive when the cab reached the ground floor. Her clothing was extinguished by firemen who arrived amid the hail of falling bodies.

The Triangle Shirtwaist Fire lasted barely an hour, yet it took 146 lives. Word of the locked doors and unsafe conditions incensed those who were already fighting for workers' rights. The disaster led the City Council to enact the most stringent fire laws in the nation. The former Asch Building still stands at 29 Washington Place as the Brown Building of New York University. The lives needlessly lost here are remembered in a small tablet that is mounted at the corner of the building.

Fire struck the Triangle Shirtwaist Company at 29 Washington Place on March 25, 1911, sparking outrage that strengthened efforts to ban sweatshop working conditions. Reformers were aided by these photographs by the only photographer who was able to sneak past the police and get shots of the devastation inside the building.

The original University Building of New York University. One of its Gothic spires can still be seen, as the Founders Monument on Fourth Street just east of the Square.

NEW YORK UNIVERSITY

Incorporated in 1831, the University of the City of New York provided a nonsectarian alternative to conservative Episcopal Columbia University. Today it is the nation's largest private university. New York University draws young people and new ideas into Greenwich Village, but the school is also a voracious neighbor that has clashed frequently with the Village community over local real estate.

Founded by Albert Gallatin, secretary of the treasury under Jefferson, the school was initially funded by John Johnston, one of the three builders of the row of houses on Washington Square North. To build its home, NYU purchased a parcel of land east of the square on Waverly Place in 1833 for $40,000. Unfortunately, this left less than $70 in the school's treasury when construction began that June. Instead of buying expensive marble cut by local tradesmen, the university made a deal with the state to buy marble cut by prisoners at Sing Sing. Prison labor was not unknown at the time, but using the state as an intermediary was; the school was getting marble for a price that no tradesman could match. Protests by stone cutters and builders were rigidly ignored by both the university and the state, precipitating the infamous Stonecutters' Riot of October 24, 1833. Though the riot was put down by the Twenty-seventh Regiment of the National Guard, it raised issues that were not resolved until the state abolished prison labor contracts in 1884. The Stonecutters' Riot, which caused thousands of dollars' worth of damage along Broadway, is now cited as the first protest demonstration by organized labor in New York State, and very possibly in the nation.

Controversy erupted again when the completed University

The present University Building at 100 Washington Square East, which stands on the site of its 1834 predecessor. When planned in 1894, its seven lower floors were leased out to provide income. The three top floors were used by the school, accounting for the building's spurt of classical details high above the square.

Dorothy Catherine Draper, 1840, the first photo portrait.

Building opened in 1835. The prestigious *Architecture Magazine* of London pronounced it "a mountain of incongruous details . . . styled as Carpenter's Gothic, though even that can give you no idea of its hideous abortions and monstrous absurdities." At home, the City Council objected to the building's encroachment upon Washington Square, although the square was barely five years old at the time and was hardly a sacred institution.

The building was partially redeemed by the distinguished tenants to whom NYU leased space. Samuel F. B. Morse took the North Tower facing the square for his experiments in telegraphy, as well as the painting for which he was better known at the time. In September 1835 he ran 1,700 feet of wire through his rooms to demonstrate electrical transmission. He patented his telegraph system in 1837 and demonstrated it here the following year, astonishing his students with the typed message that began, "Attention, The Universe." Morse also built a glass-walled studio on the adjacent roof for experiments in the new science of photography. Among his students of the daguerreotype technique was the future chronicler of the Civil War, Mathew Brady.

Daguerreotypes also intrigued the school's chemistry professor, John W. Draper. On the building's roof on December 18, 1839, Draper took the first photographic image of a celestial body, a daguerreotype of the moon requiring a twenty-minute exposure. Excited by the success of his camera—a cigar box with a spectacle lens—Draper set about attempting to make a photograph of the human form. By using mirrors he was able to concentrate enough light on his subject to cut the exposure time to fifteen minutes. By filtering all but the blue light, he kept his subject from squinting in the glare. But there remained the problem of getting the sitter to hold still that long. Draper solved that problem by attaching an iron pipe to the back of a chair; fixed to this pipe was a ring to keep the head from moving. With this elaborate device and the assistance of his subject, his sister Dorothy Catherine Draper, he took the first photo portrait of a human face on the university roof above Washington Square early in 1840.

The South Tower was rented for a time to Samuel Colt, who here worked out the design for the pistol that bears his name. Other institutional tenants included the New York Academy of Medicine and, for sixteen years, the New-York Historical Society. Painter Winslow Homer also lived here, as did America's first great architect, Richard Morris Hunt.

A BIBLIOTHEQUE ATTACK

New York University has taken over many buildings to the east and south of Washington Square, including the hotel and tower that were once affiliated with Judson Memorial Church. The Strunsky apartment block is now occupied by the law school, which has also claimed the land beneath Sullivan Street for an underground library. But no NYU structure is more noticeable or has been more vigorously opposed than the hulking twelve-story Bobst Library on the southeast corner of the square.

Objections focused on the scale of the building, but the fight over the library came to hinge on forty feet of land that its design required. That strip of land, on the east side of La Guardia Place, had been reserved by the city as part of a compromise with Villagers when sections of Wooster and Greene streets vanished to create the superblocks for the Washington Square Village towers. Now New York University was trying to buy a block of that strip, and the city was ready to sell. Villagers cried foul, demanding that the original terms of the compromise be honored.

According to Anthony Dapolito, then chairman of Village Community Board 2, the two swing votes needed to squelch the land sale were those of Constance Baker Motley, the borough president of Manhattan at that time. Her vote was expected to be against NYU, but when the votes were counted on August 26, 1966, she sided with the university. As Dapolito notes, she was elected to be an NYU trustee in May of 1968.

So the Bobst Library, designed by Philip Johnson and Richard Foster, opened its doors in 1973. Its two million books are doubtless a valuable Village resource—though Villagers sometimes have trouble getting in to use them. To this day, the strip along La Guardia Place remains largely vacant, except for the Bobst Library. And to this day, some Villagers see this building as a symbol of the vigilance required if Greenwich Village is to survive.

Recently many Villagers have sensed a softening of New York University's indifference to the needs of the community in which it is located. It is a welcome change, and one that many hope will continue.

The massive Elmer Holmes Bobst Library of NYU at 70 Washington Square South. It casts over 20 percent of Washington Square into shadow.

3 BROADWAY: "A PROMISCUOUS CHANNEL"

The bustling Broadway Strip, looking south from Waverly Place.

New York's most famous street runs straight through Greenwich Village for a mile, then angles northwestward across the rigid street grid of Midtown. The blocks of Broadway above the Village are known for elegant theaters and mammoth department stores, where rich tourists mingle with those who make their home in the street and with others who make their living there.

But the Village blocks of Broadway won the street its first international eminence. Everything that was later to be found along Broadway in Midtown first flowered here, along with the kind of grand mansions and hotels that later were built on Fifth Avenue. Raucous torchlight parades moved past refined churches and through the most brazen red-light district in town. After surveying these blocks in 1854, a magazine proclaimed Broadway the richest thoroughfare in America. It was also the most crowded, a phalanx of humanity teeming with hotels and shops, churches and saloons, homes and theaters, "all collected," stated *Putnam's Monthly*,

1 Grace Church (site of Hendrick Brevoort homestead)
2 Site of LeRoy Place
3 Colonnade Row
4 The Public Theater (formerly the Astor Library)
5 Former Mercantile Library (site of Astor Place Opera House)
6 The *Alamo*
7 Site of the Broadway Central Hotel (previously site of the Winter Garden Theatre)
8 Site of Pfaff's
9 Bayard-Condict Building
10 Site of St. Thomas' Church
11 Site of Harry Hill's
12 1 Bond Street
13 Site of the Ward Mansion
14 Stewart Apartments (site of A. T. Stewart store)
15 770 Broadway (formerly Wanamaker's store)
16 842 Broadway (Village Voice offices; site of Wallack's Theatre)
17 Site of Academy of Music
18 Site of Worrell Sisters' Theater
19 Site of Automatic Vaudeville
20 Site of Biograph Studios
21 Union Square Theatre
22 Site of City Theatre
23 Former Luchow's Restaurant
24 Union Square
25 The Palladium

"into one promiscuous channel of activity and dissipation."

After a half-century of decline, the 1967 transformation of the former Astor Library into the Public Theater signaled the rebirth of the Broadway Strip. Here West Village nonconformists met East Village hippies for cappuccino at St. Adrian's Company, shopped for torn tie-dyed jeans at the Unique Clothing Warehouse, took in a New York Dolls concert at the Mercer Arts Center, and then danced the night away at Infinity. More recently a second wave of activity along the Broadway Strip followed the 1983 opening of the huge Tower Records outlet at Fourth Street. Today Astor Place Hair Designers provides everything from crew cuts to Statue of Liberty spikes (in the appropriate shade of green), and Star Magic provides one-stop shopping for quartz crystals and spacey lighting fixtures. All this occurs within sight of the fashionable nineteenth-century church which a century ago was the scene for the wedding of the world's most famous midgets.

None of this was supposed to happen to Broadway. In fact, *nothing* was supposed to happen to Broadway. Its Village blocks were planned as its northernmost blocks; Broadway was to merge at Union Square with the Bowery and disappear. But as so often happened, the city's plans for Greenwich Village overlooked one thing: the tendency of its residents to decide such things themselves.

THE MAN WHO "SAVED" BROADWAY

Long before Broadway reached the Village area, the Bowery followed the spine of Manhattan and was the main route of travel north. Laid out in 1629, it followed a path Indians called Wickquasgeck and provided the Dutch access to the twelve farms they had established north of a marsh, or between today's Canal and Fourteenth streets.

Lower Broadway diverged from the Bowerie Road near the site of the present City Hall, ran north to the marsh, and there abruptly stopped. Once the marsh was drained, Broadway was extended north to the present Astor Place, where in 1807 it met a dead end at a small country fence. Here stood the first of two farms that Broadway was to cut through to join with the Bowery.

The first farm was the twenty-one-acre estate left by Captain Robert Richard Randall as a home for disabled seamen. But sensing the profits of development, Randall's relatives preferred to use the income of the land to open a new Sailors' Snug Harbor on Staten Island. They began leasing property between Fourth Avenue and University Place—a policy the Randall estate continues to this day. And they approved an extension of Broadway across the property, north toward the planned union with the Bowery. Only the second farm, that of Hendrick Brevoort, remained in Broadway's path.

The sixty-year-old Brevoort, an obstinate descendant of early Dutch settlers, was in several respects a proto-Villager. He still lived in the wooden house his father had built on the property, facing the Bowery at Eleventh Street. He kept a pet bear chained to a tree in his watermelon patch—presumably so that his pet deer could roam free. One room in his house was given over to his tropical birds, the first in captivity in New York and an enchanting wonder for those visitors who were careful where they stepped. Afterward, guests might wander through Brevoort's garden, mindful of the bear, and enter the freestanding building he ran as a tavern. Legend tells of a grove of trees there, much prized by Hendrick Brevoort. Legend also has him standing in that grove, fending off Broadway and city planners at the point of his blunderbuss.

Whether or not the legend is based in fact, Broadway never was joined to the Bowery, nor was the Brevoort property between them ever bisected by Eleventh Street. Broadway swerved westward at Tenth Street to run parallel to the Bowery up to the site of Union Square at Fourteenth Street. Perhaps because the projected union did not occur, this park didn't materialize until 1831, by which time Broadway had assumed the northward route of the Wickquasgeck while the Bowery vanished at the Square.

LIFESTYLES OF THE RICH AND FAMOUS

Washington Square was still a potter's field when Bond and Great Jones streets east of Broadway emerged in 1820 as the first enclave planned for the city's affluent. On these new uniform blocks established by the street grid, those unable to afford a freestanding mansion could buy into an ensemble row and have an imposing facade to call home. The first

Colonnade Row in 1890, before five of these nine houses were destroyed. Among the residents of this classic ensemble row were John Jacob Astor II and Warren Delano, grandfather of Franklin Delano Roosevelt. Guests included William Makepeace Thackeray and Charles Dickens.

of these ensemble rows, the 1827 LeRoy Place on Bleecker Street, appeared a block west of Broadway.

Colonnade Row, another such ensemble, is among the greatest architectural treasures of the Village. Built on Lafayette Place in 1832, its official name is LaGrange Terrace, after Lafayette's country estate in France—though this ensemble row is really a monument to fur trader and real-estate baron, John Jacob Astor.

In 1804 Astor took over a large tract above Great Jones Street, which he opened as Vauxhall Gardens, an early version of Central Park but run as a business for profit. It acted as a magnet drawing the rich to the area, prompting them to construct their splendid new homes on Great Jones Street. When property values peaked in 1826 Astor closed most of Vauxhall Gardens to sell off the land for development. He ran a broad road through the center of the property, three blocks without a cross street, and named his creation Lafayette Place. Lots on either side of it were offered for as much as $30,000 each, ensuring that the area would appeal only to the rich and that Astor would make a killing.

The unbroken sweep of Lafayette Place was ideal for an ensemble row, or so thought Seth Geer. He bought nine lots on the west side of Astor's new street and put up the finest ensemble row in the city. The white marble facade was unified by a second-floor terrace across all nine homes and by the twenty-eight marble columns that supported a running cornice overhang two floors above. But the enclave of the rich that was Lafayette Place was destroyed in 1900 when its southward extension brought heavy traffic to this thoroughfare, renamed Lafayette Street. A year later, half of the row was destroyed. The five southernmost houses, which had been joined in 1875 to form the Colonnade Hotel, were torn down and replaced by a warehouse for the nearby Wanamaker's department store. The name of the store is still visible across the building facade.

The four surviving houses, all designated landmarks, give a sense of the original structure, which was once compared favorably to the great ensemble rows of London and Bath. However, three of the houses are marred by ungainly skylights that break the unity of the facade—which is weather-beaten and in need of restoration—while the interiors have been subdivided into apartments and commercial spaces. At street level, 430 Lafayette has long been a restaurant, while the northernmost house, once the office of a religious publication called the *Churchman,* now houses the Astor Place Theatre, an Off-Broadway playhouse that has had a somewhat checkered career. Among its long-run hits was John Ford Noonan's *A Coupla White Chicks Sitting Around Talking* (1980), which at various times featured Eileen Brennan, Susan Sarandon, Louise Lasser, Anne Archer, and Candy Clark. At the other extreme, a

Even designated landmarks need upkeep. As this column indicates, Colonnade Row is in need of restoration, though landmarking does not mean the city will help fund the needed repairs. Maybe it should.

Facing Colonnade Row across Lafayette Street, the Public Theater operates in the former Astor Library, predecessor of the New York Public Library.

decade earlier the Astor Place housed Tom Eyen's *The Dirtiest Show in Town,* hardly the kind of fare Mr. Astor would have imagined.

VILLAGE LANDMARKS: PUBLIC LIBRARY TO PUBLIC THEATER

Like Jefferson Market Courthouse, the present home of the Public Theater was a pioneer in the recycling of old buildings to new uses—in fact, it was the first building rescued from demolition by the city's Landmarks Preservation Commission. But in contrast to the old courthouse, which was transformed into a library, the Public Theater's home was built as a library. And though appearing to be a single structure, it is actually three sections built over a period of thirty-one years into a uniform Renaissance style, reflecting the popular library's need to expand.

Washington Irving was instrumental in pursuading John Jacob Astor to bequeath funds for a free library, the city's first. When construction began two years after Astor's death in 1848, the site chosen was a plot once part of Astor's Vauxhall Gardens, one of Astor's most profitable ventures. The Astor Library opened on January 9, 1854, but it soon became apparent that the facility was too small. Astor's son and grandson took up the challenge in turn, and each funded an extension of the original building. Completed in 1881, the third section followed the example of its two predecessors in using a minimum of wood, maintaining the library's fireproof status. The most celebrated design feature was the skylight atrium in the center section, providing readers with natural light instead of candlelight, but closing the library daily at dusk.

The Astor Library closed for the last time in May 1895, and work began on linking its 250,000 volumes to the collection of the Lenox Library and the funding of the Tilden Trust, forming the New York Public Library. The old Astor Library building in the Village stood unused until 1919 when it served briefly as a club for returning doughboys. It then became the home of the Hebrew Immigrant Aid Society. After using the building for four decades as their offices and a shelter, HIAS sought smaller facilities. The building was sold to a developer who planned to clear the site for an apartment house. Once the initial payment of July 1965 was made, the old Astor Library seemed doomed.

Enter the Landmarks Preservation Commission, constituted only weeks earlier after years of debate. The Astor Library was one of the first fifteen structures considered for landmarking, and it won that designation on October 26, 1965. Meanwhile, Joseph Papp was in search of a permanent home for the New York Shakespeare Festival, which he had founded in 1954. The Astor Library seemed ideal. Papp approached the Landmarks Commission, and title to the building was transferred to the Festival. It was sensitively renovated by Giorgio Cavaglieri, who was still at work on the restoration of Jefferson Market a few blocks away.

The Public Theater opened its doors October 17, 1967, with the premiere of *Hair*. Playing in what had been the library's main reading room, *Hair* let the sunshine into the theater of the sixties, much as the glass skylight had once let the sunshine in for readers and scholars. Among the hundreds of plays and musicals that opened here were *That Championship Season, No Place to Be Somebody, I'm Getting My Act Together and Taking It on the Road, The Normal Heart,* and the hit that later moved to Broadway, *A Chorus Line.*

THE ASTOR PLACE OPERA HOUSE RIOT

The 1,800-seat Astor Place Opera House was wedged onto a plot where Astor Place and Eighth Street converge. After opening on November 22, 1847, it was acclaimed for its handsome appointments and condemned for its situation far from the homes of most theatergoers. Its management, in the hope of keeping it open, decided to drop opera in favor of less refined fare. But the new policy sealed the theater's doom and brought on the worst theater riot New York has ever seen.

British tragedian Charles Macready and company were engaged for a four-week run in May 1849. Americans at that time were not at all fond of the British in general, and they disliked

Some scoff when superstitious actors expect trouble when *Macbeth* is performed. But take one guess what was playing at the Astor Place Opera House on May 10, 1849—the night of riots that left thirty-four dead.

Macready in particular, as he was then feuding with American actor Edwin Forrest. Police were everywhere on May 10 as the audience filled the theater. When Macready entered as Macbeth, the place erupted with hoots, jeers, groans, and raspberries that stopped the performance for ten tumultuous minutes. But bad as things were in the theater, they were far worse outside.

Many supporters and opponents of Macready hadn't managed to get inside—twenty thousand of them, in fact. Ringleaders, who had been ejected from the theater, whipped that crowd into a howling mob that pelted the building with cobblestones plucked from a nearby sewer construction site, smashing several windows. Their cohorts inside seized the heavy stones and hurled them at the theater's chandelier, which rained cut glass down on the audience. By 10 P.M. the state militia and the National Guard had arrived in Astor Place amid a hail of bottles, bricks, and debris. As his terrified troups regrouped, Colonel Duryee of the National Guard cornered the embattled sheriff on the scene and threatened to withdraw and abandon the streets to the mob unless he could order his men to shoot. Though he got what he wanted, Duryee tried to avoid bloodshed by ordering a first volley fired over the heads of the rioters. This had the unfortunate effect of goading the frenzied mob into attacking the troops head on. Duryee then gave the order to fire at will.

It wasn't over until 1 A.M. At about that hour, a heavily disguised Macready left the theater through its main entrance rather than the stage door. The scene awaiting him must have been shocking. Astor Place was strewn with bodies; the wounded had been removed to the old Vauxhall Garden Theatre around the corner. The opera house was surrounded by a garrison reinforced by two brass cannons, which mercifully had not been used. The scarred theater walls and the carnage in the street so unnerved Macready that he went directly to Boston and sailed home to England. He never again appeared on the New York stage.

The riot left two hundred wounded and thirty-four dead.

In June 1850, though barely three years old, the Astor Place Opera House closed and was rebuilt as the Mercantile Library, one of several membership libraries in the city. In 1891 the library pulled down the former opera house and erected the present structure as its new home. That building still stands on the site of the opera house and is today the headquarters of a union local.

ASTOR PLACE TODAY: THE CUBE

How can you identify a true Villager? One way is to ask someone to "Remember the *Alamo*" and see if their first thought is of the black cube that stands in Astor Place.

Designed by sculptor Tony Rosenthal, *Alamo* has been a popular landmark on the Astor Place traffic island since 1967. The 3,000-pound cube is supported on a pipe sunk into a tube below ground level, permitting those with spare energy to push the sculpture around in circles. Under the "Adopt-a-Monument" program of the Municipal Art Society, the *Alamo* was restored in the summer of 1987 by the same New Haven foundry that had cast it twenty years earlier. Its adoptive sponsor is Dan Neale, who can also tell you something about the other Alamo, since he's a Texan.

The *Alamo* on Astor Place, with the former Wanamaker's store as a backdrop.

The reconstructed Astor Place subway kiosk, with Cooper Union behind it.

ASTOR PLACE TODAY: THE KIOSK

When the first IRT subway line opened in 1904, the uptown station at Astor Place had a cast-iron and glass kiosk, but the kiosk that stands on the site today is not the original one.

The last of the turn-of-the-century kiosks were removed by the Transit Authority in 1967 as part of a disastrous modernization program. Later, however, under pressure from Village groups, the TA sanctioned this kiosk reconstruction, designed by Rolf Ohlhausen after photos of the original. The eleven-ton replica was cast and constructed in Alexander City, Alabama, in 1985, and carefully trucked north to be positioned above the stairwell in March 1986. The station itself received a $2.5 million renovation, also designed by Ohlhausen, a graduate of nearby Cooper Union, and supervised by the Landmarks Commission, which had designated the station a few years earlier. Ohlhausen's plan preserved its wall mosaics and the terra-cotta plaques. These plaques were specific to each station on the IRT line so that passengers who couldn't read might identify any stop. The Astor Place plaques depict a beaver, the source of fur-trader John Jacob Astor's first fortune.

BROADWAY'S MOST HISTORIC BLOCK

A bland apartment house now standing on Broadway at Third Street gives no hint of its distinguished predecessors on this site, or of the murder here in 1872 that had local tabloids screaming.

Tripler Hall was built here in 1850 as a concert theater that offered in its brief life such artists as soprano Jenny Lind. It was renamed the Winter Garden by a new manager, noted playwright-manager Dion Boucicault. In 1859 *The Octoroon,* his drama of racism and slavery, opened here; it is often cited as the first American play to deal with contemporary issues. Here also Edwin Booth achieved a record one hundred performances of *Hamlet.* And here on November 25, 1864, the night before that historic run began, a single performance of *Julius Caesar* marked the only stage appearance by Edwin Booth with both of his brothers, Junius Brutus Booth, Jr., and John Wilkes Booth. Only weeks after Edwin Booth ended his *Hamlet* run, brother John murdered Abraham Lincoln at Ford's Theatre in Washington.

Fire leveled the Winter Garden in 1867. It was replaced by the city's largest hotel, the Grand Central, later known as the Broadway Central. Its fashionable dining hall became the last outpost of the corrupt Tweed Ring, then under attack in the press and in the first stages of its collapse. Tweed politicians under scrutiny tried to seem law-abiding to avoid any scent of scandal. But scandal was fast becoming Jim Fisk's specialty.

Fisk, the notorious robber baron of the Erie Railroad, had long flouted propriety by brazenly introducing his mistress, Josie Mansfield, to social and business associates. One of them, Edward Stokes, began his own adulterous affair with her. Furious, Fisk dragged Stokes into court on business charges. To retaliate, Stokes and Josie Mansfield threatened to publish Fisk's love letters. Charges of extortion and libel brought attention unwanted by the Tweed Ring, which had Fisk bounced from the Erie board of directors. Fisk persisted, winning indictments against Stokes and Mansfield for blackmail even as the corrupt city government was crumbling. The drama reached its vengeful climax on January 6, 1872, when Stokes followed Fisk to the Grand Central Hotel and, on a staircase just off the main lobby, shot the financier dead.

The hotel prospered despite, or because of, this notoriety—it was here that talks were held to organize major league baseball. But time and neglect took their toll on the establishment, and by the 1960s the Broadway Central had become a welfare hotel. Some glamour returned in 1970, literally through the back door, as former

**The Broadway Central Hotel at
Third Street, in 1908.**

public areas, entered from Mercer Street, became the Mercer Arts Center, a complex of six theaters and two acting schools. Its greatest success was *One Flew over the Cuckoo's Nest,* which featured William Devane and ran for over a thousand performances. By 1972, the center had established itself as an early showcase of glitter rock and new-wave musicians, with performances by the New York Dolls and Eric Emerson and appearances by performance artist Alan Vega. But an ignominious end was close at hand. Just as the afternoon rush hour began on August 3, 1973, two of the hotel's five wings collapsed with a thunderous roar into a twisted heap of splintered beams and plaster walls. Broadway was closed to traffic as firemen scrambled to pull people from the rubble. The remaining sections were soon declared structurally unsound, and the Broadway Central was pulled down in its 103rd year. We can only hope its undistinguished replacement won't last that long.

PFAFF'S: BIRTHPLACE OF AMERICAN BOHEMIANISM

Bohemians were originally just the rootless Gypsies of middle Europe, but the term was derisively extended in the 1840s to the poor artists who gathered in the side streets of Paris. In 1845, romanticized tales of the starving artist class began appearing in a Parisian magazine. Scorn turned to fascination, as readers met in print such free-living bohemians as the painter-composer Schaunard, his artist friend Marcel, and the philosopher Colline, and thrilled to the melodramatic love of the poet Rudolphe

Broadway in 1861, looking north from Houston Street. The Broadway stagecoaches Walt Whitman rode and celebrated in verse are clearly seen. At the center, just above the crosstown Bleecker Street trolley, is 653 Broadway—site of Pfaff's, the basement home of America's first bohemian subculture, which was flourishing at this time. This may well be the only photo taken before the site was cleared in 1870 to make way for the present building.

for his suffering Mimi. As a result of the success of his *Scènes de la Vie de Bohème,* author Henri Murger earned a passport into the very middle-class society his characters spurned, and he made an important discovery: the bourgeoisie would pay to safely glimpse bohemia and taste its personal freedom—and the counterculture life Murger led could be undermined by the bourgeois comforts his success made affordable. The pattern established in Paris first surfaced in America in Greenwich Village, where its impact can still be found.

In 1855 Charles Pfaff opened a basement beer hall at 653 Broadway, a few doors south of the Winter Garden, modeling it on the German rathskellers that were becoming popular in Europe. This dim, smoke-filled cave was a gathering place for a circle of like-minded rebels who here became America's first bohemians. To them it didn't matter that Pfaff's was underground. It served the best coffees in town, offered rich German beers and cheeses, and had the best-stocked wine cellar. If "respectable" people shunned Pfaff's, so much the better.

In 1858, with the help of the Pfaffians, the *New York Saturday Press* appeared—America's first counterculture publication. Its mix of radical politics, personal freedom, naïveté, silliness, realism, sexual frankness, and exuberance marked much of the modern literature and art that surfaced over the years in Greenwich Village and nationwide.

Pfaff cultivated such creative patrons as the *Saturday Press* regulars. He set up a long table for them in the deepest recess of his cellar, a vault tucked under the busy sidewalk of Broadway. The morbid works of recently deceased Edgar Allan Poe made him the group's spiritual leader, but the shining star was Walt Whitman, who was very much alive and often present.

Unlike the rest of the Pfaffians, Whitman had actually published a book! The fact that the poet himself had published *Leaves of Grass* in 1855 diminished the achievement very little in their eyes. Whitman's place of honor was not at the head of that table but off to one side, where he could observe as much as participate. Whitman may have been seated in Pfaff's itself when he wrote "The Two Vaults," an unfinished 1861 work describing

Walt Whitman in 1854, looking much as he did when he held sway at Pfaff's.

> the vault at Pfaffs where drinkers and laughers
> meet to eat and drink and carouse
> While on the walk immediately overhead pass the
> myriad feet of Broadway.

Whitman held the Pfaffians spellbound as a cult figure might. Articles about him appeared in the *Saturday Press,* along with the first publication of his "Out of the Cradle Endlessly Rocking" (1859) and "O Captain! My Captain!" (1865). Given the popularity of readings at their long table, the Pfaffians may have heard these works read aloud by their author. They may also have heard the bold homoerotic verses Whitman composed at that time, which later appeared in his augmented edition of *Leaves of Grass* in 1860. The Pfaff circle was a varied group, but it may well have been an early homosexual coterie, welcoming among their number the young men Whitman met around the corner on Bleecker Street.

Pfaffians who abandoned bohemia for the ranks of the middle class tended to live long and prosper; those keeping their bohemian ways tended to die young. William Winter rose to become a powerful drama critic. Edmund C. Stedman became a wealthy stockbroker on Wall Street, which *Saturday Press* publisher Henry Clapp always denounced as Cater-Waul Street. Bayard Taylor became a noted man of letters who, in later years, dismissed his days at Pfaff's as a silly adventure of youth. And Whitman transformed himself into America's Great Gray Poet, in part by purging *Leaves of Grass* of some homosexual references and by switching the sex of several literary lovers mentioned there.

By contrast, the contentious Fitz-James O'Brien, whose macabre tales had been favorably compared to those of Poe, was an early casualty of the Civil War; but for the frequently anthologized "What Was It?" his work was soon forgotten. Pugnacious poet George Arnold succumbed to paralysis in 1865. FitzHugh Ludlow followed Poe into murky self-exploration via opium and hashish and died of a drug habit in 1870. So-called respectable writers were quick to slur bohemians as low-life vagabonds deserving their ignominious ends. Authors of obituaries claimed bohemianism itself as a cause of death, while editorial writers suggested that the police arrest alleged bohemians on sight. One wag even scrawled a pun across Pfaff's basement wall: "C. Pfaff and die."

When its halcyon days ended, Pfaff joined the uptown march to new quarters in Midtown. In 1870 the building at 653 Broadway was demolished to make way for a store, W. & J. Sloane. Its marble facade stands there today, though a February 1979 fire gutted its interior. Lost in the blaze was Infinity disco, among the first dance clubs to cater to both gays and straights. The tall windows of the salvaged Sloane facade now conceal a modern apartment building; its entrance is around the corner at 77 Bleecker Street.

Charles Pfaff lived until 1890, when his passing was noted with respect. Not so the 1875 death of *Saturday Press* publisher Henry Clapp, who ended his days a pauper in an asylum on Blackwell's (now Roosevelt) Island. His obituaries provided another occasion for warnings on the evils of bohemia. The establishment press was still denouncing America's first counterculture years after its death. But Greenwich Village was to send many more shivers down the national spine.

An 1865 issue of the *Saturday Press,* America's first counter-culture publication. On this front page is a comic review of Dion Boucicault's hit play, *Arrah-Na-Pogue.* The review was written by Lincoln's favorite humorist, Artemus Ward (a pen name for Charles F. Browne). Another 1865 issue popularized "The Celebrated Jumping Frog of Calaveras County" and began the career of another writer, Mark Twain.

VILLAGE PEOPLE: QUEENS OF BOHEMIA

Except for its waiter-girls, Pfaff's was almost exclusively a male environment. Few women risked the censure that was sure to accompany them down the uneven stairs to Pfaff's cavernous basement. But propriety mattered little to either Ada Clare or Adah Isaacs Menken, who descended into Pfaff's and rose to become queens of bohemia.

Ada Clare used her Charleston family's wealth to escape their tedious clutches as soon as she was of age. She won notoriety soon after her arrival in New York for her love poems—decent women didn't write them, let alone get them published—and for the flaxen curls she kept cut short to emphasize her unconventional, boyish beauty. But nothing prepared New York for her flagrant affair with composer Louis Moreau Gottschalk, or for the birth of their illegitimate child. Undaunted by social slights, Ada returned from her visit to Gottschalk in Paris and boldly signed her hotel register "Miss Clare & son."

Such a woman would hardly be put off by the hard-drinking, rowdy cigar smokers of Pfaff's basement; more likely, she'd light one of those newfangled cigarettes, order a beer, and tell a few off-color stories. By whatever means, Ada Clare won the hearts of the Pfaffians, particularly those seated at the literary table in the vault. For them, Ada organized the benefit suppers, which the New York *Herald* cited as the first "surprise parties." But the Civil War destroyed her South Carolina holdings, her income, and her easy life. She returned to writing, but her 1866 roman à clef, *Only a*

Ada Clare, the queen of bohemia, in an 1866 photograph taken prior to one of her stage performances, probably as Mistress Page in Shakespeare's *Merry Wives of Windsor*.

Adah Isaacs Menken as Mazeppa, a role calculated to show off her figure and one that made her a celebrity, if not a star.

A landmark of skyscraper design at 65 Bleecker Street. This detail shows the angels used by architect Louis Sullivan that underscore the building's delicacy, remarkable when contrasted to the Archive Building on Christopher Street, a heavy, brick-faced affair completed in the same year, 1899.

Woman's Heart, was ridiculed by the establishment press and failed to attract readers.

After marrying an actor, Ada turned to the stage for income, though again her efforts were dismissed. With her husband, on January 30, 1874, Ada visited one of the agencies for actors opening near the Broadway Strip, Sanford and Weaver of Amity (now West Third) Street. Ada interviewed with them while holding on her lap Mrs. Sanford's dog, which, unknown to anyone, was rabid. The dog suddenly turned on Ada and bit her full on the face, severing the cartilage of her nose. In a Bleecker Street boardinghouse five blocks west of Pfaff's, the first queen of bohemia died in convulsive madness on March 4.

Somewhat luckier was Adah Isaacs Menken, who at least found stage success before her death in 1868 at the age of thirty-three. Like Ada Clare, she was born in the South, interested in poetry and the stage, and filled with a passion for life. She'd had a fling at all three before arriving in New York in 1859. Here she wed and became pregnant by a pugilist named Heenan, who promptly left her. Then, to her horror, Adah learned she was being sued for bigamy by her first husband, Alexander Menken. What to do? For advice she turned to a sometime Pfaffian, a drama critic, who advised her that New York offered her but one way to restore her honor: she must immediately go on the stage.

"Mrs. John C. Heenan" won considerable public sympathy at her debut in the Bowery Theatre in April 1860, despite meager thespian skills. Soon she discovered a play that allowed her to show her physical charms to great advantage and to win stardom. For reasons now forgotten, the plot of *Mazeppa* functioned chiefly to maneuver its star into being strapped virtually nude to the back of a galloping horse. New York being what it is, *Mazeppa* was instantly denounced as immoral, which made it a hit. Adah Menken toured extensively in this role, winding up in Paris, the birthplace of bohemia, where she contracted pneumonia and died.

VILLAGE LANDMARKS: A THIRTEEN-STORY SKYSCRAPER

You may not associate Greenwich Village with skyscrapers, but the Bayard-Condict Building is a pivotal work of skyscraper design.

Built just east of Broadway on Bleecker Street, it is the only New York building by noted Chicago architect Louis Sullivan and was his first solo commission. Its significance is not in its height but in its graceful facade, which substantially increased the glass window area in proportion to its solid wall, foreshadowing today's curtain-of-glass high-rises. So advanced was the Bayard-Condict Building that, six months before it was finished, the *Architectural*

Record proclaimed it as "the nearest approach yet in New York . . . to solving the problem of the skyscraper."

Weatherproofing problems forced the removal early in the 1960s of some of the ornate terra-cotta for a rebuilding of the ground floor. Despite these insensitive alterations, the Bayard-Condict Building is both an official city landmark and a designated National Historic Landmark.

St. Thomas' Church, Broadway at Houston Street, in 1837. The growing red-light district here forced St. Thomas' to move uptown. On this site today stands the 1894 Cable Building, designed by McKim, Mead & White to serve as the hub of Broadway's cable cars, now long vanished.

THE DIVES OF HOUSTON STREET

Six lanes wide, Houston Street seems to be the southern border of Greenwich Village, though until it was widened in the subway construction of the 1920s it was just another Village street—several, in fact.

East Houston was formerly North Street, laid out in 1797 as the city's northernmost street. It was joined in 1808 to the new Houston (pronounced *House-ton*) Street, and here the tale gets confusing. Stories vary as to the source of the name. Some say it was a misspelling of a local politician's name; others insist that it's a tribute to Texas war hero Sam Houston—who was only fifteen years old at the time. More likely, it derives from the Dutch *huystujn,* or "garden house," since Houston west from the Bowery was deeded to the city by the Bleeckers, who had used the dirt path to reach their garden back house.

In moving uptown, fashion afflicted Houston Street but briefly. One of its few tokens was an early masterwork of the new Gothic

Revival style, St. Thomas' Episcopal Church, which opened in 1826 on the northeast corner of Houston and Broadway. By 1866 the area was teeming with dance halls and so-called concert saloons, prompting the church congregation to remove St. Thomas' to its present site in midtown.

A loophole in the 1862 Concert Act permitted concert saloons to serve liquor provided that performers were not separated from patrons by a curtain, which legally constituted a theater. Most were basement operations to which women were admitted free, usually through a separate entrance, while men paid a quarter. Inside, the sexes mixed freely at small tables or on the cramped dance floor. Underdressed "waiter-girls" circulated unsalaried through the hall, working for a third of their bar tabs and such other income as came their way. Pickpockets also roamed freely, both in the halls and through their gambling annexes.

Not surprisingly, brawls were frequent in such places, fostered by the prizefights the halls offered as entertainment (boxing champ John L. Sullivan held his first match in a Houston Street club). The number of injuries prompted Homer Smith's club to restrict patrons to arm wrestling. But no such restrictions were attempted at Florence's, a rough joint facing St. Thomas' across Houston Street—no wonder the church left—or at Wes Allen's, which was run by a former inmate of Sing Sing.

Harry Hill's Dance Hall, the most respectable of the dives of Houston Street.

Harry Hill's

In the years after the Civil War, Harry Hill's Dance Hall developed a national reputation as a "respectable disreputable house." Harry Hill posted his house rules, which were written in verse to make them easier for patrons to remember, and as a former wrestler he was capable of enforcing them. Pickpockets were banned, as was profane language. Located south of Houston at Crosby Street, the club closed at midnight and never opened on Sundays. And while "loose" women were not banned from Harry Hill's, they knew better than to try to strike a deal while still on his premises.

As a result, Hill's attracted dance hall regulars as well as politicians, lawyers, off-duty policemen, merchants, and even judges. And if the place ever grew too rowdy, Harry Hill had only to rap with his cane for order. Invariably, he got it.

THE BROTHELS OF FRENCHTOWN

C. C. Cook
123 Mercer Street

Gentlemen should be cautious about visiting here, for the landlady puts on awful airs, and bars the door against all whom she don't fancy. Here can always be found a plenty of bad gin, and any number of low and vulgar girls, which together with the little pock marked landlady, make the place quite a bedlam.

Guide to the Harem, or Directory to the Ladies of Fashion in New York

In the 1850s, an immigrant community known as Frenchtown formed on the blocks south and east of Washington Square. By the close of the 1870s, however, most of its French families had left the area for Midtown, forced away by the growing popularity of Frenchtown as a red-light district. The former Frenchtown then became the freewheeling Latin Quarter, which for two decades offered a dazzling variety of pleasure palaces. Among them were its "cigar-store batteries," innocent-looking stores in which customers in the know might be offered "better merchandise" in a back room. There were also vulgar dance halls such as the Black & Tan Concert Hall at 153 Bleecker Street—better known as the Chemise & Drawers—where black dancing girls might interrupt their routines if the price was right.

Full-scale brothels operated openly along Greene and Mercer. Those south of Houston Street appealed to seamen and similar rough trade; those north of Houston catered to clerks, tradesmen, and the rising middle class. Still farther north were classier establishments, the finest of the lot being Josie Woods's house on Clinton Place (now Eighth Street) between University Place and Broadway. Josie moved within society while working for it—no easy task—and became acceptable in all but the highest circles.

Streetwalkers, 1860s style. If Broadway was the most famous street in 1866, Greene and Mercer streets, to the west, home to many of the city's seven hundred brothels, were the most notorious.

Such places could not operate openly without the knowledge of the police and city officials, but charges of corruption had little effect because they were unsubstantiated. Outraged, the Reverend Dr. Charles Parkhurst embarked on his 1892 campaign to unearth just such evidence. Dr. Parkhurst hired detective Charles Gardner and, disguised, undertook a tour of Latin Quarter brothels. In his eagerness he pressed his guide to the underworld to take him "someplace worse," prompting Gardner to escort Dr. Parkhurst to the Golden Rule Pleasure Club on West Third Street. The disguised minister was introduced to its hostess, Scotch Ann, and taken to a basement cubicle furnished only with a table and chairs. Moments later, the door opened to admit a young woman wearing a bit too much makeup, particularly about the chin and jaw. Disappointed, Dr. Parkhurst complained to Gardner that they had seen harlots in many clubs and that this woman was no worse than any of them. Gardner then told Parkhurst just what this "woman" really was and, horrified, the minister fled.

THE CAST-IRONING OF BROADWAY

Changes along the Broadway Strip led the rich to abandon the area as swiftly as they had seized it. By 1880, Bond and Great Jones streets had become the commercial districts they are today. This shift coincided with the heyday of cast-iron construction, making the Broadway Strip of today a northern extension of the great cast-iron district of SoHo.

Just above Houston Street is 620 Broadway, dating from 1858 and among the oldest cast-iron buildings in the city. Nearby, a 1987 renovation revealed the splendors of One Bond Street, a neglected cast-iron masterpiece built in 1871. It had been the Appleton Publishing Company, now the Appleton-Century-Crofts division of Prentice-Hall. The torch of learning, a part of the firm's original logo, still graces the entranceway to the building, recently designated a city landmark. It replaced the Bond Street mansion of Albert Gallatin, a founder of New York University.

Facing the Appleton Building across Bond Street is 670 Broadway, the 1873 home of Brooks Brothers clothiers, which incorporates cast-iron sections into its brick and sandstone facade. It has slipped into disrepair through neglect and, unlike One Bond Street, has not been renovated.

One Bond Street, just east of Broadway, among the greatest cast-iron facades in the city.

The Samuel Ward mansion at 2 Bond Street, today the site of 670 Broadway. Ward, a banker, built a windowless extension behind his 1833 home to house his art collection. It was opened to friends and art lovers and is often cited as the first private gallery in America.

BEGINNING THE LADIES' MILE

A. T. Stewart's Village store used cast iron throughout the entire building, not merely for the facade, as is true of most cast-iron structures. Shoppers were impressed by its huge central court beneath an iron and glass dome, the grandest of grand staircases, and the six steam-driven elevators, a major innovation. Stewart's further captured popular fancy the day after Christmas 1878 by becoming the first store to be fully lit by electricity.

Broadway between Ninth and Tenth streets is today occupied by Stewart House, an apartment building erected in 1961 and named for the grand department store it replaced, A. T. Stewart's, probably the largest cast-iron building ever constructed.

Alexander T. Stewart was a poor Irish immigrant who became the nation's second wealthiest man through the retail business that bore his name. Stewart began with a one-room operation in 1823 and by 1846 had expanded into his Marble Palace, the world's first department store, which still stands at Broadway and Chambers Street. Needing to expand further in 1859, Stewart leased the plot between Ninth and Tenth streets from the Sailors' Snug Harbor and began construction on his new store, which opened in 1862 as the new mecca for shoppers.

The founder's death in 1876 led to a slow decline for the business, but that pattern was reversed in 1896 when Wanamaker's took it over. This Philadelphia-based operation built a tall annex adjacent to the Stewart building and connected the two structures with a two-level bridge high above Ninth Street, which is still officially named Wanamaker Place for that one block. Under its new management, the old store found new popularity through clever marketing. Wanamaker's became Henry Ford's first selling agent. Also, a 1,600-seat second-floor auditorium offered two concerts daily; by no coincidence was the entire second floor given over to selling pianos.

Business declined in time and the twin stores closed, leaving the former annex bereft of a name and now known simply as 770 Broadway. According to the *AIA Guide to New York,* the volume of this commercial building equals that of the Empire State Building. Its basement entrance to the Astor Place subway station has long been closed, though the building's foundation still passes through the downtown platform, as subway riders can clearly see. Also, easily spotted from the sidewalk are the patched windows several floors above Ninth Street where the double-decked Bridge of Progress once joined the two buildings.

The annex survives, unlike the old Stewart store to the north. On July 15, 1956, while undergoing demolition to clear the site for the present apartments, the Stewart building burned. One of the century's more spectacular blazes closed all streets in the area for three days, along with the IRT subway, which was flooded with several feet of runoff water.

BROADWAY'S GRACEFUL LANDMARK

Broadway's crown jewel is the 1846 Grace Church, a designated city landmark and a National Historic Landmark as cited by the Department of the Interior.

Grace Church gloriously caps a two-mile stretch of Broadway north of Rector Street, which was the site of the original 1808 Grace Church. In its search for an "uptown" site, the congregation heard of the land Hendrick Brevoort had so fiercely protected from city planners. The crotchety Brevoort had died in August 1841 at the age of ninety-four, and his son Henry was offering the land to the church for a modest $35,000. On closing the deal, Grace Church also found its architect, James Renwick, Jr. How curious that so significant a commission should go to an architect who was then only twenty-three years of age and who had never designed a church before—in fact, had never designed anything before. But James Renwick, Jr., happened to be Henry Brevoort's nephew. Curious . . .

Renwick's Grace Church opened in 1846 to considerable criticism. Its white marble walls were thought vulgar, its Gothic design foolishly ornate. Even worse, gossips hinted that its spire was built of wood because faulty construction of the church itself made a stone spire impossible. But such criticism almost immediately faded, and Grace Church soon became dear to the hearts of the social elite. Gothic architecture became established, vindicating Renwick, who won such key commissions as Washington's Smithsonian Institution and the massive St. Patrick's Cathedral on Fifth Avenue in Midtown. As for Grace Church, it was a lack of funds, not Renwick's design, that necessitated the wooden spire. A marble spire finally rose above the church in 1883, where it has stood secure for more than a century.

A LITTLE GUIDANCE

Grace Church, looking north from Ninth Street. The 1961 Stewart House is at the right, and the Consolidated Edison clock tower in the distance marks the site of the 1854 Academy of Music.

An 1872 guidebook cited a Grace Church wedding or funeral as the desire of every fashionable heart. Such preeminence was no accident, but was rather the creation of Isaac Hull Brown, sexton of Grace Church for nearly thirty years. Officially a nonparticipant in fashionable society, Brown was therefore an ideal candidate to be its impartial arbiter—for a fee.

A word from Brown about a financial reversal might cause an entire family to be dropped from every respectable guest list in town. A catering firm might be sought out by the leading hostesses and might set any fee for its service, all on a word of praise from Brown. It was quite literally Brown's business to know everything that went on, and gifts to him from eligible young men, dressmakers, bakers, and jewelers were not unknown. In time the portly, ruddy-cheeked Brown amassed a sizable personal fortune of $300,000, and only one time did the Grace Church rector object to his tactics. For this the rector was sternly reprimanded by his congregation, which pointed out that his services were required but once a week while Brown served society daily. Evidently, the rector saw his position more clearly and apologized to Brown, who grandly forgave him.

Only once did Brown's actions seem transparent. In 1863 P. T. Barnum devised one of his most outrageous publicity stunts—the Wedding of the Century between a midget he'd been profitably exhibiting since 1842 and his pint-sized bride of choice. What would attract more notice than a wedding at the fashionable Grace Church? Over 1,500 people saw Charles Stratton (promoted as General Tom Thumb) wed Lavinia Warren with rival Commodore Nutt serving as best man. The details of Barnum's arrangement with Brown remained unknown, but the ceremony did not go unquestioned. One parishioner rashly asked Isaac Brown about the wisdom of hosting such a stunt. Brown merely smiled and replied, "Even little people have the right to marry in a big church."

LIVING BY BREAD ALONE

The grassy Huntington Close adjoining Grace Church, named to honor its sixth rector, was once the site of Fleischmann's Model Vienna Bakery. Fleischmann's, which stood here from 1876 to 1908, specialized in Old World pastries, rolls, coffees, and chocolates served in a leisurely manner. In summer months a canvas awning covered the front court, creating an outdoor café that enticed weary shoppers from Stewart's just across Tenth Street. By refusing to sell liquor in the café and on the main floor, Fleischmann further enhanced its reputation among women customers. But its midnight giveaway proved to be its most enduring policy.

As if to underscore the freshness of its products, Fleischmann's

"It is a small thing to get, a loaf of dry bread, but from 300 to 400 men will gather nightly from one year's end to the other in order to get it."—from "The Bread-Line" by Theodore Dreiser.

distributed unsold baked goods at midnight free of charge. As the after-theater crowd dispersed, shabbily dressed men from the city streets and flophouses gathered and formed a silent, orderly line that often stretched for blocks. After receiving their handouts and stuffing rolls and bread into their pockets, they departed as silently as they had gathered. This poignant ritual, begun in the 1880s, became the subject of several paintings and of a short essay by Theodore Dreiser, and it is popularly credited as the source of the term "breadline."

BROADWAY GOES AROUND THE BEND

Diverted from its planned union with the Bowery, Broadway bends to the west at Grace Church to create the first of its irregular blocks. Here antique dealers offer a dazzling variety of pieces ranging from ornate Victorian clocks to white plaster casts of Greek statuary. Wedged among these shops are numerous landmarks and historic sites.

The Strand on Broadway at Twelfth Street is a cavernous bookstore offering volumes long out of print as well as discounted copies of virtually every new book (*except* this one!). Facing it across Broadway is Forbidden Planet, one of the world's largest sci-fi and fantasy shops. It stocks countless comic books, model kits of alien space ships, and a handsome selection of gargoyle masks— a handy convenience for one-stop shoppers.

A block south along Broadway two nineteenth-century survivors face each other across Eleventh Street. McCreery's, a cast-iron dry goods store, became a part of the Ladies' Mile of shops in 1868 and was rebuilt as luxury apartments in the 1970s. Its landmark companion to the south is the former St. Denis Hotel, built in 1848 and once among the city's finest. Here on May 11, 1877, Alexander Graham Bell demonstrated his telephone for startled guests, speaking with someone in Brooklyn on lines that had been run across the then-unfinished Brooklyn Bridge. Since the hotel closed in 1917, the building has served varied uses and is now, like McCreery's, apartments.

The Strand is a book lover's paradise, though its claim to stock eight miles of shelves may be only as accurate as the count McDonald's keeps on the number of hamburgers sold.

THE VILLAGE FINDS ITS "VOICE"

The *Villager* has been published since 1933 and was a dependable source of community news, but by 1955 Greenwich Village could support a weekly paper of broader appeal. At least, that's what Dan Wolf thought. He talked the idea over with Ed Fancher, whom he'd met at the New School several years earlier and found himself with a partner. On October 26, 1955, the *Village Voice* first appeared on newsstands and promptly began losing $1,000 a week.

Financial support came, in part, from author Norman Mailer, who soon decided the new paper might provide him with a forum and revive his career, which was in a slump at the time. His diatribes, occasionally printed with an introduction daring readers to attempt them, invigorated Mailer's career less than they spurred debate about the *Voice*. As letters poured in demanding an end to Mailer's essays, they raised a related matter: just what sort of weekly was best suited for the iconoclastic Village of the mid-1950s? In the wake of Mailer's withdrawal from the paper in 1956, the *Village Voice* began its ascendancy as a trend-setting bastion of New Journalism.

From its ratty offices above Sutter's Bakery at 22 Greenwich Avenue, the *Voice* published essays by established writers like Gilbert Seldes, E. E. Cummings, Ezra Pound, and Katherine Anne Porter—but it was with home-grown talent that the *Voice* was to score. Columnists Nat Hentoff, Howard Smith, and Jack Newfield created their own following, and *Voice* cartoonist Jules Feiffer crystalized the new "sick" humor with his sharp observations (when a child asks whether Santa Claus exists, a Village Santa replies, "Do *any* of us truly exist?").

The weekly quickly established itself as the voice of the growing Off-Broadway theater scene. To publicize itself, the *Voice* instituted the Obie Awards in 1956. The paper is in sole control of the awards to this day. But the paper also moved from the world of greasepaint to the greasy world of New York politics. Almost from its inception, the *Voice* was a forum for activists opposed to Robert Moses' 1952 plan to build a four-lane highway through Washington Square. Among his most effective antagonists was *Voice* writer Mary Perot Nichols who, working with editor Dan Wolf, turned out to be a sharp investigative reporter. When the city banned traffic from the square permanently in August 1959, Moses was handed a very public defeat—and the *Village Voice* was regarded as a power to reckon with.

For the past decade the *Voice* has operated out of several floors at 842 Broadway, the building that replaced Wallack's Theatre in 1901. The weekly had hopscotched through several offices around the Village, from its 1959 perch on Sheridan Square to 80 University Place in 1970, the former offices of the *Evergreen Review*. The *Voice* itself has undergone several changes in policy over the years, reflecting changes in ownership. Editorial independence was first jeopardized in June 1974 when the corporation owning the *Village Voice* merged with the owner of slick and trendy *New York* magazine. Under successive managements the *Voice* has lost its unique position, but its journalistic and financial success can be credited with launching the raft of slick New York papers that now cover the downtown scene.

INVENTING "BROADWAY"

People began to associate Broadway with the theater in the 1870s when a theater district emerged in Greenwich Village. Before the century was out, Broadway and New York theater had become synonymous, the result of four decades of productions staged in the Village and on Union Square.

The city's first successful opera house, the Academy of Music, rose in 1854 on the northeast corner of Fourteenth Street and Irving Place. Publisher Horace Greeley thought it so ugly that he offered to cover the cost of burning it down. A dozen years later he got his wish, though not, evidently, a bill.

American musical comedy is most frequently traced back to *The Black Crook,* an 1866 extravaganza staged at Niblo's Garden on the northeast corner of Broadway at Prince Street. Built in 1849 on the site of a popular pleasure garden, Niblo's was joined three years later on the site by the lavish Metropolitan Hotel, making it the first theater-hotel combination built in America. *The Black Crook,* which opened at a time when hits ran continuously for only a few weeks, changed theater economics by running without a break for sixteen months.

Yet the production was an accident, fashioned by the wedding of a hackneyed drama of the Faust legend to a French ballet troupe stranded in New York when its intended theater burned. A hundred tons of scenery and elaborate stage effects were grafted onto the drama, and scantily clad girls in pink tights were added to the cast—bringing outraged ministers to their pulpits and a line of ticket buyers to Niblo's box office. Such spectacle remained identified with Niblo's Garden until 1895, when both it and the Metropolitan Hotel were replaced by the commercial structure that now stands on that site.

The theater that had burned, leaving the ballet troupe stranded, was also on the Broadway Strip. It was the Academy of Music, which opened in 1854. Six years later it was the scene of a spectacular ball honoring the dashing nineteen-year-old Prince of Wales. Even after its seats were removed to create a ballroom for 4,000, the Academy still wasn't large enough to admit all who wished to attend the social event of the century. To solve this problem, Grace Church sexton and social arbiter Isaac Hull Brown came aboard to help the committee compose its select guest list.

Rebuilt after the 1866 fire, the Academy of Music witnessed the American premieres of several operas: *Il Trovatore, Semiramide, La Traviata, Aïda, Die Walküre,* and *Carmen.* But when its limited number of prestigious boxes proved insufficient to accommodate the city's new millionaires, they organized themselves and retaliated by opening the Metropolitan Opera House in 1883, a move that wiped opera from the Academy stage within three years. It ended its days as a movie theater in May 1926, after which it was replaced by the present 530-foot Con Edison tower.

Just east of the Academy along Fourteenth Street stood Tammany Hall, the clubhouse used by "Boss" Tweed, Jim Fisk, and their political cronies. After the fall of the Tweed Ring, theater history was made here October 24, 1881, when in its ground-floor auditorium entrepreneur Tony Pastor offered the first variety show that was refined above the level of the Houston Street concert saloons. Pastor continued to present shows here for years, offering what is now called vaudeville—a word he hated, though it's forever linked to his name. It remained the chief source of light entertainment in America for the next thirty years.

Another Greenwich Village theater saw the introduction of another theatrical institution, the cliff-hanger. In 1867 at the Worrell Sisters' Theatre, 728 Broadway at Waverly Place, a play by Augustin Daly called *Under the Gaslight* left audiences breathless. Stage effects, which Daly had seen in London two years earlier, gave the impression of a train speeding across the stage seconds after the rescue of someone who had been tied to the track. Hollywood later improved the cliff-hanger, using real trains and tying the heroine to the tracks, but in Daly's version, she was the rescuer.

Wallack's historic theater on Broadway at Thirteenth Street, under its second name, the Star. It was replaced in 1902 by the present structure built by Rogers Peet & Co., the men's clothiers. Having made four decades of theatrical history, the theater made movie history in 1901 when its demolition became the subject of an early documentary film.

Daly is credited with originating the cliff-hanger, despite the British precedent; there the victim was run over, and the play flopped.

If a single theater can be credited with linking Broadway with theatrical excellence, it would undoubtedly be Wallack's Theatre on the northeast corner of Broadway and Thirteenth Street. Built in 1861 as the home for Lester Wallack's stock company, it introduced true ensemble playing to New York through classical and contemporary comedies. When Wallack's troupe moved to a new theater in 1881, the house began a second career as the Star Theatre. On its stage appeared Sarah Bernhardt, Edwin Booth, Sir Henry Irving, Ellen Terry, and Modjeska, and it remained the city's most prestigious theater until its demolition in 1901.

HOLLYWOOD ON THE HUDSON, PART 1

You might not connect Greenwich Village with motion pictures, but the advances made on Fourteenth Street were critical to film history, and only the first of several which were to occur in the Village.

In 1903 two furriers opened a penny arcade at 48 East Fourteenth Street, where the former Mays Department Store now stands. To supplement a none-too-profitable operation, the furriers added peep-show machines, which they promoted as "Automatic Vaudeville." One of the furriers was Adolph Zukor, who later founded Paramount Pictures; the other was Marcus Loew, soon to found the movie-theater chain that became the parent company of Metro-Goldwyn-Mayer. Their Automatic Vaudeville proved successful enough, and the partners opened a nickelodeon next door in 1906, one of the first theaters operated expressly to project motion pictures on a screen.

Some of the movies shown at their Comedy Theater came from the Biograph film studio a block or so away. The Biograph Film Company had built an indoor studio in a former mansion at 11 East Fourteenth Street. There they shot the films that began the careers of director Mack Sennett and actresses Mabel Normand, Mary Pickford, and Dorothy and Lillian Gish. It was in this studio that a young actor hired in 1907 soon found himself directing his first film. *The Adventures of Dollie* premiered at the Union Square Theatre on July 14, 1908, and though it showed promise, no one suspected that motion pictures would soon be revolutionized by its director, D. W. Griffith.

As the Father of American Cinema learned his craft on one side of Union Square, the Father of the Movie Palace began his own career on the other. Scots-born Thomas Lamb had studied architecture at Cooper Union, just below Union Square, and in 1909 was hired to design a new City Theatre on Union Square just east of

The penny arcade on Union Square South where the film careers of Adolph Zukor and Marcus Loew began.

The ballroom of the old Cunard mansion became home to Biograph, the pioneer film company. Today its site just west of Union Square is lost to a bland white brick apartment house.

Lüchow's Restaurant. Former Brooklyn clothier William Fox had only two design instructions: the theater had to seat 2,500, and it had to have a film projection booth, just in case. For his first commission, Lamb was therefore forced to plan, if only in part, for film. And when legitimate theater failed to draw crowds soon after the City Theatre's April 1910 opening, Fox shifted to a profitable film-and-vaudeville policy.

Fox went on to found a film studio that bore his name and that later merged with another company to form Twentieth Century-Fox. Lamb went on to design over three hundred movie palaces across the nation. Among his New York works were the Regent, the Strand, the Rialto, the Rivoli, the Capitol, and the Hollywood, all now demolished except the Regent in Harlem, which is in use as a church, and the Hollywood, now that most opulent of legitimate Broadway theaters, the Mark Hellinger. The City Theatre was demolished in 1952.

Another institution of the entertainment industry began in the Village: the theatrical agency. The first ones appeared on Bleecker Street in the 1860s. By 1875 talent agencies had invaded Union Square and were helping to turn the area into the city's first theatrical center. One innovation was the signing of star performers to long-term contracts with one agent, establishing the power stars retain to this day. Also of note is the young German immigrant who in 1885 became an apprentice at the Leavitt agency, which was run from a row house still standing at 149 West Thirteenth Street. In time the young man opened his own agency at 102 East Fourteenth Street, and the company William Morris founded there is today the world's oldest talent agency.

RESTAURANTS FOR DESSERT

The success of Italian and German opera troupes at the Academy of Music led to the rise of small immigrant neighborhoods east of Union Square. Two adventurous journalists soon discovered and wrote about these *ristorantes* and beer halls, which also attracted English-speaking New Yorkers who happily discovered European cuisine.

One of the early Italian family restaurants that welcomed native New Yorkers was Moretti's on Third Avenue at Fourteenth Street. This establishment is credited with having introduced to New York an intriguing new dish called spaghetti. Riccadona's, at 42 Union Square East, was a commercial version of an Italian family restaurant for those who were reluctant to try the real thing. But the real thing prospered on nearby Third Avenue as Buchignani's. Writer James L. Ford saw little of interest in "sirloin society," and preferred to immerse himself in gnocchi and Chianti. His essays,

Spaghetti was still regarded as an exotic dish when this photograph was taken in 1917. This meal is being served by Grace Godwin in her Washington Square South garret.

collected in 1895 as *Bohemia Invaded*, brought Buchignani's a clutch of celebrity regulars including writers Frank Norris and Stephen Crane.

James Huneker was another intrepid writer who was interested enough in bohemia to have visited Paris in search of it in 1878. Little he saw there excited him as much as his 1886 discovery of Lüchow's, a German family restaurant operating across Fourteenth Street from the Academy of Music. Its modest operations here had begun while Huneker was in Paris, and were sold by founder Otto von Muhlbach in 1882 to his head waiter, August Lüchow. On the strength of Huneker's 1886 essay, Lüchow's became the city's leading ethnic restaurant, a popularity that was spread nationwide in 1902 by an oom-pah-pah hit song called "Down Where the Wurtzburger Flows," inspired by Lüchow's best beer. Fittingly, it was under Lüchow's stained-glass skylights in 1913 that Victor Herbert pressed his fellow composers to form ASCAP, America's first society for the protection of musical compositions.

Lüchow's glittering multicolored skylights are now dark. In the late 1970s, a new management mistakenly imagined that business might improve if the restaurant left its historic home and moved to a sunken plaza in Midtown. In its centennial year, 1982, Lüchow's left Fourteenth Street—and went out of business less than four years later.

Lüchow's as it looked in 1938. One door away on East Fourteenth Street is the marquee of Thomas Lamb's City Theatre, gussied up to attract an audience. This ploy worked for another fourteen years.

Its abandoned birthplace still stands. Its musty rooms are silent where generations of families reveled amid schnitzel and schmaltz for the annual Oktoberfest, or for Christmas under a traditional *Tannenbaum,* which each year literally branched up through the ceiling. However, with the economic rebirth of Union Square in the 1980s, a developer has acquired both Lüchow's and a neighboring property, and he plans to incorporate part but not all of the old restaurant into his condominium-retail complex. Preservationists are pressuring in the hope that all of Lüchow's can be saved and that when the dust of construction settles, those historic doors will once again open on a great dining room from the square's glamorous past.

UNION SQUARE

Though it is technically one block north of Greenwich Village, Union Square developed in conjunction with the Broadway Strip to the south, not the Midtown blocks now surrounding it. Union Square's prime connections have always been with Greenwich Village.

It was conceived in 1811 as Union Place, for the projected union of Broadway to the Bowery. Because that union never occurred, the square itself wasn't laid out until 1831 and required another decade to become a fashionable address. But commercial establishments soon encroached on the square, causing the wealthy to flee the area as quickly as they had arrived. Before they did, they joined residents of nearby Lafayette Place in trying to keep the area exclusive. A lawless slum was festering at the southern end of the

As early as the 1890s Union Square became a forum for dissenting voices, and those involved in economic protests were ideal targets for the discount stores that opened on the square. S. Klein, an ungainly thrift-shop paradise, began its ramshackle occupancy of several hotels and restaurants in 1921. Seen here in 1936, the store faded from Union Square East in the 1970s. Its shell survived until 1984 when the imposing Zeckendorf Towers rose on the site.

Bowery, giving the entire length of it a very bad name. In 1849 residents successfully pressured the city to cosmetically keep the Bowery away by renaming its blocks between Sixth and Fourteenth streets. The name Fourth Avenue is still in use to this day, but the tactic didn't work—and the rich had abandoned Union Square by 1855.

At first, the commercial and theatrical ventures moving into the square were high-class affairs. In addition to the 1854 Academy of Music, the block east of the square in 1866 welcomed Steinway Hall, New York's leading concert venue prior to the opening of Carnegie Hall. Tiffany's opened its regal new shop in 1870 on Union Square West at Fifteenth Street and remained there for thirty-five years. Though stripped of its contents and its elegant cast-iron facade, the former palace of jewels still stands, unrecognizable in sterile masonry.

Another longtime survivor was the Union Square Theatre, opened in 1871 on Union Square South between Fourth Avenue and Broadway. Here in 1876 occurred the New York stage debut of matinee idol James O'Neill, whose declining years were to be dramatized by his playwright son Eugene in *Long Day's Journey into Night*. This theater was also the setting on August 20, 1883, of the first performance anywhere of a play by Oscar Wilde—though *Vera, or the Nihilist*, a premiere that the author attended, proved a disaster and barely finished out the week. Here George M. Cohan made his debut as a solo performer, soon after the Union Square began a vaudeville policy in 1893. Two years later the Union Square became one of the earliest established theaters to project motion pictures. Initially a novelty on the vaudeville bill, motion pictures completely replaced live acts at this theater in 1908. Since 1936, the theater has been closed. Its orchestra section has been replaced by shops at street level, and its upper reaches are hidden behind a brick wall erected across the proscenium arch. How much of its interior survives has long been a matter of speculation and may only be learned when the historic house is torn down for development of the site, a plan to be implemented in the early 1990s.

Also scheduled to vanish is the Palladium, the high-tech disco that opened in May 1985 inside a 1926 movie palace designed by Thomas Lamb. Built at the time the old Academy of Music was being demolished, the 2,600-seat cinema took for itself the name of the opera house facing it across Fourteenth Street, but it bore no other resemblance to the original. The building had served for several years as a rock concert venue when Arata Isozaki was asked to adapt the classic theater for use as a slick disco, which he did by honoring rather than obliterating its staid interior. To his dance floor he added such video innovations as two banks of twenty-five monitors each, programmed by computer. The Palladium also featured a private VIP club, its Mike Todd Room, which early in 1988 became Exile, a popular "juice bar" for the underage party crowd. But the potential profits of development of the site evidently doomed the Palladium to vanish in the 1990s.

With the construction of Zeckendorf Towers, a huge apartment building, as the driving engine for rebirth, a 1980s reconstruction program reclaimed Union Square Park from resident derelicts and drug pushers. Now, three days each week, from spring into the late fall, more than forty vendors truck farm goods here from Pennsylvania, New Jersey, upstate New York, and Long Island. And so a new farmers' market prospers on the square, evoking memories of similar markets that operated on this site 175 years ago, in the years before Union Square was born.

Union Square today, looking north from Broadway at Fourteenth Street.

A farmers' market returns to Union Square.

4 THE NORTH VILLAGE

The Lone Star Café on Fifth Avenue, with its unlikely emblem of the North Village.

The irregular quadrant of the Village north of Washington Square is largely residential, its sedate tone set by its main thoroughfare, Fifth Avenue. From the arch northward, the Village blocks of Fifth Avenue have offered classy features to rival their uptown counterparts: schools, churches, mansions, and museums—and a ninety-foot iguana known as Iggie. Through the 1980s, Iggie was the irreverent guardian of Lower Fifth Avenue, a shock the first time you saw her, but in short order a sight as welcome

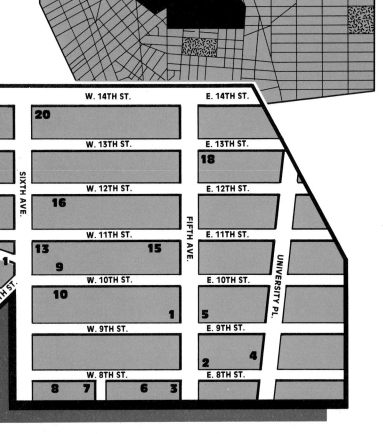

as an old friend.

Erected in 1977 over the protests of the Fifth Avenue Association, the iguana was the emblem of the Lone Star Café at the corner of Thirteenth Street—for years the city's most popular country-western music showcase. The Lone Star's success indirectly brought on its downfall—it was so successful that its rent more than tripled—and the club closed early in 1989. But while Iggie held sway, she proved the North Village wasn't as predictable as it seemed.

On one North Village street the forerunner of modern cinemas was built and is still in operation. Not far away from it a studio for artists was built that paved the way for the concept of apartment living. On Eleventh Street, a 1970 explosion turned a stately row house into an inferno and

1   Site of Brevoort Mansion

2   Site of Brevoort Hotel

3   Site of Johnston's White House (8 Fifth Ave.)

4   Site of Cedar Street Tavern

5   Site of Mabel Dodge apartment (23 Fifth Ave.)

6   Former Whitney Museum of American Art

7   Former Bon Soir (site of Van Twiller homestead)

8   Eighth Street Playhouse

9   Site of Tenth Street Studio

10   Site of Tile Club (58½ W. 10th St.)

11   Milligan Place

12   Patchin Place

13   Site of the Grapevine

14   Site of Rhinelander Garden and Garden Row

15   18 W. 11th St.

16   The New School

17   St. Vincent's Hospital

18   Former Lone Star Café

19   St. Vincent's Outpatient Building (former National Maritime Union Building)

20   Site of the original Macy's

reduced to ashes the radical idealism of the 1960s. On Twelfth Street, Jewish educators fleeing Nazi oppression found refuge in a school whose architect was also the set designer of the Ziegfeld Follies. Both the Whitney Museum and the Metropolitan Museum of Art had their origins here on blocks that have blossomed with the paintings and sculptures of the Washington Square Outdoor Art Exhibit every spring and fall since 1931.

This is a neighborhood that grew up around Fifth Avenue—and Fifth Avenue owes its fashionable reputation to the son of the man who "saved" Broadway: Henry Brevoort.

ON THE AVENUE   Seven years before Hendrick Brevoort's death in 1841, his son Henry took a muddy plot near the southwest corner of the family farm, and there built for himself a stately Greek revival mansion. Though Fifth Avenue had been planned in 1811 and built up to Thirteenth Street by 1824, it was still shabby and unpaved when Brevoort began construction on the northwest corner of Ninth Street. His understated but elegant 1834 mansion stood for a time amid rude structures of no architectural pretension, but by the mid-1840s his neighbors were among the wealthiest men in New York.

Henry Brevoort's mansion stood until 1925, when it was taken down to make way for the Fifth Avenue Hotel, which presently occupies the site. His name has remained attached to lower Fifth Avenue, first through the Brevoort Hotel, which stood for a century

Henry Brevoort's mansion at 24 Fifth Avenue, above Ninth Street. Seen here around 1850, it established Fifth Avenue as the fashionable address for the wealthy.

The Brevoort Hotel, Fifth Avenue between Eighth and Ninth streets, around 1908.

at the northeast corner of Eighth Street. The Brevoort, which opened in 1854, rambled agreeably through the four row houses from which it was fashioned. Today the name has been taken by the block-long apartment complex for which the Brevoort was demolished in 1954.

Villagers took special pride in the Brevoort Hotel, behaving as if they were all part owners. Service was always impeccable and the food superior, setting an Old World standard that few other New York hotels ever rivaled. Yet the Brevoort remained personal in its tone, a cherished bit of Paris tucked away in Greenwich Village. One of its hallmarks was a famous basement café where marble-topped tables were set into small, secluded nooks, separated by mirrored walls. Here indolent chess-playing Frenchmen were often as numerous as diners, lending to the café a Continental touch that was prized by Village radicals and the wealthier locals as well. In pre-radio days, this relaxed atmosphere was punctuated by the clatter of the café's own news ticker, which provided diners with stock market prices, news reports, and a cherished Brevoort game. As the ticker tape punched out news items, local wags reading the words aloud would amuse guests by devising fantastic or ironic endings for sentences still being typed, becoming off-the-cuff political comics.

For many years the Brevoort was owned by French-born Raymond Orteig, who bought it in 1902 a few months after purchasing the city's other leading French hotel, the Martin, which stood around the corner on University Place. Celebrating Franco-

The Washington Square Outdoor Art Exhibit, a Village fixture each spring and fall, was first held in 1931. In the background is the Brevoort, an apartment building that stands at Eighth Street and Fifth Avenue on the site of the elegant Brevoort Hotel, which it replaced.

The program for Charles Lindbergh's prize presentation at the Brevoort Hotel.

American friendship, Orteig renamed his first purchase the Hotel Lafayette, but the Brevoort retained its given name and in the 1920s played a role in an even greater link between the two countries.

Orteig announced a competition to encourage attempts at a nonstop solo flight from New York to Paris. The prize: $25,000. Several pilots tried, but honors were taken in May 1927 by a youth named Charles Lindbergh in his plane, the *Spirit of St. Louis*. A riotous ticker-tape parade celebrated the flier's return to New York, bringing him to the Brevoort Hotel where, on the morning of June 17, with air pioneer Orville Wright among the guests, Lindbergh received his prize money from a very proud Raymond Orteig.

THE WHITE HOUSE

Diagonally across from the Brevoort Hotel site is the modern apartment tower at number 2 Fifth Avenue, with the Minetta Brook fountain in its lobby. Although no plaque on the building's north wall will tell you, New York's Metropolitan Museum of Art was founded on this site, in the stable at 4 West Eighth Street, which was attached to the White House belonging to John Taylor Johnston.

Like his father, who built the glorious row houses on the square east of Fifth Avenue and founded New York University, Johnston was destined to achieve note as a builder and the founder of a great institution. In 1856, Johnston moved into the mansion he had built for himself on the southwest corner of Fifth Avenue at Eighth Street. New Yorkers came to gawk and marvel, for it was the first residence in the city to be built of white marble. However, it lacked a gallery in which Johnston could display his growing collection of great artworks. His solution was to hang the paintings on the second floor of the private stable behind his house. The spreading fame of this collection led Johnston in time to open his makeshift gallery to the public on Thursday afternoons.

In 1870 a gathering of art collectors at Johnston's White House raised the idea of founding in New York a permanent public art collection. With Johnston as its first elected president, this Metropolitan Museum of Art opened in temporary quarters at 681 Fifth Avenue, near Fifty-third Street, then took more permanent space in the former Douglas mansion at 126 West Fourteenth Street. The museum remained there from 1873 until 1879, drawing larger crowds yearly and playing a key role in attracting working artists to

Greenwich Village. Many of them remained in the Village after the museum moved to its permanent home on upper Fifth Avenue. The Metropolitan stands today as one of the premier repositories of art in the world, behind a majestic Fifth Avenue facade designed by Village architect Richard Morris Hunt.

John Taylor Johnston's White House at 8 Fifth Avenue, as it appeared in 1936. His stable, back along Eighth Street, was the birthplace of the Metropolitan Museum of Art.

THE ORIGINAL CEDAR

No one ever seemed to care that the Cedar Street Tavern was actually on University Place. Most of its regulars were just glad the bar was there, when they were sober enough to think that much.

The present Cedar Tavern is not the Cedar Tavern of fame; it's the replacement, opened near Eleventh Street in the early 1960s after its predecessor was forced to close. The Brevoort East apartments now obliterate the site of 24 University Place, between Eighth and Ninth streets, where the original Cedar thrived. And while it thrived, it was something.

It was what used to be called "a man's bar," not only because most of the patrons were male but because fists often flew in direct proportion to the number of drinks downed. But unlike other two-fisted bars, an altercation here was usually over Abstract Expressionism or Beat poetry. Beginning in the late 1950s, the Cedar was a hangout for the new divinities of American art. They may have been remote or pugnacious but they were all here: Franz Kline, Willem de Kooning, Larry Rivers, and more. Cedar regular Jackson Pollock kicked in the men's room door one night and was banned from the bar for a month. And even the Cedar's most famous patron was banished, though there are two versions of the legend: one published account has Jack Kerouac barred because he pissed into a stand-up ashtray, but Kerouac biographer Gerald Nicosia asserts it was a sink.

The Cedar Street Tavern is mentioned in the poetry of Frank O'Hara, who lived at nearby 90 University in the late 1950s. Joining him at the tavern were such writers as LeRoi Jones, Allen Ginsberg, Kenneth Koch, and at one time or another most of the hip and the cool of the day. But after it moved to 82 University the steam seemed to go out of the Cedar, and much of the action shifted to new spots in the blossoming East Village. The Cedar enjoyed a brief revival of popularity in the 1970s, when it became something of a clubhouse for staffers on the *Village Voice,* which had moved its offices into a squat building at the corner of Eleventh. Today the glory days of the Cedar are memories for those lucky enough to have been part of that scene. They had such fun at the Cedar that they might not have noticed the way its mingling of artist and uptowner conferred legitimacy on the experimental art of the day.

Village Voices

"At the Cedar, *everybody* looked unattractive."

Clement Greenberg, as quoted by John Gruen in *The Party's Over Now,* 1972

VILLAGE LANDMARKS: ALONG FIFTH AVENUE

The Church of the Ascension on Fifth Avenue at Tenth Street is prized for its architecture and its art. Built in 1841, it was the work of architect Richard Upjohn just prior to his design for the present Trinity Church at Wall Street. Fifty years after the church opened, architect Stanford White renovated its interior with the assistance of several gifted friends. Behind the marble altar carved by Augustus Saint-Gaudens rises a huge mural by John La Farge, often considered his finest work. La Farge also created several of the church's distinctive stained-glass windows using opal glass panels devised by Louis C. Tiffany.

The last mansion along lower Fifth Avenue to survive intact is the 1852 Irad Hawley House at 47 Fifth Avenue, now a designated city landmark. Built for the president of the Pennsylvania Coal Company, its faithfully restored interiors are a fitting home for the Greenwich Village Society for Historic Preservation as well as for the Salmagundi Club, America's oldest surviving arts society.

Washington Irving was among those authors to contribute to *The Salmagundi Papers,* the popular 1807 satires from which the club took its name. Irving is remembered by a gold-colored plaque that shines unnoticed on the Ninth Street side of the Brevoort apartments, recalling Irving's visits to a now-vanished house at 21 Fifth Avenue. Built by architect James Renwick, Jr., for himself in 1851, the house featured a study designed expressly for Washington Irving, who made frequent use of his friend's hospitality. Mark Twain lived here from 1904 through 1908. Here he wrote his last great fiction, *The Mysterious Stranger* as well as the fanciful memoir that was passed off as autobiography after his death. In May 1925, Twain's only surviving daughter, Mrs. Clara Grabrilowitsch, dedicated this plaque, which was saved when 21 Fifth Avenue was demolished. It still shines for those who are sharp-eyed enough to spot it.

The Village tradition of opening private art galleries to the public finds its latest incarnation at 60 Fifth Avenue, courtesy of the late Malcolm Forbes. Since 1985, the street level of the austere Forbes Magazine Building has offered one of the most lavishly designed exhibits, inch for inch, in the world. Reflecting Forbes's eclectic tastes, the display includes a rare signed copy of the Gettysburg Address as part of a collection of presidential ephemera; more than five hundred antique toy boats and twelve thousand toy soldiers are set within an animated diorama of clever design that uses mirrors for trick effects. In a separate gallery are quintessential works by such masters as Reginald Marsh, Gilbert Stuart, Edward Hopper, John Sloan, Paul Cadmus, and Andy Warhol, several of which depict Village scenes. The highlight of the Forbes Gallery is its treasures from the House of Fabergé—the largest private holding of such items in the world. Of these the reigning glories are the twelve bejeweled Easter eggs created by Peter Carl Fabergé for the last of the Russian czars. Incidentally, until Forbes purchased this 1925 building in the 1960s, it was for forty years the home of Macmillan. The publisher issued innumerable volumes from this structure, including *Gone with the Wind* in 1936.

In the 1920s, the adjacent building at 66 Fifth Avenue housed the offices of the Boni Brothers, Albert and Charles, who entered publishing by way of their Washington Square Book Shop on MacDougal Street. Initially they had joined with Horace Liveright

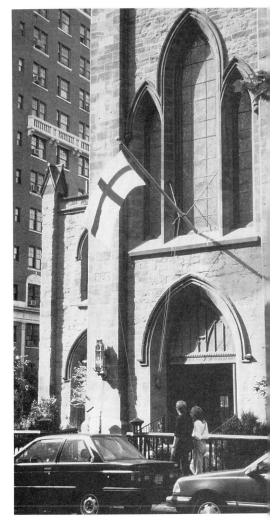

When John Tyler wed Julia Gardiner at the Church of the Ascension in 1844, he became the first President to marry in office. The bride's family, of Gardiners Island fame, lived in Colonnade Row on Lafayette Place at the time.

as Boni & Liveright. This firm published works by many Villagers, and it also devised the popular Modern Library series. By 1923, the Boni Brothers had established their own concern, which published works by Upton Sinclair, Carl Van Doren, D. H. Lawrence, and Marcel Proust, along with the Pulitzer Prize–winning *Bridge of San Luis Rey* by Thornton Wilder. In time, apartments on the upper floors of 66 Fifth Avenue were home to actor-producer John Houseman and to dancer Martha Graham. More recently, and well into the 1970s, its street level and cavernous basement were the home of the disorganized but well-stocked Dauber & Pine secondhand book shop. Today that space has been rebuilt as a computer resource center for the New School.

VILLAGE PEOPLE: MABEL DODGE

Mabel Dodge, in one of the flowing gowns she favored.

Mabel Dodge's impact on the American scene derived more from what she was than from anything she did. In her few years in the Village, she became something of a combined muse and den mother. The Buffalo-born Mabel arrived in New York with her estranged second husband, architect Edwin Dodge, in November 1912, after several years in an Italian villa above Florence. There she had become close friends with Leo and Gertrude Stein, and the subject of *Portrait of Mabel Dodge at the Villa Curonia,* a prose portrait by the poet, which won Mabel Dodge fame among the New York literati even before she moved into the second floor of 23 Fifth Avenue.

The building was then owned by an irascible ninety-two-year-old hero of the Battle of Gettysburg, General Dan Sickles, whose ground-floor apartment was festooned with patriotic bunting and filled with glass cases of military medals and swords. The decor of Mabel's suite stood in bold contrast to that of her landlord—and of almost any rooms the Village had seen. Her large parlor was a shocking white: white ceiling, white wallpaper, white woodwork, white porcelain chandelier, white bearskin rug, and white marble fireplace. The few spots of color—the silver-blue sofa and chairs, a vase of cut flowers—achieved heightened vibrancy in this setting. So did the hostess herself.

Word of Mabel Dodge spread quickly through the Village. Among the first to meet her were sculptor Jo Davidson and writers Hutchins Hapgood and Lincoln Steffens. Davidson was soon at work on a bust of Mabel while Hapgood, a noted columnist for the New York *Globe,* noticed her unique ability to foster lively discussions among others. Steffens soon encouraged Mabel to host gatherings once a week. Mabel would select a topic for unstructured discussion among guests, possibly with an occasional guest speaker. Late in January 1913, the first of these Wednesday evening gather-

The interior of 23 Fifth Avenue, as arranged by Mabel Dodge for her weekly gatherings.

ings was held, beginning what many have called the most successful salon in American history.

Typically dressed in a flowing silk gown and a great floppy hat, Mabel welcomed to her home all comers. Walter Lippmann was then a budding socialist about to issue his first book, *A Preface to Politics,* but he was poised and well educated. At the other extreme was Harry Kemp, the disheveled and manic "tramp poet" of Greenwich Village who, as many jokingly insisted, came chiefly for the midnight buffet Mabel offered after each gathering. In between was a heady mix: writer Carl Van Doren, the first prophet of the jazz era; Max Eastman, recently bounced off the Columbia University faculty and into the editorship of the stylish radical magazine, the *Masses;* Henrietta Rodman, a feminist of terrierlike determination, who fought to retain her job as a public school teacher when, like other women, she was fired when she got married; Margaret Sanger, pioneer advocate of the right of women to receive birth control information; Emma Goldman, the anarchist and writer whose very name raised the blood pressure of corporate America; poets Amy Lowell and Edwin Arlington Robinson; writers Floyd Dell and Frank Harris; painters Charles Demuth, Marsden Hartley, and John Sloan; labor activist "Big" Bill Haywood; political cartoonist Art Young; and anarchist Hippolyte Havel.

The Mabel Dodge salon marked the first time a cross section of society had gathered together to explore the social and political

The 1913 Armory Art Show, at which Americans first confronted modern art. Pictured in the foreground is Gallery A, American sculpture and decorative art. Beyond it, at the center, is Gallery R, French, English, and Swiss painting.

implications of sexual, artistic, and economic change. Socialism was a hot topic at these salons, as was workers' rights—fired, so to speak, by the Triangle disaster two years earlier. Sexual equality and free love were the topics of several gatherings, one of which ended when a Villager named Babs embraced sexual equality by announcing her availability to any man present. Another gathering offered one of the earliest public discussions of psychoanalysis in New York and featured as guest speaker a Freud disciple and translator, Dr. A. A. Brill.

The Dodge salon also played a role in two 1913 events that had far-reaching importance. One was the Armory Show, which introduced modern art and design to America; the other was a strike pageant that vividly demonstrated the political power of art. Both events occurred fifteen blocks north of the Village, but both were Village products that involved and fortified the members of the new Village community.

Mabel Dodge was one of the sponsors of the Armory Art Show, which opened February 13, 1913, not in a respectable gallery but in the musty 69th Regiment Armory, which still stands on Lexington Avenue at Twenty-sixth Street. The prime organizers of the exhibit were Villagers who had been members of the Eight, under the direction of one of their number, Arthur B. Davies. The show's 1,300 works confronted the public both with the work of these Villagers and with the new European art of Picasso, Cézanne, Matisse, Gauguin, Seurat, and Marcel Duchamp, whose *Nude Descending a Staircase* elicited howls of protest. An insular nation accustomed to sentimental representational art reeled when the social ferment seething just out of view appeared on the walls of the armory. And when the furor died down, art collector Lillie Bliss purchased the works that later formed the nucleus of the collection of New York's Museum of Modern Art.

Art wasn't the only current topic of the Dodge salon in February 1913. Silk workers striking in Paterson, New Jersey, were being assaulted by local police in an attempt to force them to end their walkout. One striker had even been murdered by the police, yet no news of the strike had appeared in any city publication other than the radical *Masses*. Mabel Dodge suggested that a strike pageant be staged in the city, an enactment of strike events spectacular enough to end the news blackout—but who would write and stage such a tremendous undertaking? Across the room, the Golden Boy of Greenwich Village raised his hand. "I'll do it," John Reed announced.

In staging the Paterson Strike Pageant in Madison Square Garden on June 7, 1913, John Reed first tasted the activism and social concerns that altered his life and marked his final few years. He drew his cast from among the striking workers themselves. He had them reenact the police riot and the murder of Modestino Valentino before a packed house of 17,000 New Yorkers. The sets were the work of one of Mabel's friends, designer Robert Edmund Jones (soon to win Broadway acclaim) and were painted by another,

"Picketing the Mills," a scene from the Paterson Strike Pageant of 1913, photographed in performance at Madison Square Garden.

When the doors below this Art Deco eagle opened in 1931, the Whitney became the first museum in the nation devoted less to preserving an artistic heritage than to creating one.

John Sloan. Mabel herself became involved on quite another level—she took John Reed as a lover.

In time their open affair proved stifling to them both, though not before it set several key events into motion. One was the next phase in Reed's career. Intent on avoiding Mabel Dodge, Reed became a war correspondent and covered first the Mexican and then the Russian revolution; the latter led him to write his journalistic landmark, *Ten Days That Shook the World*. Meanwhile, the Reed-Dodge affair was dramatized in *Constancy*, a short play written by Hutchins Hapgood's wife, Neith Boyce. It received its informal premiere on Cape Cod in the summer of 1915, in the Provincetown cottage the Hapgoods had taken. That same night saw a second amateur performance, a satire of the vogue for Freudianism by Susan Glaspell called *Suppressed Desires*. Additional performances followed that summer and the following summer, after which the players attempted a New York season in the Village, where they all lived. Few gave their venture much hope, but the Provincetown Players had made a discovery on Cape Cod in the summer of 1916—a trunkful of unproduced plays written by a youthful Greenwich Village drunk named Eugene O'Neill.

And so Mabel Dodge's final act as a muse was to inspire a theater group with which she had no contact. By the time Eugene O'Neill won his first Pulitzer Prize in 1920, Mabel Dodge was living in New Mexico, where she died in 1962.

THE WHITNEY MUSEUM

The Whitney Museum of American Art reflects the tastes of its founder, Gertrude Vanderbilt Whitney, the wealthy great-granddaughter of shipping and railroad magnate Cornelius Vanderbilt. Not far from the Washington Place site of his 1846 mansion, she turned a MacDougal Alley stable into her personal art studio. There she collected works by American artists, many of whom were friends whose paintings she bought when they were in need of funds. Adding to her initial 1908 purchases of works by the Eight, she developed a collection that by 1929 exceeded six hundred items. Convinced they should be seen by the public, she offered her collection to the Metropolitan Museum of Art which, to her astonishment, declined the offer. Piqued, she decided to open her own museum devoted to contemporary American art.

Accordingly, she purchased three row houses on Eighth Street that adjoined her studio and had them rebuilt as a single structure behind a unifying facade of pink stucco. The Whitney Museum proved an instant success. Its November 1931 opening ceremonies were broadcast live by CBS Radio. Eighth Street businesses closed amid the crush of celebrities who were invited that day to explore the Whitney's dignified presentation of works by Charles Demuth, Georgia O'Keeffe, and Stuart Davis. The Whitney remained a popular Village attraction until 1954, when a need for more space forced it to move uptown. The combined buildings at 8 West Eighth Street now house the New York Studio School of Drawing, Painting, and Sculpture. The Art Deco eagle still spreads its wings above the Eighth Street entrance—Gertrude Vanderbilt Whitney would undoubtedly be pleased.

Gertrude Vanderbilt Whitney, as painted in 1916 by Robert Henri, a member of the Eight.

VILLAGE PEOPLE: RANDOLPH BOURNE

Most shops along Eighth Street occupy the street level of former row houses. An obvious exception is the undistinguished strip of one-story shops built in 1967 from 16 to 22 West Eighth Street. Among the houses it replaced was the one in which a great thinker of this century died. Randolph Bourne pushed American intellectuals into the deep water beyond easy platitudes and wishful thinking, though he struggled against deforming physical handicaps.

Bourne's body had been twisted by a "messy" birth, then further wrenched at the age of four by spinal tuberculosis. His growth was stunted, his back severely hunched, and his facial features misshapen, but Bourne was talented and ambitious; his writings appeared in the prestigious *Atlantic Monthly* even before his 1913 graduation from Columbia University. The following year he joined the staff of the *New Republic*, which had recently been founded as a journal of social introspection. For it Bourne produced some three hundred penetrating essays on varied subjects, which made him the idol of radical Village intellectuals.

The esteemed Village philosopher and writer Randolph Bourne.

Bourne became a regular and welcome sight along Charles Street, his misshapen body partly concealed by the black cape that became his trademark. In person, as in his prose, he sparked the minds of others; introspection characterized his own development, as he detailed in his noted essay, "A Philosophy of Handicap." Yet Bourne's principal theme—the conflict between the individualist and social democracy—led him to oppose all restrictions on dissent, bringing him into sharp conflict with the rising pro-war hysteria. Woodrow Wilson's neutrality seemed to Bourne a sham, and because he insisted on saying so, he quit the increasingly hawkish *New Republic*.

Bourne's stinging attacks on government repression next appeared in *Seven Arts* magazine, giving rise to rumors that its patron, Mrs. A. K. Raskine, was supporting a pro-German publication. Stung, she withdrew her support, silencing *Seven Arts*. After the war, as America tried to sort out its values, Randolph Bourne was stricken with influenza during the worldwide epidemic that took 600,000 American lives in the winter of 1918–19. Bourne was in the care of friends at 18 West Eighth Street when he died on December 22, 1918, at the age of thirty-two. Greenwich Village, which was reeling from so many deaths, went into mourning for Bourne and for the flinty integrity that had been lost.

THE LAYERED LOOK

Some Village locations seem to have one layer of history after another and turn up through the years in various guises and situations. One such site is the southwest corner of Eighth and MacDougal streets.

Today the corner is occupied by a nondescript one-story row of shops built in 1937. Between two of these shops, a door at 40 West Eighth Street leads to the new home of the Cafe Feenjon, which moved here in September 1989, after years on MacDougal Street. But in the late 1950s and early 1960s, this basement was the hottest entertainment spot in town, the legendary Bon Soir.

In her memoir, *Enter Talking,* Joan Rivers recalled the Bon Soir as an elegant room with a receptive and sharp crowd of regulars; once you made it to this basement pinnacle, your career was on its way. That's how it was for Rivers, though her stint here was overshadowed by an unknown eighteen-year-old from Brooklyn. This young singer had just won a talent contest at the Lion, a gay bar around the corner at 62 West Ninth Street, and an appearance at the Bon Soir was her prize. It was just prior to this appearance that she changed the spelling of her name and, as Barbra Streisand, she was held over at the Bon Soir—continuing there for eleven weeks. Even so, the Bon Soir could not keep this discovery

Village Voices

"The Duplex had no stage, just an area. . . . One unisex bathroom was at the rear of the performing area [and] always, on the punch line, the toilet flushed."

Joan Rivers,
in her autobiography,
Enter Talking, 1986

to itself for long; in addition to appearances at the Duplex in Sheridan Square, Streisand soon found herself on television, in her first featured role on Broadway, and signed to a contract with Columbia Records. A color photo of Streisand in performance at the Bon Soir became the cover of her first record album, a lasting tribute to her exciting early days in Greenwich Village.

Prior to 1937, this site appears in Village history as the location of the Hotel Gonfarone, which rambled fitfully through the several wood frame houses that were built here in the early 1800s. Run for years by an Italian family, the Gonfarone cellar became an early Italian restaurant, offering the nightly table d'hôte feasts that helped popularize Italian food among New Yorkers before the turn of the century.

Those frame structures replaced an earlier layer of Village history. It was here that Wouter Van Twiller, second director of the New Amsterdam colony, had his hilltop homestead built in 1633, one that stood for more than 170 years.

THE FIRST 100% CINEMA

Ornate movie palaces were still the rule in 1928 when the Film Guild Cinema in Greenwich Village introduced the unadorned cinema design that is now the norm. Billed as "the first 100% cinema," this theater at 52 West Eighth Street used no curtain to suggest a stage. Instead, the audience was confronted by the screen, a naked white rectangle set within an adjustable black frame. Circular in shape, the frame resembled the lens of a camera—in fact, the cinema itself resembled an old-fashioned box camera, with walls that sloped inward like a bellows and a facade on Eighth Street that was designed to evoke the mechanics of a film magazine.

Though somewhat rebuilt, the interior of this movie theater still employs the design concepts pioneered here by architect Frederick Kiesler. As the Eighth Street Playhouse, it has remained for over half a century a popular neighborhood cinema.

The Eighth Street Playhouse as it appears today. Electric Lady Sound Studios are hidden below street level, where a "goofy" club once operated.

Clinton Court, extending south from Eighth Street, as it looked in 1915. One of the charming enclaves that gave Greenwich Village its reputation for oddities, Clinton Court was demolished in 1927 to make way for the construction of the present Eighth Street Playhouse.

LONG-RUN CHAMPS

Village Voices

"We progressed, my Brazilians and I, majestically up to Sheridan Square, creating a sensation of the first water. . . . We waltzed along Eighth Street, white uniforms to the right and left of us, until we came to a large sign that said 'Village Barn. Air-Cooled.' . . . Eileen kept saying that she never thought she would end up at a place like the Village Barn with a good section of a South American navy. My sister is an anti-militarist."

Ruth McKenney,
in her novel,
My Sister Eileen, 1938

The Eighth Street Playhouse could make the Guinness Book of World Records for providing the most viewings of a single film in a theater. When it took over the midnight weekend screenings of *The Rocky Horror Picture Show* from the Waverly Theatre a decade ago, it also acquired a moviegoer named Sal Piro. Soon after the film began its midnight sneak previews at the Waverly—Twentieth Century-Fox never officially released the film with a first run—Mr. Piro was among those who began talking back to the movie, duplicating its dances in the aisles, and celebrating the cinematic wedding of Brad and Janet by pelting the screen with rice. By May 1988, Piro had seen this film over 1,100 times—that's equal to seventy-five days and nights of nonstop viewing. As president of the film's fan club, he oversees the mayhem that descends on the Eighth Street Playhouse each Friday and Saturday at midnight.

Tucked under this theater are the Electric Lady Sound Studios, built in the late 1960s by rock star Jimi Hendrix. But there's something else operating under the Eighth Street Playhouse, something that's been running even longer than *The Rocky Horror Picture Show.*

Years ago this site was excavated below street level to a depth of about 100 feet to permit a club called the Village Barn to open under the movie theater. A late entry in the "goofy" club vogue, the Barn featured milk pails, haystacks, and hillbilly singers, and it remained popular through the late 1950s, when it closed. But flooding had almost kept it from opening. Subway excavation on Sixth Avenue had temporarily diverted underground streams and prevented them from seeping into the Village Barn dig. Once the subway pumps were shut off, developers of this site were forced to install water pumps to keep the Village Barn dry, and they have been in operation twenty-four hours a day ever since.

VILLAGE PEOPLE: THE MUCKRAKER OF NINTH STREET

Ida Tarbell, a pioneer of modern investigative reporting, in April 1904—a few months before her *History of the Standard Oil Company* appeared in book form.

Once upon a time, present-day petroleum giants Amoco, Chevron, Mobil, and Exxon were all a part of a single and unbelievably powerful company called Standard Oil. Its owner was corporate Goliath John D. Rockefeller, and its slayer was a tall, dark-haired woman with the unlikely name of Ida Tarbell who lived at 40 West Ninth Street.

She had been born in 1857 in Titusville, Pennsylvania, two years before the first oil drilling changed the fortunes of that sleepy town. In 1873, Rockefeller squeezed local independents, including Tarbell's father, into ruin in his ruthless drive to build an oil monopoly. It was the sort of thing this determined and intelligent woman would neither forgive nor forget, particularly after she began to make a name for herself as a writer who was adept at the new Literature of Exposure.

In 1899, Tarbell came to New York as an editor and contributor for *McClure's* magazine. She rented an apartment in the 1882 building on Ninth Street because she enjoyed the ambience of Greenwich Village, which reminded her of her formative years in Paris. After writing for *McClure's* a humanized portrait of Lincoln, she turned to John D. Rockefeller and Standard Oil for her next effort in the kind of journalism that by 1906 Teddy Roosevelt had branded as "muckraking."

Tarbell spent years researching her exposé of Standard Oil, the first installment of which appeared in the November 1902 *McClure's*. Readers were caught up by Tarbell's polished prose and carefully documented charges of pressured buyouts and illegal alliances. But this was more than the work of a thorough researcher. Evoking the 1873 ruination of her father and others, Tarbell decided to detail the actions Rockefeller had spent thirty years suppressing. She tracked down the sole surviving copy of the key documentation, which Rockefeller's agents had somehow missed, though it was hardly her only source. When published as a two-volume book in 1904, Tarbell's *History of the Standard Oil Company* required nearly 250 pages for her citations. Two years later, a reluctant federal government finally brought conspiracy charges against Standard Oil, leading to a conviction and the 1911 dissolution of the company.

Most of the infractions Standard Oil was charged with became, by 1914, the target of new and specific laws. By then, the woman who brought down Rockefeller was the president of the Pen & Brush Club, a Village arts organization with headquarters at 16 East Tenth Street. Ida Tarbell had been asked to assume the post on a temporary basis while the club straightened out some internal problems. She remained in office a bit longer than that—thirty years. Ida Tarbell again proved herself to be one tenacious lady.

Hollywood on the Hudson, Part 2

Reviewing the screenplay of Alfred Hitchcock's *Rear Window*, Paramount executives imagined the budget for its set would be low. All they thought was needed was a one-room studio apartment to serve as the hero's bachelor digs in Greenwich Village. Actually, the film required one of the largest and most expensive sets the studio had built—the interior court of an entire Village block with thirty-one additional apartments, a dozen of which had to be fully furnished. No address is given in the film for the apartment occupied by L. B. Jeffries (James Stewart), but 125 West Ninth Street is the address given for Lars Thorwald, the fictional wife-murderer played by Raymond Burr. That puts the story on a nonexistent block between Ninth and Tenth streets, as Ninth Street addresses run west no farther than number 69.

However, the Albert Hotel mentioned in the film is very real—or was. Built at the northeast corner of University Place and Tenth Street, it was named for its owner's brother, artist Albert P. Ryder. The Albert is now an apartment residence.

**NORTH
VILLAGE
NOTABLES**

The esteemed novelist William Dean Howells's decision to move from Boston to New York in 1889 signaled the end of New England's publishing primacy. Howells chose Greenwich Village for his residence, specifically the Hampshire at 48 West Ninth Street. Here he absorbed Village ambience to give color to his New York novels, including *A Hazard of New Fortunes* (1890) and *The Coast of Bohemia* (1893).

William Glackens moved from Washington Square to 10 West Ninth Street in 1919. Its top-floor studio was installed by Glackens and fitted with a skylight facade that provided this member of the Eight with the indirect northern light so prized by painters. That light was compromised in 1926, when the fifteen-story Fifth Avenue Hotel rose across Ninth Street from Glackens on the site of the historic Brevoort mansion. The hotel's tan brick gave a rosy hue to Glackens's light, and he tried everything from incandescent lamps to frosted windows to rebalance or filter his light. Nothing worked, and Glackens was still wrestling with this problem when he died here in 1938.

Etiquette (1922) author Emily Post was raised at 12 West Tenth Street. Next door is 14 West Tenth, in which Mark Twain briefly lived before his move to 21 Fifth Avenue. A few doors to the west is 20 West Tenth, in which painter Guy Pène du Bois and sculptor Frederick MacMonnies lived during the 1930s. Across the street at 23 West Tenth, the Marshall Chess Club still meets in this former

Part of the picturesque ensemble row running from 28 to 36 West Tenth Street.

home of chess champ Frank Marshall. Marcel Duchamp, the cubist star of the Armory Show, lived from 1942 at 28 West Tenth. Built in 1856, this building was part of a balconied ensemble row that ran through 36 West Tenth, the onetime home of Edward Godkin, founder of the *Nation*. Nobel Prize–winning novelist Sinclair Lewis lived at 37 West Tenth Street, and two doors west at number 41 stands the former residence of playwright Howard Lindsay and his wife, actress Dorothy Stickney. They were living here when, in collaboration with Russell Crouse, Lindsay wrote the scripts for *Anything Goes* (1934) and Broadway long-run champ *Life with Father* (1939), in which both Lindsay and Stickney starred.

Also of note is 48 West Eleventh Street, which figured briefly in the life of Oscar Wilde. His 1882 American lecture tour had been conceived as a promotional gambit for the upcoming debut of Gilbert and Sullivan's *Patience,* which satirized aesthetes in general and Wilde in particular. Wilde rested from his lengthy tour by staying in residence for several weeks at 48 West Eleventh, which has been little altered since then.

THE TENTH STREET STUDIO

The Peter Warren, an apartment building at 51 West Tenth Street, has no real connection to its namesake, an Eighteenth-century Villager whose vast estate included this small plot. But one glance at this unremarkable 1959 building may leave you yearning for the historic structure it replaced.

America hadn't seen anything quite like the Tenth Street Studio when it opened in 1856. It was the brainchild of art collector John

The Tenth Street Studio, just east of Sixth Avenue, as it appeared in 1938. Built in 1856, this haven for artists was among the earliest institutions to concentrate artists within Greenwich Village.

An artist's showing at the Tenth Street Studio, as portrayed in _Harpers' Weekly_ in 1869.

Taylor Johnston, around the time he moved into his White House on Fifth Avenue. Wouldn't artists create greater works in well-designed surroundings? This red-brick building was the result, its three floors featuring eight studios each around a central atrium providing light. Wooden doors between studios could slide open to create a makeshift art gallery for open-house visits in non-summer months.

The Studio building was the first commission for Richard Morris Hunt, the first American architect trained at the École des Beaux-Arts in Paris. Hunt later took the concepts for multiple dwellings that he explored here and expanded them in his 1869 designs for the Stuyvesant, the Eighteenth Street structure that is usually cited as America's first apartment building.

Hunt's design for the studios fostered what Winslow Homer called an "atmosphere of comradeship" when he moved into the Studio in 1872. John La Farge certainly agreed, for he remained in residence for more than fifty years. Emanuel Leutze _(Washington Crossing the Delaware)_ lived here for a time, as did painter Eastman Johnson and sculptor Augustus Saint-Gaudens. Here actor Edwin Booth posed in 1863 as Hamlet for a life-size bronze bust executed by his friend, Launt Thompson. The Studio was also the boyhood home of Alexander Calder, the inventor of the mobile, whose sculptor father A. Stirling Calder created the _Washington in Peace_ sculpture that has graced the west pedestal of Washington Square Arch since 1918.

The Studio attracted artists to other residences on this block, among them sculptor Daniel Chester French, whose immense statue of Lincoln broods within the Lincoln Memorial in the nation's capital. French took up residence at 58 West Tenth Street, a town house facing the Studio, which had its own artistic heritage. In its back house was the Tile Club, a gentlemen's club for artists, which thrived in the 1870s and 1880s. Artist and author F. Hopkins Smith left a lively portrait of the Tile Club in his novel, *The Fortunes of Oliver Horn*. Among his fellow members were Stanford White, Daniel Chester French, Tenth Street Studio residents Augustus Saint-Gaudens and William Merritt Chase, and Napoleon Sarony, father of theatrical photography, whose studio was nearby on Union Square East. Originally the clubhouse was entered from a passage under the front house, though in time 58½ West Tenth was joined to its neighbor. In that form, the joint buildings were recalled in *Those Days* by Hamilton Fish Armstrong, the noted editor who was born there in 1893 and died there eighty years later.

New York University bought the house in 1987 for a Center for Hellenic Studies, and renovations were nearing completion when fire swept the upper floors of the front house in January 1989. Though damage was great, neither the fire nor the frantic firemen damaged the enormous stained-glass window on the parlor floor, its four hundred panes a marvel to Tenth Street pedestrians. Despite the setback, work resumed and the Onassis Center was scheduled to open before the year was out.

VILLAGE LANDMARKS: TWIN ENCLAVES

Entered through separate gates on Sixth Avenue and Tenth Street respectively, Milligan Place and Patchin Place are among the most private—and treasured—New York enclaves. Yet few people know of their entwined family origins.

Samuel Milligan bought a small segment of the vast Peter Warren estate in 1799. Milligan's plot was entered from the Skinner Road, soon to be renamed Christopher Street. At some time prior to 1835, Milligan built for himself a country home on his property. Thirteen years later, when his daughter Isobel married his surveyor, Aaron Patchin, Milligan gave them the land directly behind his home, on which they built the ten miniature row houses that still bear the Patchin name. After Milligan's death, four squat row houses replaced his house in 1852, but his name is still attached to them.

Several Provincetown Players have lived in these picturesque alleys. The theater's co-founder, George Cram Cook, and his wife, playwright Susan Glaspell, lived in Milligan Place from 1913 to 1917. Provincetown playwright Eugene O'Neill lived there as well

Milligan Place in 1936, as photographed by photojournalist Berenice Abbott. Abbott knew a thing or two about Village enclaves, as she maintained a studio for years in the nook of Commerce Street.

for a time, while fellow playwright John Howard Lawson resided at 6 Patchin Place for sixteen years. Though his plays drew only limited audiences, Lawson won acclaim for his 1936 playwrighting manual, and respect for his bravery as a blacklisted and jailed member of the Hollywood Ten in 1947.

Reclusive writer Djuna Barnes moved to 5 Patchin Place in 1940, where she adopted the private life of a literary hermit; she once sent a visiting Carson McCullers away for ringing her bell without a written appointment. Across the alley is 4 Patchin Place, into which poet E. E. Cummings moved in 1923 with his new wife, fashion model Marion Morehouse. Until his death in 1962, Cummings wrote here and received such celebrity visitors as T. S. Eliot, Ezra Pound, Dylan Thomas, and John Dos Passos. When at a loss for better distraction, Cummings would occasionally throw open his window and bark across the alley, "Hey, Djuna, you still alive over there?" She was, until her death in June 1982 at the age of ninety.

After ending his relationship with Mabel Dodge, John Reed moved to Patchin Place in 1916 with his new bride, Louise Bryant. From here Reed left to witness the earliest days of the Russian Revolution, and it was to Patchin Place that he returned to begin writing his account of the events, *Ten Days That Shook the World*. His work was initially thwarted by U.S. Customs, which confiscated his notes for a year. After Reed's death in 1920, Louise Bryant remarried and moved to France, but was concerned for the safety of the notes Reed used for his book. To protect them she continued to pay rent on Reed's Patchin Place apartment for ten years after his death.

Patchinites remain closely bound to their unique enclave. One woman, Mary Trainor, moved to 10 Patchin Place as a young bride in 1870, raised seven children there, and was still there fifty-five years later when she died in 1925. By one report, she was even buried there. In 1963, Patchin residents successfully banded together with neighboring Milliganites to forestall the threatened destruction of the twin alleys for an apartment tower.

Patchin Place, as it appears today, with Jefferson Market Courthouse visible just across West Tenth Street.

The Grapevine in 1890. Built in 1838 on Sixth Avenue at Eleventh Street, this roadhouse was just around the corner from the Tenth Street Studio, which provided an endless source of artists and gossip.

OF GRAVESTONES AND GRAPEVINES

Another surviving reminder of the now-vanished extension of Christopher Street is the Shearith Israel Cemetery east of Sixth Avenue. Founded in 1805 at the juncture of Christopher Street and the Union Road, the burial ground was bisected in 1830 when Eleventh Street was cut through. The cemetery, or what's left of it, survives, still aligned to roads long since plowed under.

Next to it at 78 West Eleventh Street stands a bland 1915 apartment house, its rear wall also reflecting the odd-angled line of vanished streets. It replaced the Grapevine, a popular roadhouse built here in 1838. The wood frame structure was a hangout for early artists of the Village who came to this tavern to swap gossip. Returning to their garrets, or possibly their rooms around the corner in the Tenth Street Studio, these gossiping artists had an answer ready when asked where they got their information: "Through the Grapevine." During the Civil War, the phrase was adopted to mean "A source of unofficial military information," though it has since returned to the gossipy meaning it had when it was coined in connection with this site.

Until 1955 this ensemble row graced Eleventh Street, west of Sixth Avenue. Set back from the street, Rhinelander Gardens boasted triple-tiered front balconies with delicate cast-iron grilles.

ENSEMBLE ROWS, DEAD . . .

Rhinelander Gardens stood on the south side of Eleventh Street just west of Sixth Avenue. Built around 1854, this elegant New Orleans–style row of eight houses was the work of James Renwick of Grace Church fame. East of this row, five miniature houses formed Garden Row, an alley adjoining Milligan Place, which it greatly resembled. Both Rhinelander Gardens and Garden Row replaced a florist's garden laid out on land once owned by the prosperous Rhinelander family, hence the names.

Among the distinguished residents of Rhinelander Gardens was Theodore Dreiser, who lived at 118 West Eleventh while completing his 1925 masterpiece, *An American Tragedy*. That very address had been the setting for Edwin Booth's wedding several years earlier, while another house in the row was home to Tony Sarg, Village artist and puppeteer who designed the first giant balloons for Macy's Thanksgiving Day Parade.

Garden Row has vanished, and all but a trace of Rhinelander Gardens is gone. Public School 41 replaced them in 1955, a structure that exemplifies the stylistic sterility of Eisenhower Gothic at its worst. Only two meager reminders of the earlier structures remain. One is the bizarre shape of 461 Sixth Avenue, dating from 1852 and still reflecting the angled entrance of the now-vanished Garden Row. The only remaining trace of Rhinelander Gardens is its cast-iron grille, a section of which was preserved and incorporated into the back wall of the school. It's still there; you can easily spot it from Greenwich Avenue by looking across the school's playground. And it looks unhappy.

... AND ALIVE (MOSTLY)

Little was left after an explosion in a basement bomb factory destroyed 18 West Eleventh Street on March 6, 1970.

The present house at 18 West Eleventh Street, its skewed wall a quiet reminder of the blast two decades ago.

On the last undeveloped section of the Brevoort family farm, Henry Brevoort built seven houses in 1844–45 as numbers 14 through 26 West Eleventh Street. All but two were gifts to his five daughters. The house at 20 West Eleventh retains its original appearance unaltered, but the most famous of the seven is the one that's no longer there.

Once the home of Broadway lyricist Howard Dietz ("Dancing in the Dark," "That's Entertainment"), number 18 West Eleventh was, by 1970, the residence of James Wilkerson. His daughter Kathleen, a recent Swarthmore graduate, was at that time involved with a domestic terrorist group called the Weathermen. While her parents were in the Caribbean, she and her friends turned the basement of this staid Greek Revival home into a bomb factory.

Minutes before noon on March 6, 1970, the serenity of Eleventh Street was shattered by an explosion that blew out half the windows on the block. The entire face of number 18 was blasted off, and flames shot nearly as far as the opposite sidewalk. As horrified neighbors watched, two young women scrambled out of the inferno, one of them completely naked.

A neighbor took them in so that they could tend to their wounds while firemen battled the blaze. Dressed in borrowed clothes, the women left, saying they needed to purchase medication and that they'd return immediately. They didn't.

Firemen found a body in the debris; it was quickly identified as that of Ted Gold, an underground leader of the 1968 riot at Columbia University. Then firemen found the building's boiler—intact. Then another corpse, that of Diana Oughton. Then thirty unused blasting caps. Then sixty sticks of dynamite . . .

Kathleen Wilkerson and Kathy Boudin, the women who had fled the inferno, remained fugitives for over a year before being apprehended and brought to trial. Meanwhile, the plywood wall closing off the blast site was covered with ominous graffiti christening it "Weatherman Park." Though the Vietnam War continued to fuel the student protest movement for several years, this explosion shattered the radical elements, marking the beginning of the collapse of the entire movement. And in Greenwich Village, an architectural controversy with political overtones erupted over the replacement for 18 West Eleventh Street. Some wanted an identical Greek Revival house to obliterate all ugly reminders of that March afternoon; others insisted that serious events deserved more than a cosmetic resolution.

It was eight years before the present home was built on the site. It maintains the scale and line of its 1844 predecessor in all respects but one: at the parlor level, the facade swivels 45 degrees from the street line. This ruptured facade—half exploded and half imploded—echoes the fatal 1970 blast.

**EDUCATION
FOR
ADULTS**

There was only one thing wrong with the New School as it was organized in 1919: it couldn't survive in the real world. For its first three years, it functioned as a renegade among institutions of higher learning. No grades were given, no degrees were offered, nothing interfered with an idealized teacher-student interaction in pursuit of True Scholarship.

Founded by two Columbia professors who were opposed to the university's ban on anti-war dissent, the New School was reconstituted by Alvin Johnson in 1923 to temper its lofty principles with practicality. His success led the school to build permanent quarters to replace its original makeshift rooms in Chelsea. By 1927 Johnson had acquired a plot on Twelfth Street and selected his architect. Joseph Urban must have struck many as singularly inappropriate for the task, a man of sixty best known as the designer of the florid, frivolous settings for virtually every show produced by Florenz Ziegfeld since 1915. He had also designed the lavish 1927 theater bearing Ziegfeld's name.

Urban stunned his detractors by designing New York's first building in the bold International Style, a full year before that term was even coined. In meeting Johnson's request for a 550-seat auditorium, Urban adapted his egg-shaped Ziegfeld interior into a sleek solution to theater design that seems adventurous even today. Then, in a move worthy of Frank Lloyd Wright, Urban designed the entire building interior to conform with the International look, right down to the decor and furnishings. The New School Building at 66 West Twelfth Street was a complete environment for learning and thought, inside and out, and was quickly adopted by the intelligentsia.

Composer Aaron Copland's music courses here established him as a major force in classical composition. Martha Graham and Charles Weidman came here to perform in 1933, offering programs that encouraged Americans to take modern dance seriously. The New School introduced its first film courses in 1931, three years before New York University followed suit. Berenice Abbott taught photography here, Thomas Hart Benton taught painting, and Max Wertheimer, deviser of Gestalt psychology, explored the psyche. In later years, social scientist Claude Lévi-Strauss, economist Robert Heilbroner, composer John Cage, and writers Mario Puzo, William Styron, Gorham Munson, and Alfred Kazin have appeared before New School groups. Other speakers have included W. H. Auden, Anthony Burgess, Erskine Caldwell, T. S. Eliot, Erich Fromm, John Houseman, Eugene McCarthy, Margaret Mead, Benjamin Spock, Virgil Thomson, and Tom Wolfe.

The New School expanded into an annex built in the late 1950s to continue its commitment to knowledge. However, its finest hour was born during the horror of Nazi tyranny. When Germany ex-

The International Style made its New York debut at 66 West Twelfth Street with Joseph Urban's New School building in 1930.

Edna St. Vincent Millay, who
captivated the Village of the early
1920s, as sketched by William
Zorach in 1925.

pelled its Jewish scholars in April 1933, Alvin Johnson led a drive—in the depths of the depression—to rescue these men and women and bring them to safety in America. The New School set up its "University in Exile," consisting of many of the 178 refugees whose ethnicity or dissenting opinions were anathema to the Nazis. Acceptance of individual differences had led to the founding of the New School in the first place. Today, poised to begin its eighth decade, the New School remains true to its founding ideals, and very much at home in its Greenwich Village surroundings.

GIVING A LOVELY LIGHT

St. Vincent's Hospital has been a local lifesaver since 1849 when its doors first opened in a small house on West Thirteenth Street. In 1857 the hospital expanded to larger quarters at 143 West Eleventh Street and has since built a warren of structures across the entire west half of that city block. As the city's third oldest hospital, St. Vincent's has had its brushes with history. In 1899 it became the first hospital in America to offer automobile ambulance service. In 1911 survivors of the Triangle fire were treated here, as were survivors of the sinking of the *Titanic* the following year. More recently, its Greenwich Village location placed St. Vincent's at the forefront of AIDS treatment and care, as the deadly epidemic wreaked havoc through the 1980s.

Two poets have been linked to St. Vincent's Hospital. One is Welsh-born Dylan Thomas, who drank at the White Horse Tavern, four blocks to the west along Eleventh Street and who died in St. Vincent's in 1953. The other is Edna St. Vincent Millay. Just before the poet's birth in Maine in 1892, her mother learned that her own brother in New York had been stricken with appendicitis. When news reached Rockland, Maine, that the operation had been successful, his grateful sister named her newborn daughter after the hospital that had saved his life.

NORTH
VILLAGE
HOMESTEADERS

Verna Small showing her new neighbors the street numbers she placed on the door of 491 Sixth Avenue. As this 1945 snapshot suggests, Verna and Leonard Small were among the first post-war homesteaders on Sixth Avenue, as the adjacent row house was still used by a roofing company.

It's an enduring Village legend: the lovable-but-crazy tenants who rent unimproved apartments lacking even heating and who renovate them at their own expense, replacing an urban wilderness with a newborn neighborhood. In the case of 491 Sixth Avenue, the legend is true.

"It was, I think, an important aspect of Village history," recalled Verna Small, a Villager for nearly fifty years and chairperson of the Landmarks Committee of the local community board. "I was one of the young professionals who flocked to the Village in the late 1930s for reasons of convenience and atmosphere. Village apartments were cheap, often not improved very much, and readily available, which meant that people tended to move every year. Landlords were so eager to rent they'd offer the first month free, meaning you could cushion your rent with annual moves. You could think, This year I want to try a southern exposure, or This year I'd like a balcony. Or maybe access to the roof instead of the backyard garden. Village landlords knew the first of October was moving day, and they expected all their tenants to shift around; they took to calling it the Salmon Run.

"After the Second World War, two factors brought my husband Leonard and me back to Greenwich Village: we wanted the street atmosphere we found here, the neighborliness, and the beautifully scaled houses. The other factor was Leonard's dislike of commuting, his resolve to walk to work, a practice he continued until the day he died.

"We saw 491 Sixth Avenue the first day of our apartment search, but it looked impossible. The floor was covered with wire mesh, and there was no central heat. But it dated from 1850 or so, had a fireplace in every room, and the most magnificent fixtures and hardware. It had long been deserted, so its owner wasn't out to gouge anyone. Actually, the Rhinelander Real Estate Company was very responsible, making such spaces available at low rent to returning soldiers, getting them started in places they could improve on their own, and not exploiting them after the work was done. Someone came to show us what we needed to do, how to install and operate a kerosene stove, and I became expert at laying brick, plastering and painting walls, and scraping floors. And we uncovered one beautiful marble fireplace and other details which, being a very visual person, I suspect fostered my interest in landmark preservation. In time we rented and renovated all three floors, installed gas heat, took in tenants of our own, and over fourteen years developed it into a little paradise.

"Ultimately, the time came for it to end. We were thinking of putting in another bathroom, but the owners came to us and told us not to put any more of ourselves in, that they had a deal pending. They were very good about it, and in 1959 we left Sixth Avenue, and the building was replaced with a fairly luxurious tower, the John Adams apartments between Twelfth and Thirteenth streets.

"But I remember the neighborliness that prevailed then, so typical of Greenwich Village. One of the first things I did was to paint the front door of 491 Sixth Avenue, a light sea-green-blue, and it acted like a signal. Strangers came by and said, 'You're going to *live* in there? Well, I have four lengths of clear pine. Could you use them?' People from around the block saw the garden we put out back and came by, saying 'I have some iris bulbs. Would you like them?' The block became its own community, one that even outlived the block itself. I remember caring for a woman with a baby when there was a small fire in their studio. I had never spoken to her before, and now, over forty years later, she'll be coming to visit me tomorrow."

"TOO THIRTEENTH STREET"

Village Voices

EMPTY YOUR PURSE INTO YOUR MIND

Sign on a Village book shop, circa 1920

In education, literature, architecture, entertainment, and dining, Thirteenth Street achieved a reputation that Village writer Gorham Munson has called Montparnassian. The street even found distinction in fiction: Theodore Dreiser used the row house at 112 West Thirteenth as the home of his characters Carrie Meeber and George Hurstwood in *Sister Carrie* (1900).

Writers and editors in 1919 began referring to certain essays of dissent as being "too Thirteenth Street"—that is, too left wing—to publish. In the grip of the repressive "red scare," some publishers devised their own censorship policies so as to avoid the kind of government prosecution that had shut down the *Masses* the year before. The phrase "too Thirteenth Street" derived from the fact that the American Communist party rented rooms in a loft building at 50 East Thirteenth Street.

A THIRTEENTH STREET EDUCATION

For years it was possible to get a complete education, cradle to grave, on Thirteenth Street. One of the oldest progressive schools in the nation, the City & Country School was founded by Caroline Pratt in 1914 around the corner from its present location at 146 West Thirteenth Street. It continues to provide children with a curriculum reflecting each student's interests while fostering active rather than passive learning.

A modern apartment building at 60 West Thirteenth Street has replaced Public School 35, built here in the 1840s and popularly known as the "cradle of New York City high schools." It was the first school in Manhattan to offer a free education beyond the elementary level, and its early headmaster was one of the nation's foremost educators, Thomas Hunter. He installed the nation's first evening high school here in 1866 and made P.S. 35 the first in America to ban corporal punishment. Prior to his 1872 retirement, his graduates respectfully formed the Hunter Association, which numbered among its members a city health commissioner and a federal chief justice.

P.S. 35 was a red-brick affair that closely resembled its surviving companion, P.S. 16 at 208 West Thirteenth Street. Built in stages from 1869 through 1898, it later became one of the city's "special high schools"—the Food and Maritime Vocational High School. In 1985, however, the building was sold as city surplus. It then became New York's first Lesbian and Gay Community Services Center. Halls and rooms long abandoned now overflow with activities and meetings sponsored by gay business groups, rights activist organizations, community outreach groups, health care groups, and such varied social organizations as a gay square dancing group and Gay Vegetarians of New York.

The Jackson Square Library at 251 West Thirteenth Street was designed by Richard Morris Hunt to evoke memories of the Dutch-gabled architecture of old New Amsterdam. After being absorbed

The gabled affair at 251 West Thirteenth Street began its days as one of the city's first circulating libraries.

The former P. S. 16 at 208 West Thirteenth Street was typical of the schools built by the city in the late 1800s. This one has become the Lesbian and Gay Community Services Center, which in 1989 formed the nation's first gay and lesbian history museum.

into the New York Public Library system, it became the second most heavily used branch, featuring the largest collection of French literature and of theatrical books and play scripts. When the Jefferson Market Courthouse conversion provided the space for a much needed expansion, the century-old Hunt building became a private art gallery and residence with a cryptic name: the Great Building Crack-Up. However, the numerals across the facade, 1-8-8-7, still mark the date of its construction.

MAKING A NOISE IN THE WORLD

It's no surprise that a block with its own Parthenon should become a center of wisdom and the arts.

In 1918 the row house at 152 West Thirteenth Street became the offices of the *Dial,* a magazine dedicated to fostering literary and artistic excellence. Founded in 1880 in Chicago, the *Dial*'s editors, Scofield Taylor and Gilbert Seldes, unveiled this new policy in their first issue, which included art by Gaston Lachaise, sketches and poems by E. E. Cummings, and previously unpublished autobiographic writings by the late Village hero Randolph Bourne. In subsequent issues, Van Wyck Brooks pioneered the use of psychoanalytic theory in literary analysis with his *Ordeal of Mark Twain,* and T. S. Eliot appeared in print for the first time in America with the *Dial*'s publication of *The Waste Land* in 1922.

John Dos Passos recalled attending afternoon staff meetings in the rear garden, conducted in French over iced tea. In the discussion might be such *Dial* authors as Sherwood Anderson, Ezra Pound, and Malcolm Cowley, who might have been visiting at the time. Other literary contributors form a Who's Who of the arts of the 1920s: Virginia Woolf, Gertrude Stein, D. H. Lawrence, Archibald MacLeish, Louis Untermeyer, Bertrand Russell, Thomas Mann, E. M. Forster, H. L. Mencken, and Havelock Ellis. Contributors of artwork included Picasso, Cocteau, and Matisse. As co-editor Seldes remarked, "*The Dial* made a noise in the world" until its demise in 1929.

Noise also issued agreeably from elsewhere on the block. The *Freeman* had its offices here, in the same row house used by distinguished book publisher Ben Heubsch. Editor Albert Jay Nock encouraged the irreverent and stylish flippancies later identified with the 1920s, while maintaining a commitment to political radicalism in a very tense and repressive postwar era. The *Freeman*'s finest hour came in 1920 when Attorney General A. Mitchell Palmer embarked on a campaign of raids designed to stifle leftist dissent. To justify his actions, Palmer pointed to the noontime Wall Street bombing of September 16, 1920, in which thirty people were killed and three hundred wounded. This conveniently provided

The sedate row house at 152
West Thirteenth Street, for
eleven years the "noisy" offices
of the *Dial*, one of several
magazines published on this
block in the twenties.

Palmer with "proof" of an imminent attack by anarchist terrorists,
but when the *Dial* bravely published evidence that this was not
possible, the government fumed but charged no one with the crime.

Also published on this block was the *Liberator*, editor Max
Eastman's socialist successor to his earlier magazine, the *Masses*,
which the government had persecuted into oblivion in 1918. From
its office at 138 West Thirteenth, the *Liberator* published works by
Elinor Wylie, Ernest Hemingway, Elmer Rice, Edmund Wilson,
Vachel Lindsay, and Edna St. Vincent Millay, yet managed to seem
more strident than its suppressed predecessor. Factionalism even-

tually undermined the *Liberator,* which was subsumed in 1924 into the Communist party house organ, the *Workers' Monthly,* where it vanished in rhetoric.

It's little wonder that several restaurants and bars opened on this block and became hangouts for magazine staffers. Just next door to the *Dial* was Felix's, still in operation as Cuisine de Saigon. The *Dial* staff also gathered at Mandarin House, which occupied two basements with an entrance at 133 West Thirteenth. It is now Covent Garden, and its decor has been redesigned, but the same old wisteria vine still climbs the four floors of the building's facade. *Dial* regulars would also recognize Mario's, a speakeasy at 140 West Thirteenth, which became a legitimate restaurant when Prohibition ended. It remains one today in a sleek 1988 renovation, but its name has been changed to Grappa.

Two other noisemakers on this block deserve note. What today is Spain Restaurant, 113 West Thirteenth, was fifty years ago the famous Downtown Gallery. It specialized in the Moderns and took over the parlor floor for one of the earliest exhibits of American folk art. A century earlier, this row house was home to *Harper's* editor Henry Jarvis Raymond, who moved to nearby 134 West Thirteenth in 1847 and was still there in 1851 when he founded a little newspaper called the *New York Times.*

Village-born Mayor Fiorello La Guardia long favored a basement Italian restaurant at 126 West Thirteenth Street called Little Venice. Today it's an upscale affair called Zinno, but it achieved considerable fame between 1972 and 1979 as Reno Sweeney, the

Whether as clubs, theaters, cabarets, restaurants, offices, laundries, or even as residences, the row houses of the Village have proved themselves to be very adaptable. At 126 West Thirteenth Street, a restaurant named Zinno now occupies the basement premises that were, through the 1970s, the popular nightclub, Reno Sweeney.

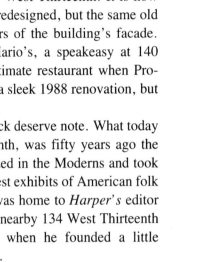

swankiest of the decade's night spots—named after the character played by Ethel Merman in *Anything Goes*. This club's owner-manager Lewis Friedman revived a moribund New York club scene by booking the likes of Peter Allen, Barbara Cook, Melissa Manchester, Leata Galloway, Jimmy Webb, Alaina Reed, Janis Ian, and Marilyn Sokol. A restrictive 1977 cabaret law eventually undercut the club scene and forced Reno's to curtail and finally suspend operations. The law was finally rescinded in 1987, a move that was celebrated a year later when forty Reno Sweeney alumni mounted a five-day festival to benefit six AIDS organizations.

A LITTLE TOUCH OF TEXAS

Its home was an old Schrafft's restaurant, built in 1938 in a modified Art Deco style. But from the minute you walked through the door, the Lone Star Café set its own tone. After opening in 1977, it remained for over a decade the city's prime venue for country-western music. Willie Nelson made his New York debut here in 1979, and Roy Orbison made his comeback here in 1981.

The ninety-foot iguana mounted on the old restaurant's roof became the bone of contention when the café opened. The Fifth Avenue Association fought it, saying it was bad for the neighborhood. Co-owner Mort Cooperman fought off the challenge successfully—so successfully that the rent increases in the area eventually priced the Lone Star Café out of existence. Faced with a 350 percent rent hike, Cooperman chose instead to close Lone Star for good. "I choose not to become an indentured servant," he reportedly quipped.

PORTHOLE TREATMENT

Running between Twelfth and Thirteenth streets on Seventh Avenue is the Outpatient Service Pavillion of St. Vincent's Hospital. It was built in 1964 and absorbed by the hospital in the 1980s as part of the expansion program that rebuilt its main facilities one block to the south. Originally this was the National Maritime Union Building, a fact that accounts for the simulated portholes in its facade. Its inverted step-pyramid shape manages to fit with curious ease into a neighborhood of homes predating it by over a century, perhaps because Villagers respond to the whimsy of this building, once described by union president Joseph Curran as the box that the Guggenheim Museum came in. Unfortunately, it replaced Cottage Row, an ensemble row from the 1850s of considerably greater whimsy and charm, which was once home to Thomas Janvier, one of the first writers to record Village history.

Seventh Avenue at Twelfth Street,
now—

—and then. Cottage Row as it
looked in 1936. Fronting Seventh
Avenue, this was the last garden
row in the Village when it passed
from the scene in the late 1950s.

A SELLER'S MARKET

In 1858 a small retail operation opened just south of Fourteenth Street. It was run by a former whaler named Rowland Hussey Macy. In time it expanded into eleven buildings and became famous as R. H. Macy's. Among its innovations was the now-traditional Christmas season toy display. Though Macy's space requirements forced its move to Herald Square in 1901, its name can still be read by the sharp eye on the rusted facade of one of its earlier buildings at 56 West Fourteenth Street.

Much as Gimbel's was Macy's Midtown competitor, a store called Hearn's was its Village nemesis. After moving into a warren of buildings on the east side of the same block of Fourteenth Street in 1878, Hearn's remained in business until 1955. Its chief impact on the Village, however, occurred some forty years earlier. Noting a decline in retail business, Hearn's joined with Cammemeyer's and O'Neill's (of Ladies' Mile fame) to begin promoting Greenwich Village as a desirable residential neighborhood. The campaign, costing by one account $15,000, was abetted by Village realtor Vincent Peppe (who found he could charge $25 rent for a $10 apartment just by installing a bathtub).

Their calculated 1915 campaign worked, bringing new residents to the Village and new business to the stores. Peppe got new tenants, and the West Village had its first brush with commercial success. This marketing of Village atmosphere proved to be a double-edged sword, however, and its success might well have changed the character of the Village had the depression not brought it to a halt.

PROMOTING EQUALITY ON FOURTEENTH STREET

From 1862 to 1876 the northeast corner of Fourteenth Street and Fifth Avenue was the site of Delmonico's, a society restaurant that offered refined European dining in New York. A banquet here in April 1868 honoring Charles Dickens played a key role in the nascent women's movement, because of who was excluded rather than who was present. In planning its guest list, the New York Press Club declined the application of one of its members, journalist Jennie June, on the grounds that women were not welcome at this prestigious event. Under her real name, Mrs. Jane Cunningham Croly invited like-minded women to her Fourteenth Street home to plan a strategy to confront this discriminatory policy. The result was Sorosis, America's first professional women's organization, founded on March 21, 1868. Its first aim was to make life miserable for the New York Press Club, and it did. The club finally sued for peace in the form of another banquet—the first New York event attended by men and women as social equals.

The old Macy's store at 204–206 Sixth Avenue, just south of Fourteenth Street. Nearly thirty years after Macy's left this block, so did its street number. When Sixth Avenue was extended below Carmine Street, the buildings were renumbered and this became a 500 block.

5 THE WEST VILLAGE

Season's Greetings to the West Village, from West Fourth Street.

In the 170 years since its irregular street pattern was preserved, the West Village has proved how you can successfully live your life and still be 45 degrees out of kilter with the rest of the world. West Villagers are as varied as the apartment buildings they live in, yet they display a remarkable, feisty unity when threatened by the outside world. Ironically, the West Village is the source of much of the innovation that made that outside world the way it is today. Here television was introduced

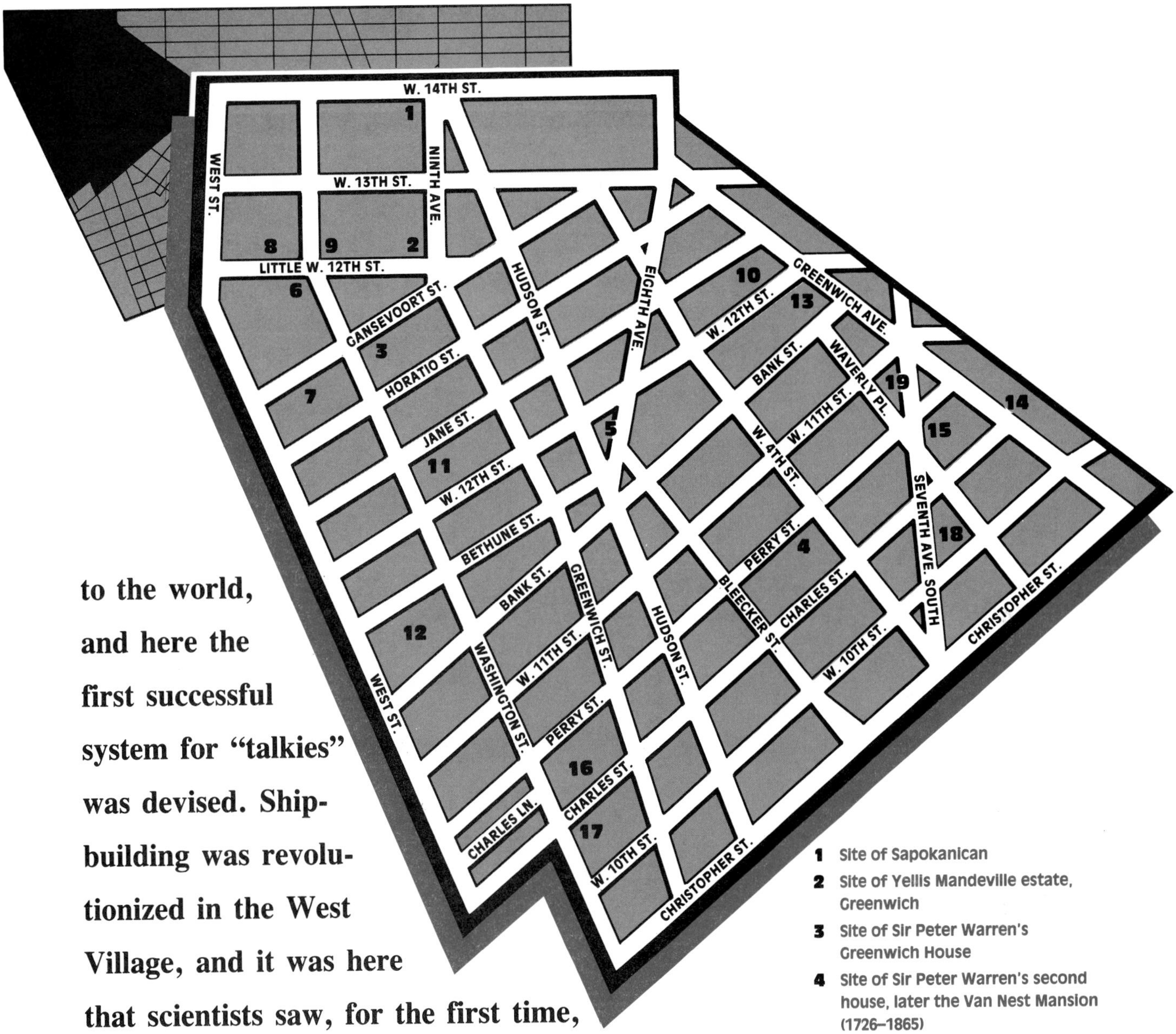

W. 14TH ST.
W. 13TH ST.
WEST ST.
NINTH AVE.
LITTLE W. 12TH ST.
GANSEVOORT ST.
HUDSON ST.
HORATIO ST.
EIGHTH AVE.
GREENWICH AVE.
W. 12TH ST.
JANE ST.
BANK ST.
WAVERLY PL.
W. 12TH ST.
W. 4TH ST.
W. 11TH ST.
BETHUNE ST.
BANK ST.
GREENWICH ST.
PERRY ST.
CHARLES ST.
SEVENTH AVE. SOUTH
CHRISTOPHER ST.
WASHINGTON ST.
W. 11TH ST.
HUDSON ST.
BLEECKER ST.
CHARLES ST.
W. 10TH ST.
WEST ST.
PERRY ST.
CHARLES LN.
CHARLES ST.
W. 10TH ST.
CHRISTOPHER ST.

to the world, and here the first successful system for "talkies" was devised. Ship-building was revolu-tionized in the West Village, and it was here that scientists saw, for the first time, "ghosts." The West Village had its own prison, its own fort, and for nearly a week back in the 1920s, its very own volcano.

Wedged between Greenwich Avenue and Christopher Street, the West Village is a district with its own distinct character. Its residential streets offer a far greater range of housing options than the more conventional and homogeneous row houses of the North Village. Until a 1910 shift in

1 Site of Sapokanican

2 Site of Yellis Mandeville estate, Greenwich

3 Site of Sir Peter Warren's Greenwich House

4 Site of Sir Peter Warren's second house, later the Van Nest Mansion (1726–1865)

5 Abingdon Square

6 Gansevoort Meat Center (site of Fort Gansevoort)

7 West Coast Apartments (former Manhattan Refrigerating Co.)

8 Site of Delamater Iron Works

9 Former Mineshaft Bar

10 247 W.12th St. (the "Village Volcano")

11 82 Jane St.

12 Westbeth (former Bell Labs)

13 Site of 91 Greenwich Ave. (office of the *Masses*)

14 Site of P.S. 26

15 *Weathering Cement Triangle*

16 121 Charles St.

17 Memphis Downtown Apartments

18 Julius' Bar

19 The Village Vanguard

property values, West Village streets faced an incursion of loft buildings, many of which have been converted into apartments in recent years. Tenements also sprang up, to vary the street scene further. Into the early 1930s heavy industry thrived here, making use of the piers along the Hudson and the shipping facilities of the former Hudson River Railroad. Over the past twenty years, the buildings that were erected during those industrial years have been transformed into luxury housing that retains rather than camouflages features of each structure's former life. The result is an understated vitality that is the hallmark of the West Village.

HOW GREENWICH VILLAGE GOT ITS NAME

The village of Greenwich was first mentioned in city records on March 28, 1713. On that date the Common Council ordered Falkert Van Hoese "of Greenwich in the Bowry division of the out ward" to remove a fence keeping his neighbor's cattle from grazing freely. Since the council used "Greenwich" to legally identify this miscreant, the name must have been established in local minds by then. But who established it, and when?

The answer can be found in the story of a West Village property near the site of the Indian village of Sapokanican. This land, south of today's Gansevoort Street, was used as a pasture by an early Dutch settler named Jan Van Rotterdam. Since his riverside *bouwerie* was south of his pasture, below the present Christopher Street, he gave his pasture the Dutch name Noortwyck—"north-district dairy farm"—a name that first appeared in council minutes in 1664. After passing from one owner to another, the pasture was bought in June 1679 by Yellis Mandeville, who had settled in the New World twenty years earlier on the verdant flatlands of Brooklyn. Not far from his Brooklyn farm was a village named Greenwyck; it appeared on maps of Brooklyn until 1673 when it vanished without a trace. Mandeville must have liked the name, for he brought it with him when he moved to Manhattan. In his will he described himself as being "of Greenwich in the county of New York." Dated September 15, 1696, this document predates by seventeen years the first mention of Greenwich in Common Council records. So, strangely enough, Greenwich Village got its name from—Brooklyn.

The block on which Peter Warren's manor house stood was opened to development in 1866 and still shows remarkable uniformity of style. These Bleecker Street row houses at the corner of Charles are elegant examples of the Second French Empire style.

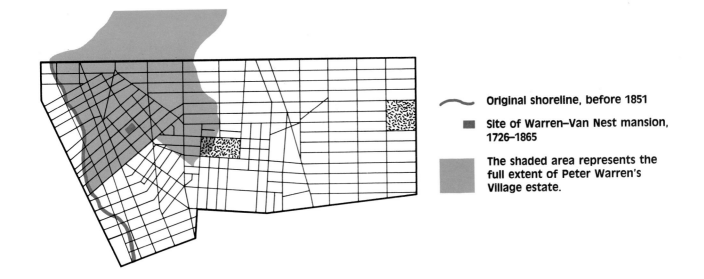

Original shoreline, before 1851

Site of Warren–Van Nest mansion, 1726–1865

The shaded area represents the full extent of Peter Warren's Village estate.

BUYING UP THE WEST VILLAGE

Sir Peter Warren was a privateer, a polite term meaning he was a pirate, and in the service of the British Crown. He must have been good at his job, for he amassed so much money he could afford to buy up the entire West Village. So he did.

The Warren estate ranged from the present Twenty-first Street all the way south to Christopher and was more or less assembled in five separate parcels, purchased over several years. The first followed Warren's June 1731 marriage to Susannah deLancey. It was a strip of old Noortwyck that featured a mansion built in 1700, which Warren dubbed Greenwich House. He expanded his estate to a full 300 acres in 1744 when he made his last and southernmost purchase. This acreage included a larger mansion dating from 1726, so Warren let Greenwich House to his brother-in-law, Oliver de-Lancey, and moved to his new home, which he called Warren House. Soon afterward, he left on one of his exploits and died seven years later in England.

His frequent absences left Lady Warren to become the leading force in the district. The school she established for her three daughters—at the present juncture of Horatio Street and Eighth Avenue—was open to children of other families in the area. She also opened her own home, Greenwich House and later Warren House, for annual children's parties. Warren House, which graced its vast acreage from atop a slope above the Hudson River, must have seemed like paradise to the locals. It was tucked into a glade of horse chestnut, willow, poplar, and sycamore trees—and there was one pear tree close enough to the house to permit fruit-picking from a second-floor window.

The Warren estate passed to Peter Warren's three daughters after his death, and their marriages provided several Village streets with names. What today is Waverly Place north of Christopher was originally Fitzroy Street, named for Ann Warren's husband, Charles Fitzroy. Her sister Susanna married Colonel Otis Skinner, who gave his name to the Skinner Road, which became Christopher Street in 1799. Finally, Charlotte Warren's marriage to the earl of Abingdon provided a name for today's Abingdon Square and also for Abingdon Lane, which ran from Greenwich Avenue to the Hudson River and is now simply an extension of Twelfth Street.

Warren's second mansion passed through several hands before being purchased in 1819 by a merchant named Abraham Van Nest. Though he lived there until his death in 1864, the grounds surrounding the mansion were cut through for development. Warren House and its stable were hemmed into a single block bounded by Charles, West Fourth, Perry, and Bleecker streets and encircled by row houses dating from as early as 1817. The mansion could not indefinitely survive pressure for development, and a year after Van Nest's death the 139-year-old Warren House was pulled down.

THE WHITE FORT

Fort Gansevoort went up in 1811 as part of the battery erected around New York Harbor when war with England grew imminent. It was officially named for General Peter Gansevoort, a hero of the Revolution. However, the whitewashed brownstone exterior gave the White Fort its popular name. Situated on landfill near a cove used by local Indians and Noortwyck settlers, it was the only fort ever built in Greenwich Village.

To permit the landfill construction of the present shoreline in 1851, the White Fort was leveled in 1849. Its site became an open train yard, which was used and then vacated by the Hudson River

As late as the 1830s, the Hudson shore south of Fort Gansevoort—known as the White Fort—served recreational uses. Thousands strolled here on warm summer evenings and bathed by day at the Knapp Tea Water Garden, which became a popular baptismal site, as this 1834 scene shows. A rare view of the White Fort itself is captured here, seen in the background just beyond the pilings of a wooden pier.

Going marketing in the 1890s meant tackling a good deal of chaos. In the foreground is the Gansevoort Market, on the site of the White Fort. Behind it, on landfill, are the Victorian sheds of the West Washington Market, built in 1887 and destroyed in 1953. On the site of these sheds now stands a former garbage processing plant, now serving as a storehouse for the rock salt spread on city streets in winter.

Railroad. In the late 1860s, New Jersey farmers, crowded out of the Washington Market on Chambers Street, set up shop in the abandoned train yard. Their success forced the city to formalize this makeshift shopping area, known as the Gansevoort Market, in 1880. Its size was doubled in 1887 when the West Washington Market was built on additional landfill across West Street.

The present meat-packing district grew up around these markets, but the markets themselves are gone. Gansevoort Market came down in 1950. It was replaced by the city-built Gansevoort Meat Center, which is still operating between Gansevoort and Little West Twelfth streets. Excavations for this center in 1949 uncovered remnants of the White Fort's foundation, which had been buried after the fort vanished ninety-eight years earlier.

VILLAGE PEOPLE: INSPECTOR 75

General Gansevoort's daughter Maria thought she'd married well by wedding merchant Allan Melvill. By 1824 they lived at 33 Bleecker Street near the fashionable Bond Street district, and they moved around the corner four years later to an even better address, 675 Broadway. But it all went sour in 1830. Melvill's business failed, and he died insane two years later. Maria fled with her children to her native Albany, where she altered the spelling of her last name to avoid creditors. Though she tried to keep her family together, her son Herman ran off to sea in 1840.

Herman Melville returned in 1844 with tales of his thrilling sea adventures and of the primitive paradise where he and his closest mate had lived as guests of a cannibal tribe. Encouraged by friends, he wrote up his adventures in a popular book entitled *Typee* (1846). Its success fostered other books in which Melville sailed on the uncharted waters of symbolism and metaphysics (which readers found obscure) and intense male friendships (which readers overlooked). He'd lost most of his following by 1851 when he produced a mystifying whaling tale called *Moby-Dick,* and the rest of it the following year with *Pierre,* which prompted some reviewers to pronounce Melville insane. From a stylish home on Fourth Avenue at Twelfth Street, Melville retreated in 1863 to 104 East Twenty-sixth Street.

Forced three years later to take a regular job, Melville became a customs inspector, measuring his life in bales and barrels at four dollars a day. During most of his nineteen years of service, Inspector 75 was stationed at 507 West Street at the foot of Jane Street, barely a block from Gansevoort Street, Market, and Hotel, all of which bore his famous grandfather's name.

On his retirement in 1885, Melville took to his study and attempted his first extended prose in years, the homoerotic reverie *Billy Budd.* He was still at work on it when he died in 1891 in obscurity. Found pasted inside his work desk was a small scrap of paper on which was written an invocation: "Keep True To the Dreams of Thy Youth."

Freight trains on West Street were preceded by a mounted cowboy who cleared the tracks ahead of the engine. One of these "Death Avenue Cowboys" is seen in this view from around 1920, posed in front of the massive Manhattan Refrigerating Company, a meat processing plant between Gansevoort and Horatio streets. The cowboys disappeared in 1934, after the train tracks were elevated, but the Manhattan Refrigerating Company building is today the trendy West Coast Apartments.

**FREIGHT
TRAINS
IN THE
SKY**

The elevated freight line today, abandoned long enough to sport saplings. The view is north up Washington Street from Charles, with Westbeth and the former Manhattan Refrigerating Company in the distance, as seen from atop the Memphis apartment tower.

Some residential neighborhoods might regard an abandoned railroad trestle as an eyesore; Villagers view their train tracks to nowhere with affection, even pride. But not all locals know the details of the origins of the trestle, and few know of its role in clearing the cowboys off West Street.

The trestle recalls the old Hudson River Railroad, an 1851 street-level line that was the brainchild of James Boorman, co-builder with John Johnston of the 1831 row of houses at 1–13 Washington Square North. The railroad found passenger service less profitable than freight, particularly as shippers were shifting their operations from East River piers to those along the Hudson. Passenger service remained the province of the New York & Harlem Railroad, with which the Hudson line was merged in 1868 to form the New York Central.

City regulations banned the line from using locomotives south of its Thirtieth Street Yard, forcing the line for years to pull its freight cars south along West Street by horse. Even after the laws were changed, locomotives had to creep along West Street, making traffic jams there only worse. As late as the 1930s, the Village piers along West Street received 80 percent of all products entering New York Harbor from East Coast ports. To lead their trains through the crush, the railroad had a cowboy on horseback precede every locomotive. They carried a red flag by day and a lit lantern by night, but their job was no joyride—as indicated by their nickname, "the Death Avenue Cowboys." And in addition to being dangerous, the job provided no real solution to the traffic and shipping congestion along West Street.

The city's solution was to remove entirely from West Street all vehicular through-traffic and railroad shipping traffic. For cars, the city built the Miller Elevated West Side Highway—four lanes that threaded perilously along the shoreline, above West Street. For the trains, a second viaduct was built one block inland—the trestle that still runs through the northern blocks of the West Village. The tracks were designed to provide, two stories above the pavement, elevated spur sidings for such West Village businesses as the National Biscuit Company, Armour Meat Packers, and the Manhattan Refrigerating Company. Tracks passed between some buildings, and in other cases extended directly into and through the buildings. In the case of the Bell Laboratories, track construction through the building required separate caissons for the viaduct, to keep the vibrations of passing trains from affecting precision experiments.

Elevated freight service on the line began in 1934, permitting the removal of tracks along West Street and ending the need for the Death Avenue Cowboys. But by then, the depression had drastically reduced commerce here, and not even the economic recovery of the war years brought shipping volume up to normal. The trestle south of Bank Street was demolished in the 1960s to permit the construction of the ambitious West Village Apartments project. Service on the elevated line reached its ignominious end in April 1980, with the delivery of three boxcars of frozen turkeys. The lacy viaduct now stands unused, an ingenious solution to an evaporated problem.

RAILROAD ART

The full-block Manhattan Refrigerating Company was built in stages in the 1910s between Gansevoort and Horatio streets on West Street. It was vacated in 1979, and its frozen innards were carved up into 234 apartments and given a trendy name—the West Coast. Its meat-storage facilities had operated for so long that it took two months for the building to thaw before the conversion could begin.

Though the adjacent elevated tracks were never used by passenger trains, one can be seen above Washington Street these days. A 128-foot mural depicting the Twentieth Century Limited was installed in eight sections across the one exterior wall of the West Coast in 1981. It was designed and executed by Sergio Kretschmann and Ed Frantz.

DINER CHIC

The beef, veal, and pork you order in Manhattan's most expensive restaurants can be seen each dawn swinging over the sidewalks of the meat-packing district of the West Village. Every weekday the cobblestone streets are clogged by 5 A.M. with refrigerator trucks unloading their cargos. Before the sides of meat are rolled into processing plants along aluminum tracks overhead, they often hang for a few moments in the morning air above sidewalks long ago stained black with animal blood. The dozens of meat-packing plants that fill the neighborhood are successors to the Gansevoort Market of a century ago. But these days some of the meat district's products don't have to travel far to a restaurant table.

Restaurant Florent opened at 69 Gansevoort Street in September 1985, taking over the R&L Diner, which had been a popular lunch spot for local meat packers since the late 1920s. Its steel and Formica decor, dating from a 1942 renovation, was wisely retained by its new owner, Florent Morellet. "I wanted a place not limited to one kind of people," Florent commented. To a simple menu of burgers and omelets, Florent added escargot and braised endive. To the sleek 1940s decor, he added mirrors, maps, and giddy souvenirs from Florida and Puerto Rico.

"We got broad press coverage right at the start," he remarked, citing every kind of publication, from *Good Housekeeping* to the funky 1980s journals of the new downtown crowd. "People of all types come here dressed as they like, without spending a lot of time or money. This is more like a French bistro than anything in New York."

Much as the recorded music shifts from reggae-rock to a Nino Rota film score, so the crowd here shifts from midwesterners to celebrities to the Manhattan party crowd. "I remember this older couple who walked in with the American Airlines magazine issue that featured us," Morellet said. "They sat down right next to a young gay couple, bizarre boys in strange outfits and dyed blue hair. The straight couple didn't mind them at all, didn't even notice them, I don't think. Which was funny, because the woman's hair was dyed that same shade of blue."

"I think there will always be a meat industry here," Florent reflected, "though as some companies move away they make commercial space available. A few advertising concerns have space here now, along with the studios taken by artists and other craft people. We have some video concerns and a photo archive in one loft, all of which brings a whole new mix of people into the neighborhood."

Perhaps that's why the meat packers have gotten used to seeing limousines outside Florent's as they arrive for work around dawn. "We are good neighbors, and they tend to ignore us, much as they ignore the celebrities who come to Florent's. One day when it was busy, Christopher Reeve came in and was seated at the counter.

Somebody pulled the waitress aside and told her she had just seated Superman, but she said, 'So what? He can sit at the counter just like anyone else.' Prince Albert of Monaco was here, and Jackie Onassis not too long ago, but nobody bothered them, which is the way they like it. I like it that way, too. Let someone bother any of my customers"—Florent grinned—"and I fix that person: I will kill them with my eyes!"

Finding His Voice

Edward Estlin Cummings started at the bottom of Thirteenth Street. P. F. Collier & Son needed someone to reply to the mail received in response to *Collier's Weekly,* the popular magazine published from offices at 416 West Thirteenth Street. Fresh from Harvard, Cummings was hired in 1917 and for $50 a week endured three months of the fractured spelling and tortured syntax that seemed to him to be a rustic national tongue. Partly from that language poet E. E. Cummings developed the "voice" that was to bring fame to him in his little Patchin Place studio.

Incidentally, the Collier's Building has outlived the publication, but its half-globe logo still presides over the building entrance. It is doubtless ignored by revelers headed home from Mars, the flashy dance palace that appeared in 1988 in an abandoned warehouse at the waterfront end of Thirteenth.

ON THE WATERFRONT

Before the meat packers moved in, the northern part of the West Village waterfront was a warren of coal yards, piano manufacturers, book binderies, lumberyards, paint factories, and plaster mills. But from the 1850s through the 1890s, the area's major industry was the huge Delamater Iron Works.

The iron works were run by Cornelius Delamater in association with the Swedish inventor John Ericsson. Here Ericsson worked on the screw propellor that revolutionized sea travel. But Ericsson is best known for designing the *Monitor,* the Union ironclad warship that preserved the blockade of southern ports to turn the tide in the Civil War. Initially derided as a Yankee cheese box on a raft, the *Monitor* introduced the revolving turret, a critical component of modern warfare. Its turret, ventilation system, and forced-draft furnace were all driven by the same engine that drove its propellor, and that engine was designed and built at the Delamater Works. Before it closed Delamater also pioneered in the construction of early submarines, the design of torpedoes, and the creation of the Delamater caloric engine, which was critical in pumping water to the upper floors of the new towers known as skyscrapers.

A Chemical Reaction

Among the first industrial companies to move to the West Village was the New York Chemical Manufacturing Company. Opening on the Hudson River at Thirteenth Street in 1823, it successfully produced vitriol, alum, saltpeter, and camphor as well as various drugs, dyes, and paints. To better use the company's assets, the six directors expanded the company charter in 1824 to permit the formation of their own bank. They stopped making chemicals and drugs in 1844, and Chemical Bank is today the fourth largest bank in America.

The Delamater Iron Works, seen here in 1863, sprawled along the Hudson waterfront at the foot of West Thirteenth Street.

WHAT BECOMES A LEGEND MOST?

The 1980s party crowd wasn't the first to discover Fantasyland in the meat-packing district, just the first to be driven there by chauffeurs. As early as the 1920s, these forbidding, dimly lit side streets were a hunting ground for homosexuals on the make as they cruised between the dangerous bars of the waterfront. The quasi-legal status of gay bars fostered a system of payoffs to the police that survived the repeal of Prohibition only to be threatened by the 1969 Stonewall Riot. A new money-maker was found in the "back room bar," which took furtive sex off the streets and brought it profitably indoors.

A precurser of the back room bar was Christopher's End, a sleazy waterfront dive that opened in the old Hotel Christopher in the late 1960s. Manager Mike Umbers was vilified as an opportunist by the fledgling gay community, but it had little clout in those days, while Umbers had nude go-go boys dancing on his bar. Christopher's End did a whopping business even before the dancers began circulating through the crowd between sets. There was little distance between that and a back room bar, but the distance was bridged in March 1970 by the Zoo, which opened at 421 West Thirteenth on the site of the Delamater Iron Works. Its "members only" policy was a legal dodge that permitted after-hours operation, though according to historian Toby Marotta it was widely rumored that the owners were making payoffs to the police. Porno films projected above the front bar fostered a do-it-yourself mentality that was carried over into the dark recesses of the club.

The clubs that opened in the 1970s made the Zoo seem tame by comparison. The Anvil, on the waterfront at Fourteenth Street, gave its runway-bar over to live sex shows that were sure to shock even its most jaded customers. Eventually the back room activity shifted from a cramped utility room to the basement, and lip-synching drag stars took over the runway to provide much-needed comic relief. A block east on Fourteenth Street at Ninth Avenue, the Triangle Building became a hotbed of activity. The Triangle opened as a conventional gay bar at street level but upstairs the Barn was anything but conventional: there was an optional clothes-check at the door—the ultimate ice-breaker. By the mid-1970s, the building's dungeonlike basement had become a private club with a euphonious name: the Sewer. Reportedly used during the Civil War to hold a cache of explosives, this dank, raw space was soon transformed into a heterosexual S&M club called Hellfire, which was written up in *Penthouse* magazine, the *New York Post,* and *The New Yorker*—yes, *The New Yorker!*

The Mineshaft opened in September 1976 as the citadel of raw masculine sex. Taking over a decaying restaurant from the 1940s, it grew out of three separate gay clubs that had been in operation there. A chaste leather bar called the Den operated at street level, while upstairs a back room club called Zodiac vied for space with the Mine Shaft Disco. Aluminum foil wallpaper gave the Mine Shaft a metallic look, and lighted miners' hats worn by humpy bartenders completed its coy atmosphere. Later, when the Mineshaft expanded, the owners retained the bartenders but banished the hats and foil along with Lacoste shirts, disco drag, and cologne.

The city shut down the Mineshaft with national fanfare in 1985, a move designed to show it was doing something about the AIDS epidemic. City inspectors loudly professed to be shocked at "discovering" what had been going on in this club at the corner of Washington and Little West Twelfth streets. By 1985, however,

MINE SHAFT Dress Code

THE DRESS CODE as adopted by the membership on the first of October 1976 will apply during 1978 & 1979.

APPROVED ARE CYCLE & WESTERN GEAR, LEVIS, T-SHIRTS UNIFORMS, JOCK STRAPS, PLAID & PLAIN SHIRTS, CUT OFFS, CLUB PATCHES, OVERLAYS & SWEAT

NO COLOGNE or PERFUME or DESIGNER SWEATERS.
NO SUITS, TIES, DRESS PANTS or JACKETS.
NO RUGBY STYLED SHIRTS or DISCO DRAG
NO COATS in the PLAYGROUND

The Zoo was quickly imitated by a dozen similar operations, among them the former International Tavern at 733 Greenwich Street. A back room that had been used in the 1950s for poetry readings provided International Stud patrons a setting for less lofty pursuits in the 1970s. Distinguished literature, however, prevailed, as both this bar and its back room were immortalized in Harvey Fierstein's 1978 play, *The International Stud*, which was later incorporated into his award-winning drama, *Torch Song Trilogy*.

The shuttered Mineshaft on Washington Street at Little West Twelfth. Although this place was a sex club notorious among gay men around the world in the 1970s, it remained unknown to many neighbors living a block or so away.

business at the Mineshaft was off. Gay men had already adjusted to the unseen killer in their midst, and in the face of tragic losses were again reinventing themselves and their sexual expression rather than abandoning the self-empowerment they had won in front of the Stonewall. But before closing, the Mineshaft heightened its legendary status by becoming—improbably—an Off-Off Broadway theater.

Early in 1983, clip-on lights dispelled the club's darkness and incense vainly battled its stale aromas for the opening of *Street Theater,* Doric Wilson's farce about the events preceding the Stonewall riot. For four months, audiences packed the place to watch a nonprofessional cast reenact the fight for gay self-empowerment, circa 1969. At this writing, word is circulating that the former Mineshaft is to be gutted and rebuilt as a Caribbean restaurant (a fate that has already overtaken the International Stud). And as of this writing, gay people show every indication of their determination to continue to reinvent themselves and to continue to move forward.

THE VILLAGE VOLCANO

To most Villagers, 247 West Twelfth Street is just the old Castle Garage, as the painted sign on its north wall announces. But it was built in 1910 as a fire-resistant, if not fireproof, warehouse. Its owners must have been very confident about its safety, because twelve years after it opened the building was used to store whiskey, rubber products, paper, and photographer's flash powder.

Fireproof? The building burned for five days and nights, starting on July 18, 1922, frequently exploding when a new cache of flash powder or whiskey caught fire. With each explosion, doors, chairs, desks, timbers, and other items were blown out the windows or through the roof. Debris rained down on the neighborhood for days, leading firemen to refer to the blaze as the Village Volcano.

The end came on July 23 with a final explosion that blew away large portions of the exterior walls. The adjacent house at 8 Jane Street was critically damaged, and two firemen were dead, but the Village Volcano was extinguished. The damaged portions of the building were patched with bricks of a different color, which are clearly visible on the upper sections of the facade today. Having functioned into the 1970s as a parking garage, the building has attained the nirvana that is the goal of every good volcano: it's now condominiums.

FIGHTING OFF PLAQUE

A plaque on the outside wall of an 1886 apartment house at 82 Jane Street marks this as the site of the country home of William Bayard, where Alexander Hamilton died on July 12, 1804, after being wounded in a duel with Aaron Burr. There's only one problem—the Bayard house never stood here.

A map drawn in 1767 places William Bayard's house just below the present Gansevoort Street. The house was not on the south side of Jane Street but north of it, close to the present Horatio Street—possibly even in its path, as Horatio wasn't mapped until 1817 or opened until 1835. But this hardly mattered to the 1936 owner of 82 Jane Street, who installed this plaque, thereby slipping his building into half a century's worth of books about the Village.

THE $6,000-PER-INCH HIGHWAY

It began in 1971 as Wateredge, a whimsy intended to develop waterfront land while creating a replacement for the deteriorating West Side Elevated Highway, then the city's second busiest artery. By 1974 it had mushroomed into Westway, a 4.2-mile Interstate Highway to be built beneath 170 acres of landfill at a cost of $1.7 billion—that's over $6,000 per running inch. Because this was to be a federal project, 90 percent of Westway's costs would have been paid by the federal government with tax dollars, even though the completed highway would benefit the city and state treasuries—a very nice deal. The problem with Westway was that New Yorkers didn't want it.

Congressman Hugh Carey of Brooklyn was elected governor in 1974, partly because of his anti-Westway position. Once elected, however, he reversed himself and endorsed the project. Congressman Edward Koch was elected mayor in 1977, in part because he opposed Westway. Once elected . . . guess what?

The old West Side Highway, built in the 1920s, had been weakened by years of inadequate maintenance, but it remained in

Villagers picnic on a typical Sunday on Morton Street Pier, 1983. The pier shed to the north was later demolished by the state, and Morton Street Pier has been allowed to fall into decay. Scenes such as this may have been pleasant, but they weren't making anyone rich. The same cannot be said of the proposed Westway, which citizen opposition has thwarted —for the present.

use until December 15, 1973, when a dump truck repairing sections of the highway actually fell through the roadway at Gansevoort Street. At that point the elevated was closed to traffic. Later, the truck was reported to have been carrying thirty tons of asphalt.

The battle over Westway dragged through a decade of court challenges and environmental studies while joggers and bikers happily used the closed highway for peaceful pleasures. Opposing three layers of government pressure were clean-air lobbyist Marcy Benstock, lawyer Albert Butzel, several ad hoc Village committees, and Village Community Board 2. Finally, in August 1985, Westway was officially laid to rest. The nominal reason for its demise? Striped bass. These fish, it was said, used the Hudson River estuary for breeding, which made the area the basis of a $200-million-a-year fishing industry.

In 1982 and again in 1985, Federal District Judge Thomas Griesa ruled that the findings supporting Westway were "marred by excessive advocacy." It seems that the government had compiled data that were flawed and insufficient and had conjured up traffic estimates that were clearly *under*estimates. The final blow to Westway was the judge's rejection of the Army Corps of Engineers' landfill permit, which rested on testimony labeled by the judge as "incredible . . . a sheer fiction."

Meanwhile, in 1983, with loud fanfare about protecting its citizens from a safety hazard, local government began demolishing the old West Side Highway, neatly preventing any possibility of its being repaired. Similarly, it allowed Village piers to deteriorate, presumably because Westway would make them unnecessary, though they had long been in use by Villagers for quiet, and free, recreation. In May 1986 the State Department of Transportation moved in and began to demolish the piers without benefit of a public hearing. As West Village residents mobilized against this maneuver, the department declared that the piers were so badly rotted that use by even a few people might cause them to collapse. It then installed around the perimeter of each pier a barricade of over 140 cement blocks weighing hundreds of pounds each. Mobilization saved the few piers that remained and forced the state to refrain from further demolition.

In August 1987, Governor Mario Cuomo and Mayor Edward Koch gave birth to "Son of Westway," the Westway substitute. "This disastrous agreement signals Governor Cuomo's intention to pursue the Westway's costly, illegal, environmentally damaging landfill and platforms for luxury development in the Hudson River," Marcy Benstock was quoted as saying in May 1988. The present schedule of the appeals process prevents any express road from opening sooner than the mid-1990s.

And there the matter rests. Stay tuned.

Elevating Commuters

Traffic gridlock gave Manhattan commuters headaches long before the invention of the automobile. Thirty years before the subway opened to provide underground rapid transit, commuters avoided gridlock by traveling above city streets on the world's first elevated railway.

Service began on the Ninth Avenue El on February 14, 1870, though in the early years the line ran north only as far as the Thirtieth Street train yards. The El initially used a temperamental cable system that was soon replaced by steam engines, which remained in service until the line was electrified in 1902. By then the Ninth Avenue El had been joined by elevated lines up Second, Third, and Sixth avenues carrying a total of 250 million riders annually.

The Ninth Avenue El ran until 1927, when it was removed as part of the plan that installed the West Side Highway and the elevated freight line. It's seen here in May 1876 from Gansevoort Street, with Little West Twelfth Street passing to the left.

VILLAGE LANDMARKS: INVENTING THE FUTURE

At Westbeth, where graphic and performing arts thrive today, television, radio, sound recording, sound movies, telephonics, and the public address system were long ago invented or perfected. For years, 463 West Street was the research facility of Western Electric and, later, the Bell Laboratories. Its landfill site, between Bethune and Bank streets, was a century ago a clutter of ramshackle residences and waterfront businesses. Western Electric bought the entire block so that it could consolidate its telephone manufacturing division in an attempt to meet rising demand. More than five thousand pilings were driven into the sandy

Westbeth, the artists' cooperative
at 463 West Street, as it looks today.

This sculpture by David Seccombe
stands in the courtyard of
Westbeth, an artists' cooperative
at 463 West Street. Resembling a
knot trying to untie itself, it's a
fitting symbol of the challenge
for artists: to solve a problem of
their own devising. Established in
1967 in the former Bell Labs, the
complex has 384 apartments—and
an eight-year waiting list. It's
often cited as the prototype for
many of New York's more recent
loft conversions.

subsoil to support the weight of the complex. At $1.4 million, the
Western Electric facility was the most costly structure in the Village
when it opened in 1899. Over the next two decades the research
division expanded, forcing the company to move its telephone
manufacturing division elsewhere by stages. By 1920, the entire
complex was devoted to research—with fascinating results.

The initial goal was cross-country phone service, which West
Street scientists achieved January 25, 1915, when Alexander
Graham Bell in New York spoke with former assistant Thomas
Watson in San Francisco. Critical to this success was the vacuum
tube, which amplified sound 130 times better than a gas-filled radio
tube. The following year, West Street scientists perfected the condenser microphone, permitting the reliable transmission of the full
range of the human voice. Armed with these devices, the scientists
built the first successful public address system, which debuted on
March 4, 1921, at the inauguration of President Warren Harding.

Not content with these achievements, the Western Electric
technicians then shifted their attention to radio, which was still the
province of ham operators. Western Electric licensed an experimental station, 2XS, which broadcast for two weeks beginning
April 22, 1920. The broadcasts offered phonograph music and
requests for comments from listeners. Enthusiastic letters arrived
from as far away as Albany, making it clear that people enjoyed
hearing broadcasts by wireless. The West Street scientists had
stumbled on a new entertainment medium. But how would the cost
of radio service be covered? For better or worse, AT&T engineers
came up with the answer: commercials.

Toll broadcasting, as it was called, began on July 25, 1922,

Pilings being sunk in 1897 for building sections of the Western Electric Labs, now Westbeth.

when WBAY took to the air. However, the weak signal from a new transmitter at 24 Walker Street discouraged advertisers from shelling out $50 to sponsor fifteen minutes of air time in the evening, or even $40 in the afternoon. The signal was strengthened when transmission was returned to West Street on August 16, by which time the station's call letters had been changed to WEAF, for the elements of Greek mythology: water, earth, air, fire. Finally, at 5:15 P.M. on August 28, 1922, the world's first commercial was broadcast from 463 West Street, promoting tenant-owned apartments in Jackson Heights. Tidewater Oil and American Express bought air time the following month, and that November Macy's paid for the first Christmas commercial even though AT&T in those days prohibited advertisers from describing product packaging or stating the selling price on the air.

The site of what is now 463 West Street, looking east along Bethune Street in 1896. Between the lumberyard in the foreground and Budd's Putty Factory ran Putty Alley, a now-forgotten Village enclave that could hardly have been the safest place to live. Little wonder that the blocks nearest the waterfront then seemed isolated from the residential Village.

A WEAF radio studio in February 1923. Note the condenser microphone on the stand to the right of the piano.

Despite such restrictions, toll broadcasting rapidly grew in popularity. In October 1922 phone lines were linked to the transmitter to provide New Yorkers with live play-by-play coverage of a football game in Illinois. Arias were soon transmitted from the Metropolitan Opera House, and the entire first act of a 1923 Broadway musical, *Wildflower*, was broadcast from the Casino Theatre. WEAF announcers and performers began receiving fan mail—after the 1925 World Series, WEAF's pioneer sportscaster Graham McNamee received fifty thousand letters.

West Street technicians knew they had a tiger by the tail, and they were none too pleased to find themselves suddenly in show business. The WEAF broadcasts took up too much of their time and interfered with other experiments. AT&T accordingly decided to withdraw from the commercial broadcasting it had invented; it sold WEAF in 1926 to the Radio Corporation of America for a million dollars. The new owners continued the station as WEAF until 1946, when its call letters were changed to WNBC, after the national network it headed. WNBC continued to operate until October 1988 when, after sixty-two years, the station and its broadcast frequency were sold by RCA's new parent company, General Electric.

By the time of RCA's 1926 purchase, WEAF had established connections with stations in other cities. This chain broadcasting dated from January 1923, when a WEAF broadcast was transmitted to Boston by telephone for rebroadcast there. As additional connections were established, Bell technicians kept track of them on a map at West Street, sketching one chain in red and the other in blue. Both the Red and the Blue Network passed to RCA in 1926 and in time became the National Broadcasting Company. NBC ran both networks into the 1950s, when a court-ordered divestiture turned the Blue Network into the American Broadcasting Company (ABC). Both began as colored pencil lines on a map at 463 West Street.

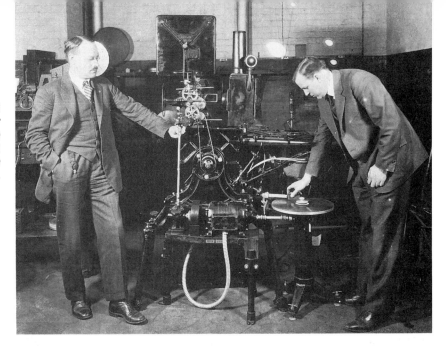

H. M. Stoller and H. Pfannenstiehl in May 1926, with their sound-on-disc motion picture projector, soon to be christened Vitaphone and to change the history of Hollywood.

The first successful sound-on-disc film projector was an ungainly device developed at West Street in 1923. It used one motor to drive both the projector and the disc player, permitting synchronous pictures and sound. Room 1109 at AT&T's West Street complex became a primitive sound stage, chosen for that function because an adjacent roof section permitted technicians to place the noisy camera on the other side of a window. The result of this project—a short film with sound—was shown at West Street for movie executive Sam Warner in 1925. The twelve-piece orchestra in the film sounded so good that Warner looked behind the screen for the live musicians. Bell technicians got a good laugh out of that.

Warner Brothers got Vitaphone out of it. With its 1926 feature, *Don Juan,* they demonstrated the commercial viability of sound movies. But the studio's initial idea was to record synchronized music only, providing the sound of full orchestras to movie theaters that could barely afford a pianist. No one considered recording the dialogue because, in the immortal words of Sam Warner's brother Harry, "Who the hell would want to hear actors talk?" Then, in 1927, Al Jolson spoke a few stray lines in *The Jazz Singer,* and Harry Warner got his answer.

AT&T cleared a section of its West Street property in September 1929 and erected the first fully equipped experimental film studio built expressly for the perfection of talkies. When it opened at 151 Bank Street the following February, its three floors contained a sound stage with monitoring facilities, a control room, a developing lab, an editing room, a screening room, and dressing rooms. Experiments here produced the improved optical sound track used by most Hollywood studios when sound-on-film replaced sound-on-disc in 1930. The former sound stage, which still stands, is now the Off-Off-Broadway Westbeth Theatre Center.

An experimental sound stage at 151 Bank Street, October 1929.

The Television, as reporters saw it on April 7, 1927. A standard telephone was used to pick up the voice. The image was received by a photoelectric cell inside a wood cabinet. The cabinet is visible on either side of the stool.

OK FOR TV

On April 7, 1927, reporters gathered in the eleventh floor auditorium of 463 West Street, above the corner of Bethune and Washington streets. There, on a cumbersome apparatus, they saw and heard Secretary of Commerce Herbert Hoover speaking from Washington, D.C. His monochromatic red-orange image flickered on the world's largest photo-electric cell—three inches wide and over a foot long. Peering into this unit, they witnessed the first transmission of synchronized picture and sound over distance—in other words, the first television broadcast.

This wasn't the kind of television technology we use today. Instead of dividing images into electronic bits through line scanning, it used a rotating disc with fifteen holes to flash successive intact images onto a photo-electric cell. In July 1929, Bell technicians used three televisions, each producing a separate monochromatic image, and by bouncing those images off a semi-transparent mirror, they focused them to produce a single full-color image. With a shot of several roses, an American flag, and a watermelon, color television was born.

After developing their condenser microphone, Bell engineers introduced full-frequency electronic recording. The success of this technique permitted them to devise the first binaural (stereo) recordings in 1930. But their oddest discovery came in 1928 when they spotted "ghosts." Long aware that radio waves bounced off the upper atmosphere, particularly at night, to produce an echo, West Street technicians were nevertheless surprised to discover that there was a television equivalent. Signals relayed back from Whippany, New Jersey, produced delayed and weak secondary images on West Street monitors. The technicians referred to them as "ghosts," and that's what they're called today, though with the advent of cable television, they are now seen by far fewer viewers. In 1929, by the way, it was Bell technicians who invented the high-frequency co-axial cable that made cable television possible.

The direct-scan television camera, on the roof of 463 West Street in July 1927. The image is focused by the glass lens and scanned by holes in the large rotating disc. This rooftop demonstration marked the first telecast using only natural light—as well as the world's first televised tennis game.

HOLLYWOOD ON THE HUDSON, PART 4

Sirens scream and tires squeal as Hollywood turns Gansevoort Street into a setting for a 1989 comedy, *See No Evil, Hear No Evil.* This scene was shot only five blocks from Westbeth, where talkies were perfected sixty-two years earlier.

Drivers, start your engines. Cue your background playback. Film is rolling, and . . . action!"

Having played a role in film history behind the scenes, it's only natural that Greenwich Village should step before the cameras to play itself in films. The odd juncture of Gansevoort and West Thirteenth streets proved ideal for a car chase in the 1989 feature *See No Evil, Hear No Evil,* starring Richard Pryor and Gene Wilder.

In the past, Hollywood movies were filmed on sets instead of on location. In 1949, for example, a section of Washington Square was built on a studio lot for *The Heiress,* the film adaptation of Henry James's *Washington Square.* In 1962, budget limitations brought cameras to actual locations on Bleecker Street for *The Greenwich Village Story.* Only four years later, crews shooting big-budget productions appeared on Village streets; for example, *Barefoot in the Park* was filmed on location in Washington Square and made use of the exterior of 111 Waverly Place. *Kojak* and *Fame* brought television crews to the Village a decade ago, and the area has recently become popular with makers of music videos: Billy Joel's "Piano Man" was filmed in the Duplex on Grove Street, and Tina Turner's "What's Love Got to Do with It?" was shot on the Seravelli Playground on Gansevoort Street, the same block used in *See No Evil, Hear No Evil.*

For another 1989 film, *The January Man,* 10 Sheridan Square—once the site of a "goofy" club called the Pirate's Den— became the scene of a vivid murder sequence. Back in 1986, the meat-packing district provided the setting for a spectacular car chase in *F/X.* Seeing such films with an all-Villager audience can be distracting, however, as it was when *The House on Carroll Street* was shown in the Village in 1988. A suspenseful chase sequence filmed in the Strand Bookstore was ruined by laughter when the characters escaped to the Cherry Lane Theatre "just around the corner"—actually half a mile away.

Film crews have taken over Village streets so frequently in recent years that a backlash has begun, but this is really nothing new. The first protests against Hollywood-on-the-Hudson were staged back in 1979, though they arose from political rather than neighborhood reasons. Angered by the anti-gay movie called *Cruising,* protesters tried to disrupt the crew filming the suspense drama, only to find themselves confronted by comic actress and director Nancy Walker. "You've got the wrong movie," she told them through her bullhorn. "You want the film down the street. This is *Can't Stop the Music*—we're the good guys." Banners high, the protesters turned around and disappeared down the block.

BANK-ABLE CREATIVITY

The Bank of New York could ill afford to suspend operations during the yellow fever epidemic of 1798, their assets being tied up in the cost of their new Wall Street offices. A plot of land near Greenwich Lane, which was then "out of town," became their insurance policy. The bank simply followed its customers to the village of Greenwich, where its employees could work in safety. When the fever returned to the city a year later, and one of its own tellers fell ill, the Bank of New York again escaped to Greenwich on September 21, 1799.

Bank Street is the result of this maneuver. According to Village legend, several New York banks operated from wooden shacks put up here during summer epidemics, leading to the naming of the lane in 1807. No traces of these banks remain. Instead, the street's serene row houses today echo the Bank Street of the 1840s. However, the Greek Revival row from 16 to 34 Bank may substantiate the legend—it's built on land sold in 1843 by the Bank of New York.

Numerous creative artists have made Bank Street their home. John Dos Passos wrote much of *Manhattan Transfer* at 11 Bank Street. That 1925 novel is an expressionist montage of New York, which was acclaimed by Sinclair Lewis as a novel of the first importance. A few doors away, a tablet celebrates Dos Passos's neighbor, Willa Cather. With her life-partner Edith Lewis, Cather took a large second-floor apartment at 5 Bank Street in the spring of 1912 and remained there until the building came down in 1927. Here she wrote her acclaimed novels of Americana, *O Pioneers!* and *My Ántonia;* her masterful portrait of virtue, *Death Comes for the Archbishop; One of Ours,* for which she won the 1923 Pulitzer Prize; and "Coming, Aphrodite!" a short story based on her Washington Square days. And at nearby 23 Bank was the home of biographer Katharine Anthony, who for thirty years lived here with her life-partner, pioneer educator Elisabeth Irwin of Little Red Schoolhouse fame.

Bank Street, just west of
Greenwich Avenue, a typical
tree-lined West Village street.

Young Betty Bacall moved to 75 Bank with her mother in 1940. She was living there when she was chosen Miss Greenwich Village in 1942, barely a year before Hollywood renamed her Lauren. West of Hudson Street is 105 Bank, to which John Lennon and Yoko Ono moved in September 1971. After renting this two-room apartment for nearly two years, they released it in 1973 to playwright John Guare.

With the profits from his father's publishing concern on Union Square, Gustave Schirmer built 69 Bank Street in 1905. Eleven years later it became the founding home of the famous Bank Street School. Initially an experiment in the education of preschool children, it grew into the Bank Street College of Education, which still reflects its Village origins despite having moved to new facilities near Columbia University.

A decade before the Bank Street School went north, the famous HB Studio moved into its permanent home at 120 Bank. The training of actors in classes independent of a school or a theater was something of a new concept when Herbert Berghof arrived in New York in 1939, a refugee from Nazi rule. Since the move to Bank Street in 1959, Berghof and his wife, actress Uta Hagen, have numbered among their students such actors as Anne Bancroft, Robert De Niro, Al Pacino, Bette Midler, Christopher Reeve, Matthew Broderick, and Lily Tomlin.

"THIS IS NOT OUR WAR"

The home of Willa Cather wasn't the only noted building that was lost in 1927 when the present apartment house at One Bank Street was constructed. Also demolished was 91 Greenwich Avenue. In 1918 the government claimed this small brick house had been the center of a conspiracy against the United States. Actually, it was nothing more than the editorial offices of a magazine that routinely tweaked the nose of business and government. The *Masses* was a ten cent monthly that advocated workmen's compensation, safe working conditions for miners, the right of women to vote and to receive birth control information, and the formation of a world peace organization. In the words of historian Albert Parry, it was "a magazine for liberals published by radicals."

The *Masses* first appeared in January 1911, edited somewhat casually by a Dutch-born socialist named Piet Vlag. When revenues dwindled and its patron withdrew his funding, Vlag allowed the *Masses* to suspend publication. However, its contributing writers and artists decided to keep it going themselves, and for their new editor chose Max Eastman, recently bounced from the Columbia University faculty because of his radical political views. A torn scrap of paper was slipped to Eastman in August 1912: "You are

Village Voices

"Here [in Greenwich Village] a woman could say damn right out loud and still be respected."

Art Young,
in his autobiography,
On My Way, 1928

elected editor of the *Masses*—No pay." Five months later the magazine was reborn in Eastman's image—radical, witty, and slick. Its political courage paved the way for two decades of little magazines, while its style and polish set the stage for its apolitical successor, *The New Yorker,* which appeared eight years after the *Masses* died.

By moving its office from 150 Nassau Street to 91 Greenwich Avenue in June 1913, the *Masses* became in fact what it already was in spirit, a product of Greenwich Village. The *Masses* published John Reed's "War in Paterson" essay, forcing other papers to cover the bloody strike in that city. It also published John Sloan's acerbic cartoon of a fat cat tycoon wondering when some striker would get shot to prove he was serious. It skirted the post office ban on mailing birth control information by publishing the addresses of clinics. And when wealthy contributors questioned its editorial policy, the *Masses* ran a cartoon in which skunks donated money to find out what was making their neighborhood stink.

Contributors—literally, for contributors seldom were paid—included Upton Sinclair, Carl Sandburg, Sherwood Anderson, Jo Davidson, Randolph Bourne, Susan Glaspell, and even Pablo Picasso. But the journal's sense of mission did not foster internal harmony—quite the reverse. One famous exchange involved managing editor Floyd Dell and the anarchist Hippolyte Havel. Outraged to learn that a democratic vote determined what the *Masses* published, Havel protested that poetry was the product of the soul. "How can you vote on a poem?" he bellowed. Dell tactfully reminded Havel that he had helped Emma Goldman with her radical periodical, *Mother Earth.* "And you voted on submissions to *Mother Earth,* didn't you?" Dell asked. "Yes," Havel hotly replied, "but we didn't abide by the results!"

A far more serious rift occurred in 1916 when President Woodrow Wilson, who had been reelected on a peace platform, pushed America into World War I a month after his second inauguration. A nation that had crooned "I Didn't Raise My Boy to Be a Soldier" in 1915 was now singing "Over There." War fever had even managed to infect iconoclastic Greenwich Village in June 1917, when the week-long Alley Fiesta was held in MacDougal Alley to benefit war relief organizations.

The *Masses,* seeing the greed that the flag-waving concealed, proclaimed what a militaristic government wanted no one to know. John Reed quoted Congressional reports to prove that "preparedness" organizations were run by steel mill owners, munitions manufacturers, and shipbuilders. Reed listed them by name. Profiteers who feared the rising labor movement were seeking a profitable refuge in international war, cloaking their scramble for spoils in patriotic platitudes. In the July 1916 issue of *Masses,* Reed named

America's enemy: it was not Germany but "that 2 percent of the United States that owns 60 percent of the national wealth." Like all Reed essays on the subject, it closed with his benediction: "This is not our war."

For their trouble, *Masses* contributors were accused of being pro-German and worse. After the August 1917 issue was banned by the Post Office under the Espionage Act, the government claimed the *Masses* was no longer a monthly and revoked its mailing permit. It pressured subway and elevated newsstands to stop carrying the *Masses,* and these tactics led to its demise in December 1917. Four months later, the government charged Max Eastman, Floyd Dell, Art Young, and John Reed with "conspiracy against the government for interfering with enlistment," a charge that could carry twenty-one years' imprisonment. Their trials, in April and September 1918, resulted in hung juries, after which—the war having ended in November 1918—the charges were quietly dropped.

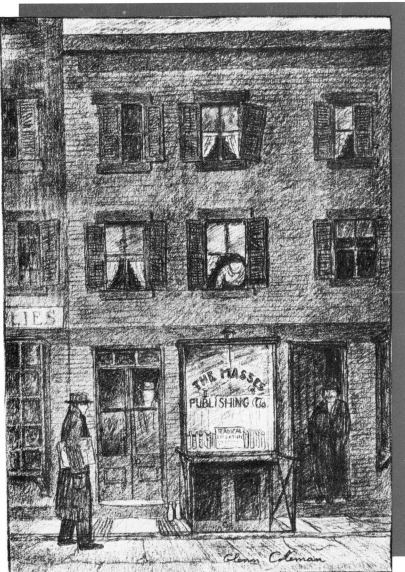

The offices of the *Masses* at 91 Greenwich Avenue, drawn for its June 1914 issue by contributing artist Glenn O. Coleman.

A video store now occupies the ground floor at 91 Greenwich Avenue. Its stock includes *Reds,* Warren Beatty's 1981 film biography of John Reed. But unlike the Willa Cather site around the corner, no plaque recalls the *Masses* or its editors' valiant struggle to live by the principles other Americans so glibly espoused. Political dissent remains the bulwark of the Village mentality today, and even though dissent is no easier now than it was then, the *Masses'* editors might be somewhat pleased to learn how many of their positions are now supported by federal law.

"MAIN STREET"

Between the clashing street grids of the North and West Village, Greenwich Avenue runs like a truce. It conforms to neither pattern; no adjacent street is its parallel companion, nor does any street—except for one accommodating block of Tenth—cross it at a right angle. It retains a residential character, though it has been widened into a major traffic route and most of its surviving row houses are occupied by shops at street level. It's the closest thing the West Village has to a Main Street where residents run into one another and cluster to chat, a casual street that offers sidewalk dining and window shopping.

Greenwich Avenue was known as Greenwich Lane until 1843. It is the only surviving segment of a path that, prior to 1828, continued east of Sixth Avenue and connected with Astor Place. That path was one of the five Indian paths through the forested area that became Greenwich Village, which means that people have been running into one another along Greenwich Avenue or its predecessors for at least 350 years.

One of the most curious events in the history of Greenwich Avenue occurred on what is now a school playground at the head of Charles Street. On November 20, 1851, in the school that stood on this site, a teacher grew suddenly faint and asked a student for a glass of water. The request as relayed became an appeal for water to extinguish a fire. Before teachers could intervene, panicked students stampeded down the stairs to escape the nonexistent blaze. But the main doors of P.S. 26 opened inward, and in the crush this made it impossible for anyone to get out. Some students were trampled to death in the melee, others suffocated. Still others ran back upstairs and jumped from second- or third-floor windows—many of them to their death. The fire that hadn't occurred claimed more than forty lives, and this led the state government to act within six weeks to require doors of public buildings to open outward—a legislative landmark.

Among the public buildings in the Greenwich Avenue area was the Jefferson Market Courthouse complex in the 1870s. The court-

Looking north up Greenwich Avenue in 1914, from the platform of the Sixth Avenue El station at Eighth Street. Trolley tracks disappear at the left onto Christopher Street. At right is a section of the Jefferson Market jail, later replaced by the Women's House of Detention and, since 1973, a garden.

house itself, now a branch library, is on Sixth Avenue, but some of the adjoining buildings stood along Greenwich Avenue. All of them are now gone. A jail designed in Venetian Gothic style was demolished in the 1920s and replaced in 1929 by the fourteen-story Women's House of Detention, which stood there until 1973. That structure's modified Art Deco details were not its most interesting feature. That distinction went to the colorful brigade of hookers who gathered nightly across the avenue between Christopher and Tenth streets to shout to their incarcerated friends, who would then yell down from the windows of their jail cells. When the city could find no use for the building after it closed, an intense campaign led to the present "English country garden," planned in 1975 by landscape designer Pamela Berdan, a Village resident.

Another garden grew on Greenwich Avenue for over ten years before yielding to development in the mid-1980s. The triangle formed at Seventh Avenue and Twelfth Street is now an underground service center, built as part of the $80 million expansion program that St. Vincent's Hospital completed in 1987. Originally the plot was cluttered with ramshackle residences. One at 86 Greenwich Avenue was the home of Provincetown Playhouse director James Light, who turned it into a combination office and dormitory for people who were associated with the company. Later, from 1921 through 1970, the block was entirely taken up by the 3,000-seat Loew's Sheridan, the only movie palace ever constructed in the West Village. After the theater was torn down, delays in hospital construction prompted St. Vincent's to allow Villagers access to the site, with the understanding that the garden they planted could not bloom forever. And it didn't.

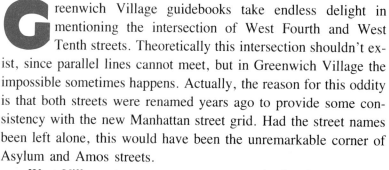

REAL PEOPLE

Greenwich Village guidebooks take endless delight in mentioning the intersection of West Fourth and West Tenth streets. Theoretically this intersection shouldn't exist, since parallel lines cannot meet, but in Greenwich Village the impossible sometimes happens. Actually, the reason for this oddity is that both streets were renamed years ago to provide some consistency with the new Manhattan street grid. Had the street names been left alone, this would have been the unremarkable corner of Asylum and Amos streets.

West Village streets were, as a group, the last in Manhattan named to reflect their origins. There was, for example, an asylum on Asylum Street. The Orphan Asylum Society was formed in 1806, the first institution of its kind in America. It stood east of what is now Fourth Street between the present Bank and Twelfth streets. When the asylum was demolished, Asylum Street was renamed in 1833 and became an extension of Fourth Street. Nearby Bethune Street honors Mrs. Joanna Bethune, a Villager who served for years as one of the asylum's directors.

Neighboring Jane Street is said to have been named for the landowning Jaynes family, then later altered by another Villager, Mrs. Jane Gahn. Revolutionary War General Horatio Gates is remembered in Horatio Street, while Perry Street honors Oliver Hazard Perry, a commander in the War of 1812.

Eleventh Street was laid out in 1799 by Abijah Hammond, for whom it was originally named. Hammond Street bisected Hammond's farm, a fifty-five-acre tract carved out of the old Peter Warren estate—and which, in that year, Hammond decided to sell off to developers. A survivor of his efforts is a brick-faced wood frame house at 282 West Eleventh Street, built in 1818 and little altered since then.

Similarly, Richard Amos held a strip of the old Warren estate running west of Bleecker Street between the present Christopher and Perry streets. By 1809, this fiesty survivor of the Revolution saw development was more profitable than farming. He ceded to the city the land that was to become Charles and Amos (Tenth) streets—with a catch. His farmhouse, which stood in the projected path of Amos Street, was not to be disturbed for five years. By 1815 Amos had moved into a new home a few feet to the south, at what is now 685 Greenwich Street. At that point in time the present Tenth Street was cut through. Amos remained in his Greenwich Street house until his death in 1837 at the age of seventy-seven. That house stood until 1906, when it was demolished so that the present PATH substation could be built.

By local legend, Christopher and Charles streets are said to be named for a trustee of the Warren estate, Charles Christopher Amos. However, until 1936 the north side of Charles Street from Bleecker to West Fourth was known as Van Nest Place, recalling the last owner of Peter Warren's manor house. This name posed two problems: it was confusing to have different names for opposite sides of the same street; and there was another Van Nest Place in the Bronx. This was too odd even for the Village, and residents finally requested the change of name.

Weathering Cement Triangle on Seventh Avenue South at Waverly Place, an artistic experiment and a legal nightmare.

ANOTHER TRIANGLE TANGLE

Artist Terry Fugate-Wilcox designed his *Weathering Cement Triangle* to demonstrate a process. As it turns out, he succeeded—though the process his work demonstrated wasn't the one he intended.

Fugate-Wilcox's fifteen-foot white triangle was installed in 1983 on Seventh Avenue near Waverly Place on a plot left over from the 1915 Subway Cut. Under its surface the artist embedded small bits of steel, bronze, brass, copper, and iron, "laid down in a weeping willow pattern," Mr. Fugate-Wilcox explained. As these fragments rusted over time, a willow-tree pattern would become

Memphis Downtown, at 140 Charles Street, alerted Villagers to the dangers of construction on the waterfront.

visible, and what had begun as a snow-white sheet would be changed by the weather into colors that would complement the Village itself. That was the plan, but light rainfall undermined the natural process and a storm of controversy arose. What had started as sculptural art turned into a five-year legal performance piece.

The tiny triangular plot, technically 159 Seventh Avenue South, was purchased from the city for $450 by the artist's wife, Valerie Shakespeare. Though several agencies of government were aware of the project, other agencies saw the work as setting a precedent for unauthorized alterations within a historic district. There were other problems. "It brought about complaints from neighbors," Landmarks Commissioner Gene Norman commented. "It was being used as a convenient scaling point to gain access to adjacent apartments, to peep into them, all sorts of mayhem."

Supported by the local community board, the city sued Ms. Shakespeare as the owner of the property for $1 million—even, according to Fugate-Wilcox, briefly issuing a warrant for her arrest—while, at the same time, *Weathering Cement Triangle* was given mention in a book about the notable sculptures of New York.

"Greenwich Village *is* change," Fugate-Wilcox insists, and change is what his triangle is designed to show. "It's important that the Village be allowed to continue to change. So I'm trying to see if the courts will uphold the city's right to ban artworks in a historic district, even if it's on private property."

Spray-paint graffiti washes off the triangle's treated cement surface, but the legal tangle persists. Though it is slated for removal to continue weathering in Old Wick, New Jersey, the legal questions raised by Fugate-Wilcox's triangle continue to weather through the city's legal system. As with the Westway controversy, stay tuned.

SOMETHING BORROWED, SOMETHING BIG

The lopsided cottage at 121 Charles Street looks like a valiant survivor of the Village of long ago. It's a survivor, all right, but one that was transplanted in 1967 from the Upper East Side. Demolition on York Avenue at Seventy-first Street uncovered this farmhouse, long hidden inside a block surrounded by tenements. The little house, known as Cobble Court, was slated for demolition until its resident-owners Sven and Ingrid Bernhard won a reprieve and hatched a plan to move their home to a vacant plot on Charles Street. On Sunday, March 6, 1967, in a driving rain, their ramshackle home was trucked intact through the city streets—even the court's ancient cobblestones were uprooted and transported. Now located within the protective boundaries of the Village Historic District, it stands as a testament to the persistence of the Bernhards,

This house, which was transplanted from the Upper East Side, made it to 121 Charles Street just in time to be included inside the Village Historic District. Its exact age is unknown, though it is generally thought to date from the early 1800s.

who at the time of the move were, appropriately, travel agents.

A few steps to the west, just outside the historic district, is another recent arrival on Charles Street, a 230-foot condominium tower known as Memphis Downtown. Designed by architect Carmi Bee, it opened in November 1986 after considerable negotiation and turmoil, yet it has been assimilated into the Village landscape with surprising ease. "The Village has always been a mixture," Mr. Bee commented, "but despite their diversity Villagers all respect the quality of their environment. We went to great lengths in using design components to minimize the scale of the Memphis: adding the horizontal bands, rounding the corners, and giving functional elements at the top a whimsical quality." The remarkably slender tower extends to the 1980s the observation that Greenwich Village features exemplary architecture of every decade from the 1790s to the present. Yet even Bee senses the danger to the Village that the success of the Memphis may represent. "Today the Memphis functions the way a church spire might have on the low line of a cityscape in Europe. But three or five such towers on top of one another would be oppressive and self-defeating. Clearly, it is the waterfront area of the Village that is threatened, a soft market which, in the next decade, will be critical in whether the character here survives or is forever altered. Attention has to be paid. I don't think the Village can support even one more tower."

WRITERS OF THE WEST VILLAGE

Village Voices

"I signalized my solidarity with the intellectual life by taking an apartment in Greenwich Village. . . . There seemed no other place in New York where a right-thinking person might live."

Lionel Trilling, as quoted in *Literary New York*, 1976

Theodore Dreiser's experiments in literary realism reached a peak in July 1914 after his move to 165 West Tenth Street. Having boldly probed the life of streetcar tycoon Charles Yerkes in *The Financier* and *The Tycoon,* Dreiser turned to a subject he knew more intimately: himself. For *The "Genius,"* his lacerating depiction of the creative life, Dreiser used superficial details from the life of Village painter Everett Shinn to create Eugene Witla, a stand-in for Dreiser. Critical abuse greeted the novel on its October 1915 publication, and the following year the Society for the Suppression of Vice successfully banned it as obscene. A decade after Dreiser's 1919 departure, 165 West Tenth Street was demolished and replaced by a two-story commercial taxpayer fronting Seventh Avenue South, now housing the Taste of Tokyo restaurant.

James Agee took the ground floor of 38 Perry Street in 1933. Here he conceived and began writing the works that won him belated fame. An autobiographical novel, *A Death in the Family,* won him a posthumous Pulitzer in 1958. His portrait of sharecropper life, *Let Us Now Praise Famous Men,* was ignored when it was published in 1942, but it won praise when it was reissued in 1960.

Thomas Wolfe wrote several fictional portraits of Greenwich Village, always taking care to disguise the exact locale. While he was teaching at New York University in the 1920s, Wolfe lived at the Hotel Albert on University Place; it became the Hotel Leopold in *Of Time and the River* (1935). The scruffy studio he described in *The Web and the Rock* (1939) was at 13 East Eighth Street, not on Waverly Place. After moving to the West Village in 1925, he wrote *Look Homeward, Angel* (1929) at 263 West Eleventh Street, but he placed that house on Twelfth Street in a later novel, *You Can't Go Home Again* (1940).

Golden Eagle Press was a one-man operation run in the twenties and thirties from the basement of 48 Charles Street. There S. A. Jacobs was able to meet the exacting typographic demands of poet E. E. Cummings, who gave Jacobs the plum task of printing *him AND the critics,* a pamphlet distributed at the Provincetown Playhouse during the run of Cummings's experimental play *him.* Jacobs also did much of the typesetting for the noted Depression-era publisher Covici-Friede.

The West Village has been home to many other writers, including playwright Edward Albee, who wrote his first successful play, *The Zoo Story* (1958), on a rickety kitchen table at 238 West Fourth Street. Earlier in the 1950s, novelist William Styron lived at 45 Greenwich Avenue. Experimental novelist Thomas Pynchon worked on *Gravity's Rainbow* (1973) in the shadowy recesses of tiny Charles Lane. All but unknown, this alley runs a short block inland from the waterfront and is thought to mark the northern boundary of the 1797 state prison property. As Village enclaves go,

"Auntie Mame," royally ensconced at the Village Nursing Home, 1977.

it's probably the most rustic and the least known, which made it perfect for Pynchon, whose fabled reclusiveness makes J. D. Salinger seem as gregarious as Mayor Ed Koch.

However, the most famous literary name associated with the West Village belongs not to a writer but to a character. The 1839 house at 72 Bank Street was bought by Marion Tanner in 1927. It later became the setting of a 1955 novel by her nephew, Edward Everett Tanner III. If none of this sounds familiar, you may instead recognize the author by his pen name, Patrick Dennis, and Marion Tanner by the fictional name he gave to the most famous aunt in literature—*Auntie Mame*. An international best-seller, the novel was adapted as a Broadway comedy, a motion picture, a Broadway musical, and a film musical. Marion Tanner, who remained on Bank Street until 1964, was occasionally exasperated by the fame of her doppelgänger: "I don't especially like Auntie Mame," she was once quoted as saying. "I think I'm much nicer." Marion Tanner died in 1985 at the Village Nursing Home on nearby Abingdon Square at the impressive age of ninety-four, but Auntie Mame lives on.

**ALL
THAT
JAZZ**

Three clubs in the 1950s made the West Village the place to go to hear the best jazz in town. Their origins were as varied as their destinies proved to be, but for a few upbeat years they were collectively something else, man.

Julius' is reputedly the oldest continuously operated bar in the West Village, dating from 1864. Its front room is inside 188 Waverly Place, an 1826 wood frame house that became a small grocery in 1840. At some point in time it was expanded back into 159 West Tenth Street, an adjacent 1845 house that now provides the street address for Julius'. It also provided the back door used when the club was a speakeasy during Prohibition. This bar's live jazz performances may have begun then, along with the inexpensive burgers cited as "peerless" in a 1959 Village guidebook. They still are, though in the 1960s the live music was replaced by a jukebox—also peerless—when Julius' was transformed from a part-time to a full-time gay bar, the role in which it continues today.

Jazz also wailed during the fifties at Nick's, across Tenth Street at the corner of Seventh Avenue South, in an irregularly shaped 1923 building. During its heyday, the interior of Nick's looked like a cross between an English pub and a hunting lodge. Moose heads impassively surveyed the college crowd that packed the wooden booths carved deep with initials and obscenities. Dixieland was the draw, though in time the steaks at Nick's became as renowned as Julius' burgers. By the late 1960s, Nick's had become Your Father's Mustache, a parody of an 1890s ragtime club. After several derelict years, the building vanished almost overnight in January 1989, and its wedge-shaped plot was cleared for development. Elevated above two floors of retail and restaurant space there will soon be an enclosed, landscaped courtyard to be shared by seven condominium units. The low-rise project is to open in 1990, leading some of Nick's regulars to wonder whether a new restaurant there will restore jazz and the moose head to the site of their old haunt.

The youngest of the jazz clubs in the 1950s, the Village Vanguard, had opened its door in 1934. Of the three West Village clubs mentioned here, it's the only one that's still going strong. It's also the oldest continuously operated nightclub in Manhattan, having been run by founder Max Gordon for over half a century. He started the place himself in the basement of number one Charles Street, then moved it in 1935 to 178 Seventh Avenue South when a speakeasy there folded in the wake of repeal. Initially the entertainment in Gordon's new basement spot was poetry read by Village eccentrics Joe Gould, Maxwell Bodenheim, and Harry Kemp under the scattered direction of poet-emcee Eli Siegel. The gradual shift toward jazz began with folk music. Performing at the Vanguard in those days were legends like Leadbelly, Burl Ives, and the Weavers (Pete Seeger, Lee Hayes, Ronnie Gilbert, and Fred Hellerman). A

Julius' on West Tenth Street, a lively spot since 1864, is decked out for Gay Pride Day, 1988.

later wave of folksingers included Peter, Paul and Mary, the Kingston Trio, and Woody Guthrie. Calypso took the stage early in its 1950s revival, notably when an unknown Harry Belafonte played the Vanguard. Irwin Corey, Woody Allen, and Lenny Bruce brought their varied styles of stand-up comedy to Vanguard crowds as well.

But it was jazz that made and maintained the Vanguard, with performances by such legendary talents as Miles Davis, John Coltrane, Erroll Garner, Art Tatum, Coleman Hawkins, Dinah Washington, Charlie Parker, Thelonius Monk, Betty Carter, Art Blakey, Charles Mingus, Bill Evans, Dexter Gordon, Maxine Sullivan, Anita O'Day, Dizzy Gillespie, Sonny Rollins . . . the list can go on and on. Without question, the long-run record at the Vanguard is held by the big band that has played at the club on Monday nights since 1966. Organized by Mel Lewis and Thad Jones to provide Broadway musicians with a place to wail on their night off, the band has given over 1,200 performances to date. But it's not the only tie between the Village Vanguard and Broadway.

In 1938 the Vanguard launched the careers of the Broadway and Hollywood writing team of Betty Comden and Adolph Green and of actress Judy Holliday. These three joined with John Frank and Alvin Hammer to form the Revuers, a troupe that created and performed topical satires in the manner of the mini-rep companies that later flourished on *Saturday Night Live*. By Betty Comden's later account, their greatest challenge initially was devising opening numbers that would allow them to wear their coats—the Vanguard was, at that time, unheated.

In 1943 their fortunes were changed when Hollywood beckoned. The Revuers were summoned west to appear in a Carmen Miranda musical called *Greenwich Village*—only to see their specialty numbers wind up on the cutting room floor. After returning to New York, Comden and Green won lasting success on Broadway when they wrote the script and lyrics for their first musical, *On the Town* (1944), to a score by their friend, sometime-Villager Leonard Bernstein. Judy Holliday rose to Broadway stardom two years later in *Born Yesterday*. A decade later, the three former Revuers were reunited for the Broadway musical *Bells Are Ringing,* Holliday's greatest stage triumph and the basis of a 1960 film. Sadly, Holliday died of cancer in 1965. Comden and Green went on to write the screenplays for *Singin' in the Rain* and *The Bandwagon.* They also worked on two projects set in the Village: *Wonderful Town* (1953)—the musical based on *My Sister Eileen*—and the film version of *Auntie Mame* (1958).

Village Voices

"Max Gordon has been a catalyst by which thousands upon thousands have known resoundingly memorable evenings of music and mordant comedy on his premises."

Nat Hentoff,
in his introduction to
Max Gordon's autobiography,
Live at the Village Vanguard, 1982

The Village Vanguard, the jazz club at 178 Seventh Avenue South, looking much as it did when it moved here in 1935. After the May 1989 death of its founder, Max Gordon, the Village Vanguard continued operating under the direction of his widow, Lorraine Gordon.

THE VILLAGE HALLOWEEN PARADE

The Greenwich Village Halloween Parade began some twenty years ago as an arts project funded through Westbeth. Its artists created an extravagant street pageant intended to amuse the younger residents of the West Village. But as the crowds along the parade route grew larger each year, the Halloween Parade grew into an annual event that draws the whole city into participation—the West Village answer to Mardi Gras.

Most of the West Village is closed to traffic, as hordes of people turn the streets into an open-air party. Despite the brisk autumn weather, there is always a great emphasis on ribald vulgarity, along with as much good-natured nudity as the streets can bear. Much of this madness winds up on television news broadcasts as comic relief, which has made the parade a national event.

The 1987 Greenwich Village Halloween Parade—from the ridiculously sublime to the sublimely ridiculous. At right, Rollerina, New York's official fairy godmother, puts in her traditional appearance. Eric Staller's Lightmobile is a Volkswagen festooned with 1,600 computerized lights flashing in sequence. His *Bubbleheads*, at left, is a striking bike illusion for four, unmasked by the flash camera.

VILLAGE PEOPLE: GRIFFIN GOLD

Griffin Gold, in the Eleventh Street offices of the People With AIDS Coalition.

More than any district of Greenwich Village, the West Village suffered heavy losses during the AIDS epidemic of the 1980s. "Store for rent" signs became a common sight on Christopher Street, though small gay-owned businesses were hardly the only economic losers. Several million dollars had turned the crumbling Hotel Christopher into the sleek River Hotel in 1983, intended to attract wealthy gay tourists, but after limping along the building became Bailey House in 1987, a city-owned residence for homeless AIDS patients.

The spirit that fostered the gay activism of the 1960s was revived in the 1980s to confront a new challenge. One of its most remarkable creations was the PWA Coalition, founded in 1985 by a group of people with AIDS. According to Griffin Gold, president of its board of directors, it is rare among service organizations in that it's composed of the people it is created to assist.

"The mission of the Coalition is the fostering of self-empowerment," Gold remarked. "Just last week a fellow came by and complained, 'My doctor makes me take medicine that makes me sick.' I said, 'Your doctor *makes* you take it?' 'Well, he says it's the best thing for me. What should I do?' So I told him if he wanted a doctor who would tell him *not* to take that medicine, I'd give him the phone numbers of three. But *he* would be responsible for selecting his doctor.

"One of the few silver linings to AIDS is learning to take responsibility for yourself, learning not to surrender power over you to others. That's why I'm not a 'victim' of AIDS, as the press too often insists. I am a person with AIDS—a term that eliminates a 'victim' mentality, a term that, like 'black' or 'gay,' has been coined by the people involved. Self-determination fosters self-empowerment.

"In some places, people can be very intolerant of differences, but not here. Greenwich Village *is* tolerance. I have a certain safe feeling here I might not have elsewhere in this city. For example, if I'm walking down Christopher Street and run into some kids who are out to 'fag-bash,' I know if the police come they'll be from the Village, from the Sixth Precinct, and as a gay man I'll be treated with respect.

"Greenwich Village is also about diversity. My block association includes retired women and widows, some gay men, some families . . . not exactly a group you'd expect to find together in one room. But we all care about our neighborhood, so who's gay and who's straight? Who cares? That might have mattered to me when I was in college, but not anymore. I guess that's part of growing up.

"Not that the Village is without problems. A case is now pending in which a barber at the NYU Medical Center refused to cut the hair of PWAs. Representing the Coalition, I spent three months negotiating with the hospital's public relations department and all they offered was another barber. I said, 'Look, if I run a restaurant where twelve waiters refuse to serve blacks and I hire one who will, I am *still* discriminating. It's not just a matter of providing the service. It's providing the same service to everyone in the same manner at the same time and the same price. It is the right to equal treatment, and I want my rights!' Now, imagine a 'victim' saying something like that!"

"Greenwich Village as we know it and love it would not exist today had it not been designated a historic district in 1969. It would be totally changed, an enclave of high-rise apartments that would have been built at the end of the 1960s. But as constituted, the Greenwich Village Historic District has been a spectacular success."

—Gene Norman, former chair,
Landmarks Preservation Commission

**ON
LANDMARKING**

Residents of the West Village were instrumental in getting the city's Landmarks Preservation Law passed in 1965. In the wake of the demolition of Pennsylvania Station in 1963, all New Yorkers saw what Villagers had long known—that a neighborhood has the right to influence its own destiny. Exercising that right was seldom easy, but Villagers had been doing it since 1818 and had recently saved their beloved Jefferson Market Courthouse. The struggle to save that one Village building, begun at Margot Gayle's 1959 Christmas party, now expanded to a concern for other structures and went citywide in an attempt to establish a legal system for landmark protection. As Kent Barwick commented, "There is a plausible relationship between the kitchen of Margot Gayle and the successful drive for a landmarks preservation law in New York."

Villagers had already organized in an attempt to limit further construction in their neighborhood. The result of their efforts was impressive: as a 1961 zoning change encouraged development elsewhere in Manhattan, Greenwich Village was "down-zoned"—a major victory for local activists. And as the Landmarks Preservation Law became reality, last-minute pressure from Villagers and residents of Brooklyn Heights forced the addition of the historic districts category. The residential nature of the Heights made it relatively easy for that area to win the distinction of becoming the city's first historic district in 1965. To Greenwich Village fell the

"Real-estate interests and some merchants were apprehensive about loss of property values through landmarking, seeing it as a force which creates stasis. But it's been well documented that the protection of Village qualities has contributed to the value of the property. When properly used, landmarking is a machine for refining the way we deal with change."

—Kent Barwick, chair,
Municipal Art Society

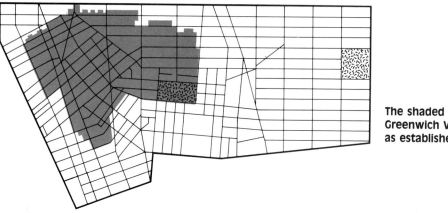

The shaded area represents the Greenwich Village Historic District, as established by law in 1969.

tougher task of establishing the need for comprehensive preservation of a sector that was a mix of the residential and the commercial. It wasn't easy.

Hearings on Village designation began in December 1965, barely eight months after the Landmarks Commission was established by law. Commercial and real-estate interests in the Village fought to exclude the avenues from designation. They also supported a counterproposal to create eighteen separate historic districts in the Village. These districts would have offered no comprehensive protection from development and would have possessed no clout.

Instead of waiting for Landmarks Commission researchers to provide data, Villagers flooded the hearings with documentation on the historic value of the area's structures and streets. Hearings continued through February 1967, but pressure from Village residents never flagged. On April 30, 1969, their efforts were rewarded as, with the stroke of a pen, 2,035 structures were placed under the protection of one comprehensive landmarked district that included virtually all of the West Village from Sixth Avenue to Hudson Street.

Excluded was the entire Village waterfront, which was thought to lack the residential character of the blocks within the Village district. In the wake of the Westway struggle, Villagers have

The stylish new Historic District markers, like this one on West Fourth Street, are hopefully high enough to elude scribblers.

awakened to the need to guard their waterfront and have rallied to bring it under landmark protection. Instead of attempting to win an expansion of the Village district, however, they are seeking designation for a separate and contiguous Waterfront Historic District in a grass-roots campaign similar to the landmarking movement of the 1960s.

Meanwhile, the lamppost signs that mark the boundaries of the Village Historic District—long since faded or removed—were replaced with colorful new markers in September 1988.

"I always knew Village streets were beautiful and interesting, but until I became active in historic preservation I didn't know the difference between a Federal and a Greek Revival. Now I can look at a lintel or the size of the window-panes and know the decade a house was built. It amuses me to be, in a way, an urban bird-watcher, which provides pleasure comparable to knowing the difference between a chickadee and a sparrow."

—Verna Small, chair,
Landmarks Committee
Community Board 2

6 THE SOUTH VILLAGE

The Feast of San Gennaro on Mulberry Street, one of the summertime treats in the South Village.

Pack several thousand people onto a narrow Village street, set up a Ferris wheel and a shrine to the Virgin, and then fill every inch of pavement with food stands packed with zeppoles, lulus, napoleons, and those greasy sausage heros that'll sit on your stomach for days— and what do you have? Three times each summer, you have the street festivals of New York's Little Italy. The barkers in the game booths keep up their cheerful spiel, insisting their games of skill are easy to win, and inevitably you'll spot

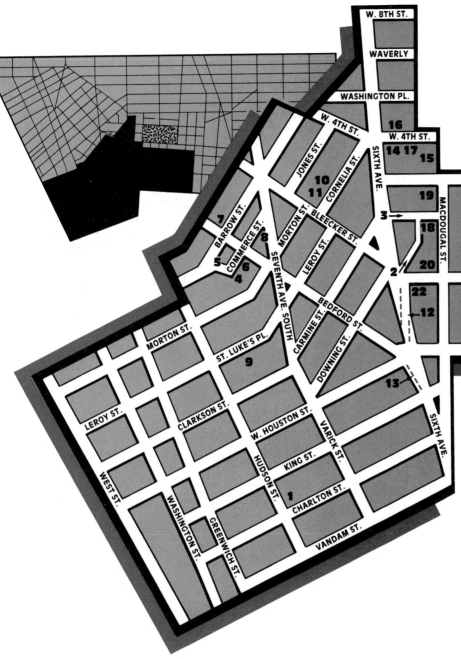

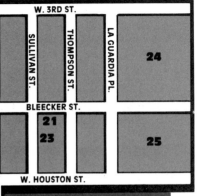

1 Site of Richmond Hill
2 Minetta St.
3 Minetta Ln.
4 Cherry Lane Theatre
5 39 and 41 Commerce St.
6 77 Bedford St.
7 Chumley's
8 Former PureOil Gas Station
9 James J. Walker Park (former Hudson Park)
10 Former Caffe Cino
11 Cornelia Street Café
12 Site of Hancock St.
13 Site of Congress St.
14 Site of the Golden Swan (the "Hell-Hole")
15 Site of 133–139 MacDougal St. (the Provincetown Playhouse, the Liberal Club, the Washington Square Bookshop, and Polly Holladay's restaurant)
16 147 West 4th St.
17 150 West 4th St. (formerly the Mad Hatter, the Samovar, and the Pepper Pot)
18 Minetta Tavern
19 Caffe Reggio
20 Former San Remo
21 The Atrium (formerly Mills House)
22 The Little Red Schoolhouse
23 Sullivan Street Playhouse
24 University Towers
25 Washington Square Village (*Bust of Sylvette*)

a few people wandering around with stuffed giraffes under their arms. But the real challenge is to make it through this dieters' nightmare without buying any food.

These Italian street fairs are the emblem of the South Village. But so are the coffeehouses of Bleecker Street, which have changed little since the beatnik heyday of black turtlenecks and existential poetry. The South Village is typified by the secluded enclave of Commerce Street, but also by the stern red-stone bluffs of the NYU buildings. Charlton Street is quietly residential, ancient, and no less typical of the South Village than the lively crowds that gather along Sixth Avenue to watch the impromptu basketball games on the outdoor courts at Third Street. Your impression of the South Village may have started with a visit to one of its many Off-Broadway theaters or with a sitting with one of the sidewalk portrait artists who spend their summers on Sixth Avenue near Fourth Street—they're licensed by the city and, in only one sitting, can do *very* good work.

The South Village offers a number of distinctly different impressions, a disparity that is curious in view of the fact that it began as a single property—the seventeenth-century *bouwerie* of Wouter Van Twiller. It subsequently became a black community, then an Irish community, and then a French community. For nearly a century now it has been the family-oriented Little Italy. Our walking tour through time and space will evoke the South Village of history and legend as well as the neighborhood of today. It will include a speakeasy everyone knew about that actually did have a secret, and the famous Liberal Club that actually permitted women to attend dances without wearing corsets. And it begins with a hill owned first by a freed slave and later by the richest man in America.

RICHMOND HILL

In 1644 a hill covering seven acres became of the earliest parcels in the colonies to have a black owner. Though many black squatters had lived on Wouter Van Twiller's *bouwerie*, Symon Congo, a freed slave, was granted ownership of those seven acres by Van Twiller's successor, William Kieft.

Known as Ishpatanau (Devil Hill) to the Indians, the land passed through several different hands after Congo's death. It was acquired in the 1750s by Trinity Church and added to their vast Village holdings. In 1767 some twenty-six acres of Trinity property were leased by a British major, Abraham Mortimer, who chose Symon Congo's hill as the site of his three-story mansion, which he named Richmond Hill. With its own stable, coach house, and garden, it twice became a military field headquarters during the Revolutionary War, once for the British and once for George Washington, just before he was forced to abandon New York to British control in 1776. Washington returned to this house as a guest in 1789, when he was the nation's first President. At that time Richmond Hill was the first official residence of the Vice-President, though only John Adams spent his term of office living here.

After the federal government left New York, Richmond Hill

George Washington slept
here—though Richmond Hill's
later owner, Aaron Burr,
doubtless tried to forget that
fact. The site of Richmond Hill is
now a historic district, though
the mansion itself is long gone.

became home in 1794 to a senator, future Vice-President, and sharp-shooter—Aaron Burr. He established the mansion as the cynosure of society, but his fashionable days were cut short by his 1804 duel with Alexander Hamilton. At that point, public opinion turned against Burr, forcing him to abandon Richmond Hill and leave unrealized his 1797 plan for its development. The estate passed from Burr's creditors to the sharp-eyed John Jacob Astor, who knew a profitable investment when he saw one. Astor decided to implement Burr's development plan, but saw money still to be made from the mansion itself. Instead of demolishing Richmond Hill, Astor decided to move it. On December 21, 1820, the fifty-foot-square brick mansion was rolled on logs some fifty-five feet down the hill in about forty-five minutes. Then the hill was leveled and Charlton Street was cut through the property. Here Astor planned to build the Federal row houses planned by Burr. The transplanted mansion first failed as a tavern, then as a resort, and finally as a theater. It was demolished in 1849.

The row houses fared far better. Today they constitute the Charlton-King-Vandam Historic District, the greatest concentration of surviving Federal row houses in the city. The seventy-two structures include one unbroken Federal row at 27–39 Charlton, the city's longest. Next to this row, at 25 Charlton, is one of the (many!) Village residences of Edna St. Vincent Millay.

Artist Glenn O. Coleman captured the atmosphere of Minetta Street in this 1913 sketch. For years a black ghetto, it retains a touch of mystery to this day, as it twists to follow the route of Minetta Brook, which was moved underground in the 1820s.

"LITTLE . . . WHATEVER"

Ethnic communities have long been a feature of the South Village. The first was a black community sizable enough to earn the area its first ethnic nickname, Little Africa. In what is now the middle of Sixth Avenue across from the south end of Minetta Street, the nation's first black Roman Catholic church opened in 1833. It served a community that had already seen the 1821 opening of the nation's first black theater, the African Grove on Mercer and Bleecker streets, and the 1827 publication of America's first black newspaper, *Freedom Journal*.

As late as 1865, fully a quarter of the city's black population lived within a few blocks of Minetta Street. That population dispersed as the century waned, but the alleys at the center of the Minetta ghetto deteriorated into a dangerous slum into which few whites walked. One who did was a young Village writer, Stephen Crane, who was drawn to the area by the very qualities that kept others away. His 1896 essay, "Stephen Crane in Minetta Lane," contains a vivid description of this "small and becobbled valley between hills of dingy brick." He describes Pop Babcock's dive in which "sin shone from every corner, like a new headlight." Here such denizens as No-Toe Charley, Blood-Thirsty, and Black Cat were involved in brawls that nightly stained Minetta sidewalks red.

Such violence forced other clubs from the area, notably one that had opened around the corner on Minetta Lane in 1883, running midblock through to Third Street. Ike Hines had left the Hicks and

The Bleecker Street French Bakery
at 159 Greene Street, 1879.

The Grand Vatel, of Bleecker
Street, 1879.

Sawyer Georgia Minstrels to open this basement club that bore his name. In its lively, informal setting, black performers were free to mix with their audiences, marking the beginning of cabaret entertainment, according to Perry Bradford in his 1965 history, *Born with the Blues.*

Little Africa was succeeded by Frenchtown, an immigrant French community that appeared in the South Village in the 1850s. As the 1880s began, the blocks around Greene and Third streets came to be known as the Latin Quarter, and as "tourists" invaded and the area was commercialized, its resident families fled. An 1879 sketch from *Scribner's Monthly* shows the Grand Vatel, a popular French restaurant on Bleecker Street. Though it stood on the fringes of Frenchtown, it smacked less of sin than of ribaldry and naughtiness. The Grand Vatel was depicted in *The Midge,* a popular novel of 1886, though the author, H. C. Bunner, changed its name to the Charlemagne of Houston Street.

No matter. The Gay Nineties counterparts of today's yuppies read *The Midge* and flocked to the Latin Quarter, where they treated the French residents who remained as if they were performing seals. In short order, clubs such as Au Chat Noir on West Broadway and Washington Square's Café de Paris became parodies of themselves.

A small Italian community appeared in the South Village even before the Civil War ended, and the city's first Italian church opened at 153 Sullivan Street in 1866. The community grew rap-

A grocery on Houston Street, 1879.

idly; though there were fewer than forty thousand Italians in all of America in 1880, by 1910 fully half the residents of the South Village were Italian-born. Some row houses south of Washington Square were subdivided to pack several families into each of them, but most were demolished to make room for high-density tenements that offered few amenities. Landlords' abuses of poor immigrants were curbed by the city with laws in 1887 and 1901, which required such basics as windows, fresh air, and running water. The streetscape of the South Village is still dotted with these structures, still referred to as "Old Law Tenements" and "New Law Tenements" by neighborhood old-timers.

The early years of this century produced a "literature of reform" that shocked readers who had been unaware of the plight of the disadvantaged immigrants and the abuses that were rampant in business and housing. Community organizations were formed, inspired by Jane Addams's Hull House, which had opened in 1889 in Chicago. Each group aimed to better conditions among the immigrant poor. In 1902, Mary K. Simkhovich opened a settlement house in rented quarters at 16 Jones Street. It proved so successful in community care that in 1917 Greenwich House constructed its own permanent home at 27 Barrow Street. Today the Georgian-style Greenwich House offers child-care programs, drug counseling services, a music school, a lecture series, adult education courses, and a senior citizens' center.

CORNERING LEGENDS

In the best tradition of Greenwich Village, Barrow Street runs west of Seventh Avenue only to intersect with its parallel companion, Commerce Street. Their juncture, one of the most picturesque corners in the city, is home to the historic Cherry Lane Theatre. Its name clearly suggests that a street called Cherry Lane ran somewhere near here. A walk back to the corner of Commerce and Bedford streets will bring you to a tablet on the side of an apartment house. On it you will read that Commerce Street was once a country lane named for the pink-blossomed trees that line it. You may conjure up an image of that lane, on which the nearby 1821 Federals rose—particularly if you read this plaque in the spring, under the influence of the one young cherry tree growing in front of the theater.

Unfortunately, the legend is as bogus as the one about George Washington and *his* cherry tree. The whole Cherry Lane story was the invention of William Rainey, whose "confession" ran in the *Herald-Tribune* in 1964 at the time of his death. Rainey, who was programming director of NBC Radio and the Voice of America, had once been a member of a plucky group of Villagers who were determined to start a neighborhood theater. In 1924 they took on an abandoned box factory at 38 Commerce Street that had been built as a brewery in 1836. As their renovations proceeded, a young reporter appeared to ask about the group's plans. She also asked what the theater would be named. Rainey faltered. The group had made no final choice, though they'd joked about a "Cheery Lane" theater after hearing one sour London critic's suggestion that the famed Drury Lane be renamed the Dreary Lane. The joke seemed too silly to tell a reporter, however, and so Rainey blurted out the name this theater still uses. He even concocted a tale about having found an old map of the area giving Cherry Lane as the original name of

The legendary "twins" at 39 and 41 Commerce Street, a cozy Village nook of considerable charm. The Cherry Lane Theatre is at right, the source of a widely believed legend that is quite untrue.

Commerce Street. And so the reporter had her story, and Greenwich Village had a legend that many people still believe.

Other legends cling to this Village corner like ivy, and several of them are untrue. One concerns the twin houses at 39 and 41 Commerce Street, which were supposedly built by a sea captain for his two daughters who refused to speak to each other. This tale has several variations, all of them charming—and all of them untrue. Both houses were built in 1831, four years after Commerce Street was extended to join Barrow. Their builder, a milkman named Peter Huyler, was the original tenant at 39 Commerce. Both remained simple two-story Federals until 1873, when their distinctive mansard roofs were added.

Washington Irving is often reported to have lived at 11 Commerce Street. He did not. That was his sister's house, and he was merely a frequent visitor. Neighboring 17 Barrow bears a tablet identifying it as "Aaron Burr House." Untrue: the 1826 Federal rose long after Burr had left the area. And the bend in Commerce, Barrow, and adjacent streets reflects the 1633 boundary of Wouter Van Twiller's *bouwerie*—not, as some would have you believe, a bend in the path of Minetta Brook, which is several blocks away.

Some Village legends are true, though. The oldest house in Greenwich Village is the 1799 Isaacs-Hendricks House at 77 Bedford Street. Its plot was once part of the Elbert Roosevelt farm, which was being sliced up for development beginning in 1794. Joshua Isaacs bought this land for $225, then lost it to creditors within two years. It passed to Harmon Hendricks, a noted copper supplier who provided Robert Fulton with the makings of the copper boilers he used in his steamboat experiments. One such boiler powered Fulton's *Clermont* on August 17, 1807, when it left the Christopher Street pier at the state prison for its historic journey up the Hudson to Albany. The wood frame Isaacs-Hendricks House has twice been remodeled. Its brick face was an 1836 addition, and its third floor was added in 1928. The former farmhouse remains a treasured Village landmark and a rare survivor from the eighteenth century.

Another legendary house, just next door at 75½ Bedford Street, is destined to be forever identified with Edna St. Vincent Millay, even though the poet lived here for little more than a year in 1923–24. Only 9½ feet wide—the narrowest house in New York City—it was built in 1873 in what had been the carriage entrance to stables located inside this block. Under its steep-pitched roof, the poet collaborated with Deems Taylor on *The King's Henchman*, a rare American opera in that it has been performed at the Met. On a less prestigious note, 75½ Bedford appears in the 1957 film, *Bachelor Party*. If further distinction is needed, note that John Barrymore lived here briefly.

At the corner of Bedford and Commerce streets is the 1799 Isaacs-Hendricks House. Next to it, filling what was once a narrow carriageway, is 75½ Bedford Street, which was for a short time the home of poet Edna St. Vincent Millay.

"I KNOW THIS GREAT PLACE IN THE VILLAGE THAT YOU'LL NEVER FIND UNLESS I TAKE YOU THERE"

For over sixty years, people have slipped through an unmarked door at 86 Bedford Street into what seems to be a small carriage house. Most reappear an hour or so later, though some never emerge—not from this door, anyway. It might seem sinister to the uninitiated, but neighbors know this to be an entrance to Chumley's, one of the most celebrated secrets of the Village.

Lee Chumley had been a soldier of fortune, a writer, a laborer, and a covered-wagon driver before Sam Schwartz hired him to manage the Black Knight, Schwartz's speakeasy facing the Provincetown Playhouse across MacDougal Street. In 1926, Chumley took space on the second floor of 86 Bedford Street, initially to edit and publish a radical workers' journal and to hold secret meetings of the IWW. By 1928, he had taken over the onetime blacksmith's shop at street level and turned it into a speakeasy of his own. The Bedford Street entrance became a concealed back door, while another secret entrance appeared in Pamela Court, a secluded residence entered around the corner at 58 Barrow Street. According to legend, the door at 86 Bedford Street was used only when cops enforcing Prohibition appeared in Pamela Court. They'd be held there just long enough for Chumley to tell his customers to "eighty-six it," meaning "clear out!" The phrase is still popular slang.

With its inviting atmosphere and a fireplace fashioned from the blacksmith's forge, the speakeasy soon attracted a literary crowd, which Lee Chumley encouraged by inventing a tradition. He encouraged authors to bring dust jackets of their new books to be mounted on the walls above the initial-carved oak booths. After six decades the jackets are still there. Works by Chumley regulars Upton Sinclair, Floyd Dell, and John Dos Passos share equal billing

Village Voices

"We have a tremendous respect for this place," says Steve Shlopak, co-owner of Chumley's since December 1987. "But that's as it should be. Do you realize there've probably been more Pulitzer and even Nobel Prize winners through here than any place in this city? Possibly even in the nation?

"The few changes we're making are designed to maintain our links with Chumley's traditions, so we don't mind the expense of doing things right. We want to turn Chumley's over to future generations as we think Lee Chumley would have. Sure, we're the present owners, but we think of ourselves as stewards—husbanding this place for the time being. We plan to be here for quite a while, but we know Chumley's itself will go on far longer."

On the Roster at Chumley's

John Steinbeck
Ernest Hemingway
Eugene O'Neill
Sinclair Lewis
William Faulkner
Arthur Miller
Edna Ferber
Thornton Wilder
James Agee
William Styron
John Cheever
Malcolm Cowley
James Farrell
Mark Van Doren
Carl Van Vechten
Edna St. Vincent Millay
Norman Mailer
Alfred Kazin
Dwight Macdonald
Margaret Mead
Anaïs Nin
Simone de Beauvoir
J. D. Salinger
Gay Talese
Allen Ginsberg
Jack Kerouac
Gregory Corso
Horton Foote
Maxwell Bodenheim
Theodore Dreiser
E. E. Cummings
Dylan Thomas
Calvin Trillin
Edmund Wilson

with such now-forgotten works as *Hat-Check Girl* and (my favorite) *The Eaters of Darkness*.

Two years after Prohibition ended in 1933, Lee Chumley died of a heart attack, prompting a surprise appearance at the Bedford Street door. A forty-two-year-old woman walked in and announced herself to be Henrietta Chumley, widow of the restaurateur, who had long been thought to be a bachelor by both his patrons and his staff. Few thought Mrs. Chumley could make a go of bar management, but she managed to keep a tight hold on the place for twenty-five years—and managed to keep herself even tighter. From her favorite table next to the fireplace, Mrs. Chumley nightly presided over restaurant affairs, knocking back manhattans between hands of solitaire until she put down her head and passed out. Regulars grew used to the sight of her, unconscious, seated in their midst. After closing each night, a waiter would rouse Mrs. Chumley and maneuver her to her second-floor apartment at 54 Barrow Street—until one night in 1960, when waiters found she'd been sitting among her customers for the better part of that evening, dead.

The pudgy little woman who wore too many rings was gone, but such subsequent owners as Ray Santini and, later, Bill Bigelow kept the place much as Mrs. Chumley left it. "I think she forced us to," Bigelow recalled. "We put in a video game in the seventies, and it was nothing but trouble. That's when our old jukebox started acting up. Once the video game left, the jukebox was fine again, and we later heard that the new owners of that video game never had trouble with it. Then there was the chess game back in the sixties that brought on a quarrel, and one player stabbed the other to death. That was the end of chess, except for one night a few years later when the bartender and a waiter took the old chessboard out just before closing and started playing. They got into a terrible fight over it, but fortunately stopped playing before there was real trouble. And there's been no chess here since."

As a speakeasy, Chumley's wasn't really a secret from the police, but its upstairs activities may have been. The restaurant kitchen was connected to the apartment upstairs by an oversized dumbwaiter whose platform is large enough to carry two people. Its apartment exit is now closed, but the dumbwaiter is still there, as are some electrical wires that suggest that a now-inoperative buzzer once terminated in that same apartment. It all seems more elaborate than IWW meetings would have required, and gives credence to rumors of a second-floor casino, rumors that a few old-timers in the Village have heard. If they're true, the "secret" speakeasy may simply have been a cover for the real secret—a second-floor gambling casino, perhaps unknown even to Mrs. Chumley.

Little changed in over sixty years, Chumley's is a living example of an actual speakeasy, not the Hollywood version of one. Its literary patrons have left dust jackets in their wake, some of which can be seen on the walls below the "specials" board and above the booths at the right.

VILLAGE PEOPLE: SANDRA AND ROBERT WAGENFELD

Sandra and Robert Wagenfeld found their dream house on Bedford Street in 1982. There was just one problem: the backyard of this 1821 Federal had long ago been exposed by the Seventh Avenue Cut, and there in 1922 the PureOil Company had built a miniature gasoline station. One of several that appeared in the Village at the time, the twelve-by-fourteen-foot structure operated until 1972 when its pumps were removed and it became an auto repair shop.

When the Wagenfelds inadvertently bought it, the long-deserted station was in considerable disrepair. They decided to demolish it and replace it with a garden, but the Landmarks Commission intervened. As a structure within the Village Historic District, it could not be demolished without their approval—which they were not about to give.

Initially the Wagenfelds thought the restriction nutty, but they had to comply. Rather than live with an eyesore in their yard, they began remodeling the station the Commission Report termed "a simulated Italian Renaissance chapel," turning it into a combination office and guest house. They had the plumbing, heating, and electrical wiring rebuilt and restored the slate roof, insulation, and windows. All work was approved by the commission, which even

The former PureOil Gas Station at 48–52 Seventh Avenue South was restored in 1984, making it one of the newest Village curiosities.

The vine-covered door of historic 6 St. Luke's Place.

had a say in the exterior color scheme. The concrete station plaza was removed—a real chore, since it was thirty inches thick. The sunken gas tank was filled with sand—but, incredibly, it first had to be drained of decade-old gasoline. Finally a fence was installed along Seventh Avenue to offer privacy and security while providing the visual access to the building the commission required.

After two years (and some $100,000), Sandra Wagenfeld moved her financial consulting work into her new office, which proved surprisingly delightful as a work space and a boon to her business. The process had been arduous, the red tape frustrating, but the finished product is a gem, a curio beginning a new life as part of Greenwich Village lore because of the willingness of the Wagenfelds to be the ultimate good sports.

SITCOM FAME

Since they were built in the early 1850s, the fifteen row houses of St. Luke's Place have been considered among the city's finest. Mayor James J. Walker lived his term of office at 6 St. Luke's, in a house bought by his father in 1891. Though scandal and corruption forced him to resign in September 1932, the house retains the "lamps of honor" that traditionally designate the official residence of a New York mayor.

Author Theodore Dreiser moved to 16 St. Luke's Place in 1923 and there wrote most of his classic, *An American Tragedy*. He also continued his battle against censorship, most notably with a strategy session attended here by H. L. Mencken, Carl Van Vechten, Horace Liveright, and F. Scott Fitzgerald. Also present was writer Sherwood Anderson, who lived a few doors away at 12 St. Luke's. Other residents of the row over the years have been poet and editor Marianne Moore and writer-director Arthur Laurents *(Gypsy, West Side Story, The Way We Were)*.

But the most famous residents of St. Luke's Place live here only in the minds of tens of millions of TV viewers. They would recognize 10 St. Luke's Place as the home of the Huxtable family on *The Cosby Show*. Though exterior shots of this house appear in each episode, the program itself is shot at the Kaufman Astoria Studios in Queens, far from St. Luke's Place.

WAIT UNTIL PARK

Since 1946 it's been a dusty neighborhood softball field on St. Luke's Place, but for fifty years before that it was Hudson Park, a glorious sunken garden of marble terraces designed by the noted architectural firm of Carrère & Hastings. For nearly a century before that, the present ball field was a cemetery for St. John's Chapel, which stood below nearby Canal Street until its demolition in 1918. It was through this cemetery that Edgar Allan Poe wandered in 1837, while residing around the corner at 113½ Carmine Street, and here that his moody mind fashioned his 1838 novel, *The Narrative of Arthur Gordon Pym*.

The cemetery, which extended across the present-day St.

Until 1946 Hudson Park was the pride of St. Luke's Place.

Luke's Place as far as Morton Street, is responsible for the one-block gap in Leroy Street. When the cemetery was laid out in 1801, Leroy Street began at Hudson Street and ran west three short blocks to the Hudson River. East of the cemetery, something called Burton Street ran a block and a half to Herring (Bleecker) Street. Burton was renamed Leroy Street in 1845, around the time St. Luke's Place was cut through the cemetery to connect them. However, the one-block-long St. Luke's Place has always gone by that name. It was not—as legend suggests—a name devised by Mayor Walker to avoid living on dull Leroy Street.

Mayor Walker's name has been appropriated by the ball field, which can be seen in the 1967 film, *Wait Until Dark,* where it serves as the roost of the sadistic thugs who terrorize a blind Audrey Hepburn in her apartment—at 4 St. Luke's Place.

MAKING MAGIC

The storefront at 31 Cornelia Street doesn't look like a significant historical site. For years its windows have been barricaded closed, its recesses serving as storage space for the Pink Pussycat Erotic Boutique over on Fourth Street. But 31 Cornelia Street is the site of the legendary Caffe Cino, and is historically important as the birthplace of Off–Off Broadway.

It was a typical coffeehouse of the "beat generation" when it opened in December 1958. Cappuccino cost forty cents and was artfully served in shaving mugs. The artworks on the walls were changed monthly, and the occasional poetry reading served to distract patrons from noticing how uncomfortable the cramped, dimly lit tables were. What made Caffe Cino unique was its owner, Joe Cino, who was less interested in making money than in creating a testing ground for those in the arts—or, better still, for those about to be. Among those to emerge as "Cino writers" were Lanford Wilson, Sam Shepard, Robert Patrick, William Hoffman, Tom Eyen, and John Guare.

"Joe never read your script," playwright Doric Wilson recalled. "He just asked your astrological sign—something *nobody* did in the fifties—and then gave you the date for your performance. If your sign in any way affected the date you got, Joe never let on. He was good at sizing people up, and I think he just used that to get them talking."

The shift from art gallery to performance space began in 1959 when one poetry reading included scenes from Oscar Wilde's play, *Salomé.* As other play excerpts followed, traces of theatrical staging began to appear in the tiny club. Doric Wilson's *And He Made a Her,* presented on March 23, 1961, was the first play written expressly for staging there. That amateur performance marked the

The vest-pocket Caffe Cino, at 31 Cornelia Street, the birthplace of Off–Off Broadway.

beginning of both Off-Off Broadway and the modern gay theater movement.

It was followed by *Babel, Babel, Little Tower,* "in which my actors took tables away from the patrons," Doric Wilson remembered. "They were used as the set, although it proved an inconvenience that cut into business. But Joe didn't care; all he cared about was having a good play."

The Caffe Cino fostered irreverent experimentation free of any commercial constraints. Cino himself made sure of this, making of his café walls a vast mural of faded photos and treasured junk items. When the mood struck him, Cino was given to baring his bottom and announcing, "On with the show!" If the theater has changed enough since the fifties to make Cino advances now seem tame, it is only because the barriers were first breached in that tiny room. "No play ran over forty minutes," playwright Lanford Wilson recalls, "because that was as long as anyone could hold out on those tiny chairs. But exciting things happened in that room; for example, unless I'm mistaken, I was the first playwright to get the word 'fuck' spoken on an American stage, with *So Long at the Fair* (1963) . . . though Jack Gelber may have slipped 'fuck' into *The Connection* a few years earlier—I'm not really sure, because I can't imagine him passing up such a wonderful opportunity."

Uptown crowds were drawn to the Cino by 1964, resulting in the first Cino "long-runs": Lanford Wilson's harrowing portrait of an aging homosexual, *The Madness of Lady Bright;* Tom Eyen's comedic roller coaster, *Why Hanna's Skirt Won't Stay Down;* and

George Haimsohn's spoof musical, *Dames at Sea,* which later enjoyed a lengthy commercial run Off Broadway and made a star of Bernadette Peters. But the Caffe Cino's days were numbered when its founder attempted suicide on March 31, 1967. Despite the efforts of Cino loyalists, 130 of whom rushed to St. Vincent's Hospital to give blood, Joe Cino died three days later. His theater café survived barely a year after his death.

"Joe Cino was like everyone's uncle," Lanford Wilson remembers, "like everyone you wished people would be like. He created a place only so he could turn it over to you. He said, 'This is my room. . . . Make magic!' "

Joe Cino in front of his ever-changing wall collage at the Caffe Cino.

VILLAGE VOICES

The Cornelia Street Café had a haphazard beginning, according to co-owner Robin Hirsch, but he feels it's the only survivor of the café-art scene of the fifties and sixties. "Charles McKenna, Raphaela Pivetta, and I spent two months building this place, which opened as a single room with a pathetically small investment. Initially we knew nothing about running a café, and we opened with only a cappuccino machine and a toaster-oven." Operating since 1977 at 29 Cornelia Street, the café has since burrowed its way into adjoining rooms much as did tearooms in the 1910s. "We've since installed a real kitchen, and actually have become more of a restaurant. But I miss those early café days," Hirsch recalls in an impeccable British accent he insists has softened to mid-Atlantic. "The vitality now seen in rock clubs was to be found then in cafés, but we still have our Sunday Night Series, which recalls those early, freewheeling days."

The Cino spirit may well return to Cornelia Street under Hirsch. "We're installing a cabaret theater downstairs, something I've wanted to do since the beginning. I think there's a European tradition of café theater that is akin to environmental theater, where you're fighting the seduction of food and drink—so you have to be good!" Hirsch sees it as similar to the concentration needed by the writers—several of whom are quite well known—who hole up daily in the café to work. "In the readings, the concerts by our Songwriters Exchange, and the plays staged here, I've found more freedom producing in a café than I ever could find in a formal theater," Hirsch says with contentment. Citing the thousands of writers and artists who've worked there, Hirsch quite rightly calls Cornelia Street Café an arena for the arts.

ANOTHER UNKIND CUT

Sixth Avenue south of Carmine Street is a late addition to the Village landscape, cut through in the late 1920s by the city to permit construction of the city-owned Independent subway line. Much as the IRT construction a decade earlier had produced the through-route called Seventh Avenue South, the IND cut opened the Village to through-traffic where a maze of streets had been. The odd angle of the Sixth Avenue cut produced the otherwise inexplicable plazas to be seen today below Bleecker Street. One such plaza indicates the remains of Hancock Street, which ran between Bleecker and Houston; the location of its east curb is suggested by the surviving buildings that once lined it, though Hancock Street itself is gone. Similarly, Sixth Avenue absorbed Congress Street, a one-block wonder between Houston and King streets. It also wiped out Clark Street, which once ran between Spring and Broome. Once the cut was completed, all Sixth Avenue addresses were altered to reflect its new point of origin, making tricky the accurate identification of street numbers in guidebooks and literature written before 1928.

In some respects, the Sixth Avenue construction was harder than its Seventh Avenue counterpart. For one thing, the Sixth

Unlike the east side of Sixth Avenue, its west side remains largely intact, and many of the row houses in this 1868 view south of Waverly Place are still standing. At the corner of Washington Place is the 1834 St. Joseph's, the oldest surviving Roman Catholic church in Manhattan. Farther south and too dark to be clearly seen here is the 1807 Dutch Reform Church, built four years before Sixth Avenue replaced the dusty West Road. That church no longer functions, but the shell still stands and is now the Waverly Theatre.

John Sloan captured his doomed neighborhood in 1928 in *Sixth Avenue Elevated at Third Street.* The lost east side of the avenue can be seen through the El girders. At the left, Sloan hints at structures still standing today, the Jefferson Market Courthouse, the pillars of St. Joseph's, even a bit of the face of what now is the Waverly Theatre. Also visible in shadow at the left is the Cornelia Street tower into which Sloan had moved his studio in 1912. Three years later he moved across Sixth Avenue to the corner of Washington Place, where he remained until subway construction forced him out the year he painted this superb study of a neighborhood.

Avenue Elevated was still running overhead. The spindly iron stilts that supported its tracks had to be shored up before cut-and-cover digging could begin. And then, in order to prepare for the triple-decked station at West Fourth Street, workmen had to dig more than eighty feet below the surface. Before they could do so, the structures on the east side of Sixth Avenue, from Eighth Street south to Minetta Street, had to be demolished. For this reason, no nineteenth-century structures have survived on that side of the avenue.

VILLAGE VOICES

Ermanno Stingo remembers Hancock Street as a block-long affair that teemed with people and traffic. "Remember, there were few through-streets connecting Bleecker and Houston before Sixth Avenue went through."

Stingo was born at 5–7 Hancock in 1917, what today is 270 Sixth Avenue. "I suppose you'd call the building a tenement, but we kept it well and I remember it as quite cozy. Downstairs at street level was an old-fashioned café run by my great-uncle, with a pool table and those tall spittoons, and tables for playing cards, drinking coffee, and eating pastries. Out front, pushcarts were everywhere, wagons loaded with watermelons and bananas, which were a treat then, because you couldn't find them everywhere.

"The man who brought us ice in the summer brought coal in the winter. There was no electricity in our building, but we had gaslights everywhere that gave a beautiful soft light. The hall always smelled of soap because the woman next door to us took in laundry. We had someone come in to do ours, a woman named Lucia. She also sold alcohol—a lot of people did during Prohibition—and people mixed it with water, sugar, and extracts to make their own liquor at home. My father also had a crusher and a barrel and bought crates of grapes each fall to make wine.

"I remember every Election Day Hancock Street was closed off, and crates and packing boxes were piled as high as a second-floor window for great bonfires. I remember them vividly. And I also remember being taken by my mother to the cavernous Fugazy Theatre, which stood at the bottom of Hancock at Houston Street. Once, just after we paid our dime admission, some man pulled a gun and held up the box office. Mother dragged me down the aisle and hid me behind the piano. I remember the pianist went right on playing, as if nothing had happened.

"We moved away a few years before Hancock Street vanished, but our building was spared. Sometimes I look up at the room I was born in and wonder who lives there now. But whoever it is left a Christmas wreath in the window right through the year. Maybe it's better not to know."

ICE CREAM AND BOOZE

Today the 1829 Federal at 355 Sixth Avenue is Les Fleurs, a florist's shop, but in 1872 it was a popular ice cream parlor run by E.A.G. Intemann. He took advantage of the experiments in ammonia refrigeration being conducted in 1870 by the Jefferson Market at its annex at 70 West Tenth Street. For the market, ammonia refrigeration meant reduced reliance on the huge cakes of ice required to keep its meats fresh in summer months. For E.A.G. Intemann, it meant that he would be able to make ice cream

The west side of Sixth Avenue, between Washington Place and West Fourth Street. These row houses gave over their street levels to stores in the 1850s when Sixth Avenue became a shopping district for the wealthy residents of Washington Square. Two of them are little-known historic sites.

at the counter before his startled patrons' eyes and serve it in new ways. One of his innovations was ice cream served in soda water, a novelty that Intemann's son later recalled as the true introduction of the ice cream soda—four years before it won wide popularity at the Philadelphia Exposition of 1876.

Two doors north, at 359 Sixth Avenue on the street level of an unpretentious 1832 Federal house, is a popular burger joint called McBell's. In 1922 this was the Red Head, a speakeasy popular with local collegians and with Sonia, the Cigarette Girl, who visited here frequently during the final months of her eccentric life. After a brief subsequent stay in the basement of 88 Washington Place, the Red Head made its move to Midtown, where for over sixty years it prospered under its new and more famous name—the 21 Club.

THE CANTILEVERED COURT

The Sixth Avenue block between Washington Place and Waverly Place remained a parking lot through the 1970s, partly because there were weight limitations on land that is directly above the subway. Also, this block lies inside the historic district established in 1969. As a result, any development proposal for the site had to be reviewed by the Landmarks Commission. That review process gave local residents and preservationists ample opportunity to kill one plan for the plot—a multiscreen movie theater.

In 1985 a proposal by local developer Philips International was approved by the commission and preservationists. The result, Washington Court, is a success by almost any standard. The twenty-

Sixth Avenue, looking south across Village Square from the Jefferson Market Courthouse. The cantilevered Washington Court is the brick affair on the far side of Sixth, at center just above the tree's top branches.

eight condominium units in the $20 million structure sold for $500 a square foot, a good 20 percent higher than the prevailing rate at the time for comparable space on New York's Upper East Side. The cachet of the Village led to a waiting list of six hundred prospective buyers.

Neither preservationists nor buyers gave much thought to the subway station running under part of Washington Court, but architect James Stewart Polshek did. He selected materials to keep the building as light as possible. Still, the entire structure rides on a huge steel-frame cantilever, which shifts its weight away from the Sixth Avenue side.

A rare photograph of the Golden Swan, which stood on the southeast corner of Fourth Street and Sixth Avenue.

THE ORIGINAL CAST

When the Sixth Avenue subway construction claimed a bar at the southeast corner of Fourth Street, some Villagers were glad to see it go. A weather-beaten sign over its door bore the faded image of a swan in flaking gold paint. Another swan, stuffed and ratty, presided over the back room from within a glass case, where it sat ignominiously on wood slabs painted to represent lily pads. Sawdust covered a floor littered with rickety tables and even more rickety patrons, for whom daylight was that thick gray illumination that sometimes penetrated a filthy window.

This was the Golden Swan, though seedy regulars referred to it as the Hell-Hole. One of many Irish bars in the Village before World War I, it was a harmless, good-natured place for all its sinister gloom, a place in which Village celebrities were as welcome as local bums. One patron was both a celebrity *and* a bum: a tubercular young man of twenty-seven named Eugene O'Neill was one of the resident drunks here in 1915.

John Sloan and Charles Demuth sketched the interior of the Hell-Hole, and Hutchins Hapgood borrowed one of its regulars for his novel, *An Anarchist Woman*. But Eugene O'Neill found more here than atmosphere. The Hell-Hole brought the dramatist in contact with people who shaped his view of life and who later emerged as characters in O'Neill's searing barroom drama, *The Iceman Cometh*.

The most colorful of the lot was Hippolyte Havel, the anarchist who later served briefly on the editorial board of the *Masses*. Emma Goldman had met Havel in London in 1899 while she was on a lecture tour. The Hungarian-born Gypsy told her he'd been booted out of Vienna because of his anarchist preaching, a fact that heightened his fiery appeal in her eyes. They became lovers, and it was with Goldman that Havel first came to America in 1900. He turned up nine years later in Greenwich Village as an arrogant headwaiter-cook-dishwasher for Polly Holladay. A native of Evanston, Illinois, she had opened a freewheeling Village restaurant at 137 MacDougal Street, and like Goldman, she took Havel as her lover. He gained quick fame among Villagers for his ability to spot uptowners as soon as they entered Polly's—and for his habit of loudly calling them bourgeois pigs while taking their order. Once described as a man who thought in German, swore in English, and drank in all languages, Havel did much of his drinking around the corner from Polly's at the Hell-Hole, where he became the model for the character of anarchist Hugo Kalmar in O'Neill's play.

The bar setting of *The Iceman Cometh* is based on a downtown waterfront bar O'Neill frequented in 1912, but like most of the play's characters, the bar's proprietor has a Hell-Hole source—Tom Wallace, an ex-prizefighter who lived in a room above the bar. Some people said that Wallace had not been outside for nearly twenty years. He kept a player piano in the Hell-Hole, though its nickels were often pilfered by regulars who couldn't afford a mug of beer. Wallace kept a pig in the basement one autumn, throwing scraps and other garbage down the stairs to fatten it for Christmas. It's doubtful the animal made it that long, since drunken Hell-Holers dragged it upstairs one night and poured liquor down its throat until it ran madly around the bar, screeching.

The character called Don Parritt was based on Polly Holladay's brother, Louis, whose January 1918 death shocked Hell-Holers and cast O'Neill into deep despair. Having sworn off booze for the sake

The denizens of the Golden Swan, better known as the Hell-Hole, as captured in an etching by John Sloan.

of a girl, Louis hit the bottle hard when she ditched him. He even managed to get his hands on some heroin. His all-night debauch ended at Romany Marie's at 133 Washington Place. There Louis Holladay had a seizure and collapsed, unconscious. Romany Marie managed to reach Polly, who arrived minutes after her brother's death. Only by swearing to the police that Louis had been having "heart trouble" were the Hell-Holers able to avoid an investigation.

O'Neill included himself in *The Iceman Cometh* in the guise of Willie Oban. He also made use of Happy, the collector for a laundry chain and a Friday night regular at the Hell-Hole. After Happy's visits abruptly ended, word filtered back that he'd stolen a week's receipts and vanished. From this event O'Neill fashioned the catalyst for his play—the boisterous salesman he named Hickey, who was making one last visit to the bar before being arrested for killing his wife.

The most important influence on O'Neill in those days was Terry Carlin, a self-taught philosopher whose views were absorbed by the playwright as the "hopeless hope" of his greatest dramas. At fifty, Carlin was a father figure for O'Neill. In the 1915–16 winter, the two sank into a shared life of flophouses and nihilism during which O'Neill heard often of Carlin's mistress Marie. Several years later, the playwright conjured her up when fashioning Anna Christie. Carlin was also responsible for taking O'Neill to Cape Cod for the summer of 1916. It was there that the second-season Provincetown Players found him and the remarkable play, *Bound East for Cardiff*, which began his career.

At first, the Hell-Hole made only one concession to Prohibition: the Sixth Avenue window was boarded up. In time, however, the bar degenerated into a scruffy soda parlor and was swept away by the subway construction of 1928. By then, O'Neill was Broadway's leading playwright and a three-time winner of the Pulitzer Prize. His evocation of the Hell-Hole, *The Iceman Cometh,* was not very successful when it opened on Broadway in 1946; its towering reputation today derives from the environmental production at Circle in the Square in 1956, at their Sheridan Square theater just up Fourth Street from the corner where the real Hell-Hole once stood.

HITCHING PEGASUS

With *Bound East for Cardiff,* the Provincetown Players had their first hit, and this strengthened their resolve to try a winter season in Greenwich Village. Prime movers George Cook and John Reed rented the parlor floor of a row house at 139 MacDougal Street, a few doors south of Washington Square, and there the Provincetown Players made their New York debut on November 3, 1916. A makeshift stage twelve feet square faced tiered wooden benches to seat 140. But though the triple bill offered the O'Neill play along with one-acts by Floyd Dell and Louise Bryant, only twenty-seven people attended on opening night.

Nevertheless, the Players persisted, aided greatly by their

Eugene O'Neill is on the ladder at left, helping to set the stage for the 1916 Provincetown Players premiere of his *Bound East for Cardiff.* At right, holding a pole, is Provincetown co-founder George Cram Cook, and seated at center is Hippolyte Havel, the fiery anarchist of Greenwich Village.

neighbors. Polly Holladay's famous restaurant was next door at 137 MacDougal, in the basement beneath the Liberal Club. The club was a self-proclaimed "meeting place for those interested in New Ideas," and in 1916, that meant all of Greenwich Village; at times it seemed as if the entire Village population was packed inside the Liberal Club's two parlors. Next door to the south was the Washington Square Bookshop, which Charles and Albert Boni had opened at 135 MacDougal with Albert's college tuition money. In the hope that increased browsing would mean increased business, they broke through the walls, creating a doorway between their store and the Liberal Club. They were disappointed to encounter only increased "book-borrowing," but the brothers remained too fond of the doorway to seal it up.

These cultural centers provided audiences for the budding theater group, and even a few participants. Feminist Ida Rauh, wife of *Masses* editor Max Eastman, appeared in so many early productions that she became known as the Eleonora Duse of MacDougal Street. Writer Djuna Barnes acted in several plays and ushered for several others, including her own offering, *Kurzy of the Sea*. A 1917 Vassar graduate found her way to the auditions for Floyd Dell's play, *An Angel Intrudes,* and walked away with the lead. In short order, Edna St. Vincent Millay also had Dell's heart, and their affair later formed the basis for her poems, "Weeds" and "Journal." More immediately, Millay wrote *Aria da Capo,* which the Provincetown premiered in 1919. By that time, she'd been joined at the theater by her sister Norma, who also found romance on MacDougal Street. There Norma met actor Charles Ellis (of the Drick Rebellion sextet), whom she soon married and with whom she appeared in 1924 in the original cast of *Desire Under the Elms,* at the Greenwich Village Theatre on Sheridan Square.

As its second season in New York ended, the Provincetown Players had done well enough to want larger quarters, but they were reluctant to leave MacDougal Street. Here good luck and good neighbors were again with them. Their landlady, Jenny Belardi, owned—in addition to the Liberal Club and Boni bookshop buildings—an old stable at 133 MacDougal that had been used most recently as a bottling plant. The Players rented it for $400 a month. They put a scenery shop and dressing rooms in the basement and installed offices and a dining room on the second floor. Scenic designer Cleon Throckmorton filled the former stable with benches seating two hundred, facing a real stage. But one vestige of the equestrian past was retained. A hitching post still hung from the wall; above it one of the Players, Donald Corley, painted an idealistic inscription: "Here Pegasus Was Hitched."

And here history was made. Here in 1919, in a move almost without precedent for a white-run theater, O'Neill's *The Dreamy*

Village Voices

"I recall [little] of that first performance now except the last scene. . . . Suddenly there was a clap of thunder and a frightening rumble that vibrated throughout the building. I thought the rain had caused the roof to cave in. It was the audience. It was applause."

Bette Davis,
in her autobiography,
The Lonely Life, 1962

The original Provincetown Players
stable-theater at 133 MacDougal
Street, as it appeared in 1936.

Kid rejected the stereotypic roles that had long been written for
blacks. Here in 1920 O'Neill's experimental drama *The Emperor
Jones* opened, making a star of black actor Charles S. Gilpin. And
here outrage greeted O'Neill's controversial 1924 play, *All God's
Chillun Got Wings,* a tension-ridden premiere that launched Paul
Robeson on his career.

Word circulated during rehearsals that with this play O'Neill
had gone too far. His portrait of a racially mixed couple was so
realistic that white actress Mary Blair, newly wed to writer Edmund
Wilson, actually kissed Robeson, who played her husband. The
Salvation Army called for the play to be banned, as did the Society
for the Suppression of Vice and the Ku Klux Klan. On the afternoon
of the opening, the mayor revoked the license under which several
child actors were allowed to appear in the play. Director James
Light countered this move with a vow that he would read the
children's lines himself rather than let their absence scuttle the play.
Then the theater received a bomb threat. When the curtain rose, the
walls of the theater were lined with policemen. But despite such
handicaps, the play ran for five months. During that run, it was
moved to the Greenwich Village Theatre, where it appeared on a bill

Village Voices

"The first evening I was in the Village I was taken to call upon a beautiful girl dancer who kept a pet alligator in her bathtub; she bade me let it bite my finger, saying it wouldn't hurt me; I obeyed her trustfully, but offered the alligator the little finger of my left hand, just in case; and the amiable reptile nipped it very gently. The next morning Henrietta Rodman came to call, and asked me to write a play to produce at the housewarming of the Liberal Club."

Floyd Dell,
in his autobiography,
Homecoming, 1933

with *The Emperor Jones*—the first performance for Paul Robeson in a role that was associated with him for the rest of his life.

When O'Neill went on to Broadway, the Provincetown had to struggle to survive. *In Abraham's Bosom* did well, winning for author Paul Green the 1927 Pulitzer Prize. A year later audiences flocked to see E. E. Cummings's mystifying *him,* but its $6,000 cost and cast of thirty rendered it a financial failure for the theater. A few Provincetown cast members later found fame in films, particularly Ann Harding and Miriam Hopkins. And a plucky young actress named Bette Davis made her New York stage debut there in a March 1929 play, *The Earth Between.*

If audience response was any measure, however, the most popular Provincetown actress was Christine Ell. When she was not walking her leashed leopard cub through Washington Square, Ell ran the Players' second-floor dining hall and appeared on stage in walk-on roles. She often timed her work upstairs to allow herself to sprint down the back stairs to the stage, speak her few lines, and then rush back to her kitchen. Her every appearance prompted an eruption of cheers and applause from Provincetown regulars, leaving other members of the audience in the dark as to who this beautiful redhead was.

On December 14, 1929, a few weeks after the stock market crash, the Provincetown Players gave their final performance. Other theater groups followed them into the old stable, but none of them lasted long. In the 1940s the four Jenny Belardi properties were completely rebuilt, forming apartments and NYU Law School offices. A new Provincetown Playhouse was also built to replace the old stable. Most recently it housed Charles Busch's long-run comedy hit, *Vampire Lesbians of Sodom.* But the glory days of the Provincetown Players have long since ascended into myth, much as Pegasus seems to have returned to the sky after his MacDougal Street hitching post was removed.

NEW IDEAS

The Liberal Club might have stayed up near Gramercy Park where it was born had it not been for a public school teacher named Henrietta Rodman. Her ideas were often too liberal for some members. They believed women should have equal rights, and so did she; but Henrietta Rodman also believed women should have access to information about birth control, a subject she sometimes discussed with her students. And if that wasn't enough to get her in trouble with the Board of Education, she also protested the board's policy of dismissing women once they were married. Men could continue teaching after marriage, she pointed out. Why not women?

WHEN LIFE IS VERY STRENUOUS AND SPIRITS ARE WAY DOWN
YOU'D BETTER GO TO POLLY'S IN LITTLE GREENWICH TOWN
FOR THERE THE CLANS ARE GATHERED - ITS THERE YOU'LL FIND 'EM ALL
THE ARTISTS AND THE WRITERS RANGED ALONG THE WALL.
MISS POLLY TAKES THE MONEY AND MIKE SAYS HE JUST CAN'T
WAIT ANY FASTER ON THE FOLKS IN POLLY'S RES-TAU-RANT
                                                        J.T.B.
GREENWICH VILLAGE - NEW YORK   24
                                          JESSIE TARBOX BEALS

**For this unique glimpse inside
Polly Holladay's restaurant, we
can thank Jessie Tarbox Beals.
A pioneer photojournalist, Beals
opened her own studio in the
Village in the early years of this
century, in a row house still
standing as the present 473 Sixth
Avenue. As with this shot, her
images were often sold for use
as postcards, which accounts for
their rarity today.**

Such notions made Henrietta Rodman notorious, but in the fall
of 1913 her liberal positions influenced two disputes within the
Liberal Club and fractured the five-year-old organization. Her en-
dorsements for free love inspired one married club member to take a
mistress, who then moved in with him and his wife to the dismay of
other members. Then Rodman insisted that the Liberal Club admit
blacks, something many members resisted. Unable to imagine a
racist Liberal Club, Rodman and her followers broke from the
Gramercy Park contingent and established their own Liberal Club.
They found space at 137 MacDougal Street above Polly Holladay's
restaurant, which seventy years earlier had been the home of
Nathaniel Currier, of Currier & Ives.

On MacDougal Street the Liberal Club came into its own.
During its short heyday before World War I, it offered dances (to
which uncorseted women were admitted), lectures on birth control
by Margaret Sanger, play readings, and exhibits of cubist art. The
club rooms were also used for the bimonthly meetings of Heterodoxy, a now-forgotten women's organization that, in its time, did
much to advance feminist activism. Though Heterodoxy continued
through the late 1930s, the Liberal Club disbanded in 1919 after
Polly's Restaurant moved to new quarters around the corner.

VILLAGE LANDMARKS: 147 WEST FOURTH STREET

Though it doesn't look like much, the austere 1849 row house at 147 West Fourth has had several brushes with history. Its ground floor is the Volare restaurant today, but in 1919 this was the second of Polly Holladay's three Village operations and the only one that can still be visited. A few years after her 1921 move from this house to Sheridan Square, the parlor floor here became the Whitney Gallery, one of the precursors of the Whitney Museum.

During the nineteenth century, this had been the private residence of noted *Evening Post* editor William Cullen Bryant. And in November 1918 another journalist lived here briefly while writing his masterpiece. To avoid callers at his Patchin Place apartment, John Reed rented the top floor studio here to finish his eyewitness chronicle of the Russian Revolution. He finished it two months later, and *Ten Days That Shook the World* shook the world when it was published by Horace Liveright in March 1919. Soon afterward, Reed returned to the Soviet Union, where he died of typhus on October 17, 1920—the only American to be honored with a burial along the Kremlin wall.

John Reed, the Golden Boy of Greenwich Village, in Provincetown during the summer of 1916. A few weeks later, he was back in the Village on MacDougal Street, co-producing the play that marked Eugene O'Neill's New York debut. A year after that he was in Russia witnessing the revolution that was the subject of his masterpiece, *Ten Days That Shook the World.*

"NWOD EHT TIBBAR ELOH"

The ramshackle buildings at 146 to 150 West Fourth Street are the remains of the Pepper Pot, which opened here in 1921. A combination tearoom and restaurant, the Pepper Pot ranged aimlessly through these three buildings—a house dating from 1871, an old gristmill with its basement treadle still in working order, and a stable possibly dating from the 1780s. The Pepper Pot occupied the combined sites of two previous operations, the Mad Hatter and the Samovar.

The Mad Hatter, the first Village tearoom, had opened in July 1916 in the basement of 150 West Fourth, under the present Washington Square Coffee Shoppee. Though its famous Alice-in-Wonderland entrance sign, "NWOD EHT TIBBAR ELOH," has long gone, the clapboard facade of the building is still visible in

No one is quite sure how old parts of these wood shacks may be, but the Washington Square Coffee Shoppee is on the site of the Mad Hatter, the first of the Village tearooms. These structures are just outside the protection of the Landmarks District.

part. Next door, a back house at 148 West Fourth presently operates as a yoga center, but in the years after World War I it was the Samovar. This rather inaccessible restaurant bested the Mad Hatter with its own descriptive tag line: "Through the Alley, Up the Stairs, & Over the Roof." This former studio had been converted into a restaurant by Christine Ell, who evidently figured she could be earning good money for the restaurant services she provided for the Provincetown Players. Her hunch was right, and as the Samovar it became immortalized in doggerel: "Samovars twinkle, ukeleles tinkle, Villagers drinkel."

**PARTY
TILL
YOU
DROP**

Accounts vary as to how Robert Clairmont became "the millionaire poet" of Greenwich Village, but they all involve Pittsburgh industrialist Sellers McKees Chandler. According to one version, Clairmont was a pool attendant who once saved Chandler from drowning, leading the grateful steel magnate to write Clairmont into his will and then conveniently die. A less dramatic version has Clairmont simply teaching Chandler how to swim, though that could hardly have warranted a bequest of $350,000.

However he got it, Clairmont came to New York in 1926 to

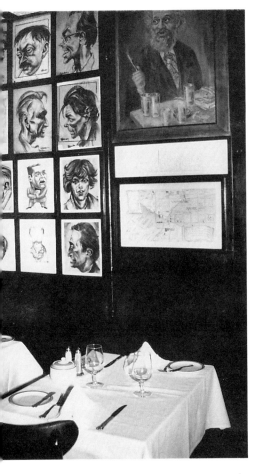

The Joe Gould shrine as it appears today, in the front dining room of the Minetta Tavern. In addition to its Village caricatures, the tavern has a dandy Village mural in its back room—and a surprising history in its basement.

study journalism at Columbia, but after Wall Street investments tripled his wealth a formal education seemed unnecessary. Clairmont took a studio at 143 West Fourth Street and became a fixture of the mad whirl of the Village of the late 1920s. What began as simple parties thrown by Clairmont for friends ballooned into freewheeling affairs that could cost upward of $10,000 each and might last for days. The guests were often people Clairmont didn't know, and occasionally people he never even saw, since he developed the habit of leaving his apartment in mid-celebration. He'd return a day or so later and find the party still in progress or half his books and clothing gone.

One party was thrown in January 1928 when Clairmont wasn't even in town, and that one got him evicted. Hans Stengel, famous for his tart caricatures of Village life, invited friends to Clairmont's apartment for a "Saturday night blowout." The guests found black candles flickering everywhere and noticed that Stengel was in a strangely somber mood. Then the party's tone lightened and remained cheery until midnight, when Stengel locked himself inside the bathroom. When his guests forced the door, they found the cartoonist had used his belt to hang himself. His unexplained suicide became even more grisly a few days later when friends found his last drawing, a cartoon sketch of his bathroom hanging.

A sober Clairmont moved to 61 Perry Street and was just emerging from his gloomy mood when the stock market crashed and took $800,000 of his money with it. Reduced to living in a municipal boardinghouse, Clairmont remained good-natured about the financial prank fate had played on him. "Education," he told an interviewer, "can be expensive."

VILLAGE PEOPLE: PROFESSOR SEA GULL

For forty years Joe Gould was a familiar figure on MacDougal Street, a short, bearded, and disheveled panhandler who professed a strong belief in democracy: "I believe everyone has the right to buy me dinner." Many of those dinners were bought at the Minetta Tavern, still a popular restaurant at 113 MacDougal Street. For that reason, an oil painting of Joe Gould occupies a place of honor in the tavern's vivid wall display of Village caricatures. Gould often entertained his dinner host with recitations of the world's greatest poetry as translated by him into Sea Gull, a bird language he claimed to have mastered. But "Professor Sea Gull" wasn't the fool many imagined him to be. A 1911 Harvard graduate, he had refused to join an exodus of some Village intellectuals to Europe in 1922. "Why bother?" Gould reasoned coolly. "There I'd only meet second-class Americans, while here I meet first-class Europeans!"

Joe Gould always carried a scruffy red folder or two. Over the years, his *Oral History of the World* grew to several thousand manuscript pages, many of which were dispersed to local landladies in lieu of rent. When his *History* was sold, he would assure them, he'd return to make good on his debt and redeem his pledge; then he would shuffle off to another furnished room to repeat the process. The Village must have seemed like a vast literary pawnshop to him. After his death in August 1957, however, no literary masterwork emerged; in fact, not even a few scattered pages surfaced, leading some to consider Gould's *History* a hoax designed by him to provide rent-free living.

But portions of Joe Gould's *Oral History of the World* have since turned up. Gould's manuscript files were found by Israel Young, owner of the popular Folklore Center, which opened just across MacDougal from the Minetta Tavern around the time of Gould's death. Page upon page records, in verbatim transcripts, the mundane exchanges overheard by Gould across the backs of restaurant booths and along the sidewalks. In style, they suggest the "transcript" tone of today's *Interview* magazine, differing only in the absence of any meaningful content. The manuscripts remind 1950s historian John Tytell of an early version of the tape-recorded interview—done without access to a recorder.

And yes, they are written in English—not in Sea Gull.

Born in Greenwich Village. Unlikely, but true.

THE READER'S DIGEST

THIRTY-ONE ARTICLES EACH MONTH FROM LEADING MAGAZINES—EACH ARTICLE OF ENDURING VALUE AND INTEREST, IN CONDENSED AND COMPACT FORM

FEBRUARY 1922

"Is the State Too Vulgar?"

As magazine articles go, an essay title like this must have seemed promising to many liberal Villagers in February 1922— if its phrasing was oddly genteel. A quick glance beyond the table of contents revealed the truth: "Is the State Too Vulgar?" was actually an essay on the theater, with a typographic error in the word "stage." It appeared in the historic first issue of the *Reader's Digest,* which in cumulative sales has since become the best-selling magazine of all time. The magazine was the brainchild of DeWitt Wallace, and its first home was a rented basement at 113 MacDougal Street, under a speakeasy that later became the Minetta Tavern. The *Digest*'s quick success led Wallace to leave the Village after the first few issues, but its point of origin remains here, beneath the Joe Gould shrine.

Contents

Remarkable Remarks 4
How to Keep Young Mentally 5
Prison Facts 7
The Story of the Premature Peace Report 9
Untying the Apron Strings 11
What Do You Know? 13
Whatever is New for Women is Wrong 15
The Difficulty of Being Unsuspected 17
"Rich as Crœsus" 18
Watch Your Dog and Be Wise! 19
Henry Ford, Dreamer and Worker 21
Love—Luxury or Necessity? 23
Time Telling—Past, Present and Future 25
The Philippines Inside Out 27
What Kind of a Husband are You? 29
The Future of Poison Gas 31
Useful Points in Judging People 33
Progress In Science 35
The Firefly's Light 37
Wanted—Motives for Motherhood 39
Vilhjalmur Stefansson 41
Today 42
Can We Have a Beautiful Human Race? 43
Advice From a President's Physician 45
Research and Everyday Life 47
A Peasant on a Painted Train 49
To Bore or Not to Bore 51
Is the State too Vulgar? 53
Hart of The World 54
Printing and Its Early Vicissitudes 55
Northward the Course of Empire 57
Advertising and Health 59
Don't Growl—Kick 61

Published Monthly by
THE READER'S DIGEST ASSOCIATION
No. 1 Minetta Lane, New York City
EDITORS
Lila Bell Acheson, DeWitt Wallace, Louise M. Patteson, Hazel J. Cubberley
25c a Copy, $3.00 a year
Application for entry as second-class matter is pending.
Copyright, 1922, by the Reader's Digest Association.

**BEATNIK
COUNTRY**

The postwar complacency of the late 1940s lulled many into a life of conformity, but not the young writers and artists who gathered in the South Village in those years. Attracted by the low rents, they talked philosophy over chess games and listened to folk music at a new coffeehouse called Edgar's Hobby. Often they gravitated to the San Remo, a neighborhood bar dating from 1925 whose working-class regulars were none too pleased by the invasion of intellectuals. Brawls at the San Remo were frequent—not only among patrons but between patrons and bartenders—but the Beats were not about to back down.

In May 1953 six artists and writers got together and opened Rienzi, a coffeehouse of their own at 107 MacDougal Street. They wanted to create their own environment rather than be dependent on the whims of local club owners. The idea caught on, partly because an artist-owned coffeehouse required no liquor license, no dealings with state bureaucracy, no payoffs for protection. The Rienzi and its successors became central to a burst of activity unlike anything the Village had known in thirty years. Folk music gave way to bebop and bongos, art exhibits to environmental interiors, poetry readings to performance art and café theater. The South Village became Beatnik Country, a world unto itself that achieved worldwide fame.

Poetry readings were a fixture of the Gaslight Café in the basement of 116 MacDougal (where the Scrap Bar is now—a punk Day-Glo version of the tourist trap). All the Beat poets read

MacDougal Street in its heyday. Seen here in 1967 are the Café Feenjon, Rienzi just beyond it, the Café Wha?—and hordes of one-night Villagers.

One of the classic coffeehouses today. Caffe Borgia, at Bleecker and MacDougal streets, is little changed since its glory days of the 1960s.

here at the Gaslight, from Allen Ginsberg to Lawrence Ferlinghetti, and the place became so typical of Beatnik Country that TV journalist Mike Wallace brought a camera crew here for his beatnik profile. That broadcast did little to cut down on the tourists and gate crashers, leading owner John Mitchell occasionally to stand at the door with a loaded gun at hand, serving as an effective bouncer. The Gaslight Café turned up in *The Greenwich Village Story,* a low-budget verité-style feature film shot in the South Village in the summer of 1962.

Among the locations used in that movie was the San Remo, which had long since been converted from a rough-and-tumble bar into a benign coffeehouse. A decade earlier, the San Remo had turned up in *Go,* John Clellon Holmes's 1952 novel, which introduced the Beats to American fiction. That book marked the debut in print of the term "Beat Generation," which Holmes attributed to Jack Kerouac. Kerouac would later incorporate the San Remo into his own fiction, transposing it to San Francisco for his novel, *The Subterraneans,* in 1958. By then the popularity of the Remo had begun to wane. The coffeehouse was soon done in entirely by a glossy puff piece written by Mary McCarthy. According to Ronald Sukenick's memoir, that *New York Post* article sent Kerouac, Paul Goodman, Jackson Pollock, and John Cage scurrying from the gawking uptowners who descended on the place. The northwest corner of MacDougal and Bleecker, once occupied by the San Remo, has hosted a succession of restaurants in recent years, the latest being Carpo's Café.

The years have been kinder to the other corners of this intersection. MacDougal's dates from the late 1940s and still operates as a coffeehouse, as does Le Figaro, which appeared a few years later. What today is the Caffe Borgia was formerly the Scene, a hip poetry spot that became a coffeehouse in the early 1960s. Its interior mural of the Borgias has weathered the years well, its impassive faces providing a link to the beatniks over whom they once watched.

All of these famous remnants of Beatnik Country were styled after the Caffe Reggio, the first European-style coffeehouse in Greenwich Village, which opened at 119 MacDougal Street in 1927. It's still there, its huge paintings, pressed-tin ceiling, and shining espresso machine showing little sign of change after six laid-back decades of operation. Long identified with young people, the Reggio provided the backdrop for the first presidential campaign speech of John Kennedy in 1960 and was used as a location by Paul Mazursky to re-create the youthful Village of the fifties for his 1975 film, *Next Stop, Greenwich Village*.

Café theater began along these blocks in the mid-1950s, initially in the former stable at 106 West Third Street that Rick Allman fashioned into Café Bizarre. In an environment best described now as cliché beatnik, weird masks hung on the walls, bongos drummed incessantly, cigarettes and reefers created a thick purple haze, and Beat poetry was barked through loudspeakers. Here Allman created a freewheeling club that seemed open to almost anything. His eccentric menus became a topic of conversation, and he had so many requests for them that he began to sell them as souvenirs. One item on those menus was the Voo-doo-It-Yourself Sundae, $2.50— served with a small doll and toothpicks. As café theater at the Cino eclipsed the shows at the Bizarre, Allman shifted to stand-up comedy. Now the site of the Bizarre is occupied by a dormitory for the NYU Law School, which cleared the block in 1984.

Caffe Reggio, on MacDougal Street since 1927.

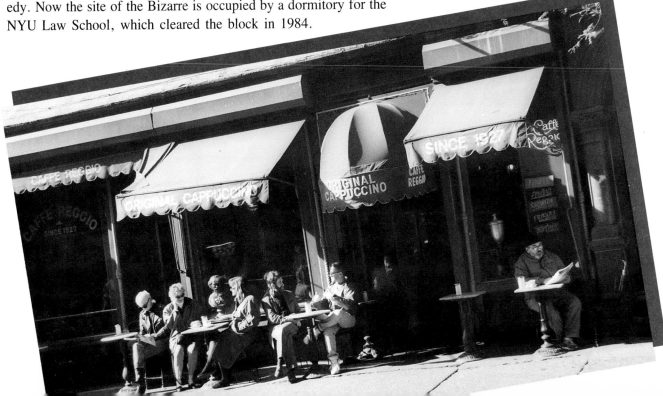

Stand-up comedy shared the spotlight with music at the Bitter End, the most prestigious club in the South Village and still going strong at 147 Bleecker Street. Among the comedians who worked this room early in their careers were Bill Cosby, Woody Allen, Richard Pryor, Joan Rivers, George Carlin, and on one of their Monday talent nights, Dick Cavett. The music acts that took center stage included Cass Elliott; Peter, Paul and Mary, for an entire year; Carly Simon; and a moody kid named Bobby Zimmerman, soon better known as Bob Dylan. More recently, the Bitter End has hosted such up-and-comers as Bette Midler.

A similar mix has thrived across the street at the Village Gate. It opened in 1958 in the basement—formerly a laundry—of the 1892 Mills House, now an apartment house called the Atrium. Encouraged by his success as a concert producer, Art D'Lugoff looked for his own space and found his way to 160 Bleecker Street. Built to provide inexpensive housing for the down and out, Mills House was, in 1958, merely a run-down flophouse. As a result, D'Lugoff negotiated a low-rent forty-eight-year lease extending to the year 2006. Blessed with this security, he has expanded his operations within the building from one venue to three, and augments concerts with Off-Broadway productions. Among his attractions have been singers Odetta, Harry Belafonte, Pete Seeger, and Nina Simone as well as jazz greats Dizzy Gillespie, Charles Mingus, Thelonius Monk, and John Coltrane. The Village Gate hosted the first New York appearance of Aretha Franklin, and such Off-Broadway hits as *Macbird, Jacques Brel Is Alive and Well . . . , One Mo' Time,* and *Beehive.*

Yet for all the activity of those soon to be famous, the most intriguing performer in Beatnik Country was the house favorite at Epitome, a dive at 167 Bleecker Street. His act consisted of scatological poetry, which he read with his head stuck through a toilet seat. History leaves unmentioned what he did for an encore.

FROM
BED
TO
VERSE

Maxwell Bodenheim was something of an embarrassment to the Beats. His gaunt, seedy figure suggested the downside of bohemian disaffection—not the sort of thing an idealistic rebel would want to consider.

Bodenheim was down and out during the 1950s, but back in the mid-1920s, this native Missourian had been a celebrity. His instant fame was the result of a book he had written called *Replenishing Jessica,* a briefly banned tale of a young woman and her inability to refrain from having sex. Its first-year sales of thirty-thousand copies brought a number of enterprising hopefuls to Bodenheim's door at 34 Washington Square in search of literary advice or anything else

Elisabeth Irwin's Little Red Schoolhouse has operated for sixty years on Bleecker Street and is still reinventing the teaching process.

they could negotiate. First was Gladys Loeb, only eighteen but madly in love with the twenty-eight-year-old author. When Bodenheim discouraged both her literary efforts and her amatory advances in June 1928, she stuck her head into the oven and turned on the gas. Her landlady found her just in time and turned her over to her father, who dragged Gladys back to the Bronx.

Virginia Drew wasn't as lucky. After spurning her, Bodenheim personally escorted her to the subway and then promptly left for a vacation in Provincetown. Little did he know the police were searching for him. Miss Drew, it seemed, had wound up not in her home in the Bronx but floating in the Hudson River.

Not that Bodenheim declined all comers—quite the contrary. He developed a slightly greasy reputation as a ladies' man, but even this had unfortunate results. One affair had a grisly ending in August 1928, in a freak subway wreck a hundred feet south of the IRT station at Times Square. A hundred people were injured and sixteen were killed, among them Bodenheim's latest flame. His passionate love letters to her were in her purse when the train's last car was sheared in half, and press reports of the accident made much of the bloody pages they found strewn across the tunnel.

The 1929 market crash reduced Bodenheim to life as a bum, a life that was only briefly improved years later by the publication of his memoir, *My Life and Loves*. On February 6, 1954, Bodenheim was shot to death in a flophouse dispute and, in a final burst of roller-coaster glory, was posthumously honored by the Beats who had shunned him in life. His photo was mounted above the bar at the San Remo, a fitting if tardy recognition of their spiritual predecessor. But Bodenheim would have taken the gesture in his stride, particularly if his spirit sensed that before the 1960s were out, Beats Jack Kerouac and Neal Cassady would both be dead from abuse of alcohol and drugs. As Bodenheim himself put it, what was Greenwich Village but "the Coney Island of the soul"?

BEYOND "PROGRESSIVE"

Its goals were thought radical at the time, but Elisabeth Irwin was smart enough to choose a deceptively old-fashioned name. She named her new progressive school the Little Red Schoolhouse, and it's still there in the building at 196 Bleecker Street, which Irwin opened in 1932. But its origins predate the school itself by over a decade.

Irwin began teaching in New York's public schools around 1916, according to Little Red's present director, Richard Fitzgerald. "By 1919, she'd set up an experimental first grade at P.S. 64 on the Lower East Side, and she taught six other experimental classes over the next two years. Her ideas were new. One of them was to tailor the curriculum to the individual child. When public funds for her program were withdrawn in 1931, the parents of her students rallied around her and bought for her the old chapel at 196 Bleecker, which was to become her school.

"Irwin believed that children learned better by doing than by being told, and she instituted the first field trips for elementary students anywhere in the country. She also pioneered psychological testing here. All very advanced at the time, though since then traditional education has absorbed many of her methods.

"Today," Fitzgerald noted, "we hold her legacy dear, though we don't limit ourselves to it, point for point. We continue to promote critical, independent thinking among our students, and we believe that they benefit from diversity. We try to keep tuition low for just this reason, and maintain an extensive scholarship program that disperses over $500,000 in financial aid annually. And we now have a variance from the state since we exceed the mandated curriculum. I don't know if there's a name for what we offer at Little Red, but I know it's very good."

Though virtually no shows other than *The Fantasticks* have played the Sullivan Street Playhouse, older Villagers recall this as Jimmy Kelly's, a popular night spot that for years served up light entertainment with supper. And almost no one today remembers the blacksmith shop that occupied the basement of 181 Sullivan Street early in this century.

A FANTASTICK SUCCESS

A girl, a boy, a little moonlight, and a wall—unlikely ingredients of theatrical history. But *The Fantasticks* had a few other things going for it, notably a deft score by Tom Jones and Harvey Schmidt, a gifted cast, inspired staging by Word Baker, and Lore Noto, a producer who, like the two fathers in the show, "never said no."

Reviews after the May 3, 1960, opening of this show were decidedly mixed. Co-author Jones left the cast party early, only to be sick in a cab in the middle of Central Park. The press agent advised producer Noto to close the show after the Sunday night performance, advice that wasn't taken. For week after week the fate of the production hung by a financial thread, but its audience slowly began to grow as a result of word-of-mouth praise. A corner was turned when the show caught on with theater people, and by summer's end it was sometimes sold out—a heartening development, even though "sold out" at the Sullivan Street Playhouse meant an audience of only 153 people.

That was more than thirty years ago, and since then *The Fantasticks* has circled the globe while still giving performances on Sullivan Street. The original cast included Jerry Orbach, Kenneth Nelson, Rita Gardner, and "Thomas Bruce" (author Tom Jones). Subsequent actors seen on Sullivan Street have included David Cryer, John Cunningham, Bert Convy, F. Murray Abraham, and, as the Boy's Father through most of the 1970s, producer Lore Noto.

SOUTH VILLAGE NAME-DROPPING

The unassuming structure at 85 West Third Street is a landmark site in the history of detective fiction. It was known as 15 Amity Street when Edgar Allan Poe lived here in 1845 and here wrote *Facts in the Case of M. Valdemar,* one of the earliest examples of the form. Today the building is Poe House, and the property of the ubiquitous NYU Law School, but in recent years it was a fraternity house, and during the 1970s, it housed the Gold

Mori's at 144 Bleecker Street was an early Italian restaurant—it opened in 1884—and one of the first restaurants to draw a theatrical clientele. Actors were led here by a Village resident, noted actress Minnie Maddern Fiske.

Bug, a popular gay dance bar named after another Poe tale that reputedly was written here. However, it is best remembered as the home of Bertolotti's, which for seventy years was a family-run Italian restaurant.

The top floor of nearby 172 Bleecker Street was rented in 1941 by budding film reviewer James Agee. He still held this apartment at the close of that decade while he was at work on his screenplay for *The African Queen*. A few doors east at number 144 is the Bleecker Street Cinema, long one of New York's leading revival houses. It was here that Aidan Quinn's character worked as a projectionist in the 1985 film, *Desperately Seeking Susan*. But this building's greatest fame was achieved before it became a movie theater. Originally this was Mori's, an Italian restaurant that opened in 1884. Its exterior was redesigned in the 1920s by skyscraper architect Raymond Hood. Until it closed in the 1930s, this family restaurant was a Village favorite. The forty-foot mural along its east wall was as famous in its day as the Caffe Borgia murals were a few generations later. Unfortunately, the cinema's plasterboard walls have hidden the mural for the past forty years.

NOW YOU SEE IT, NOW YOU DON'T

The Nucciarone Funeral Home at 177 Sullivan Street is briefly seen at the beginning of *Moonstruck,* the Oscar-winning 1987 film. But don't go looking for it. On the morning of November 11, 1987, this five-story structure collapsed, becoming in seconds a twisted pile of rubble. In addition to claiming one life, the collapse took from New Yorkers the 1882 birthplace of the city's most beloved mayor, Fiorello La Guardia. A plaque on the building's facade commemorating La Guardia's birth was recovered and will be returned to the site when new construction allows.

This isn't the most elusive South Village site to be seen in *Moonstruck*. For over twenty years, *Moonstruck* author John Patrick Shanley enjoyed dining at the Grand Ticino Restaurant at 228 Thompson Street, and decided to write it into his script. However, the actual restaurant appears in the film in name only. Interiors were shot on a replica set built in Montreal, because the actual 1929 interior of the Grand Ticino was too small to accommodate cameras and crew. Exterior shots actually feature the facade of Scarlet, another Village restaurant blocks away on the corner of West Fourth and West Twelfth streets. To further confuse things, the filmmakers covered over the street sign there and turned West Twelfth Street into Hicks Street, which is actually in Brooklyn Heights.

The Grand Ticino proudly publicizes its participation in the film, but don't be disillusioned by the facts. After all, *Moonstruck* is a romance, and facts aren't everything when you're in love.

**A
PABLO
AMID
PABLUM**

It looks like a Picasso and it is, the only outdoor sculpture in the city designed by the Master in a non-museum setting. Set in the middle of University Village in 1970, the thirty-six-foot-high *Bust of Sylvette* stands on the site of Frenchtown, the red-light district of a century before.

To make room for this complex of towers, the blocks east to Mercer Street were wiped away in two stages. Though the last vestiges of Frenchtown were lost, urban renewal was originally planned as a far larger project, one that meant to level much of the South Village. In the face of this plan, an ad hoc consortium of seventeen community organizations joined Community Board 2 in a successful campaign to limit the scope and location of the plan proposed by local power broker Robert Moses. He had lobbied vigorously to have the South Village declared a slum—with good reason. The $3.5 billion in funds that he controlled, and the power its spending conferred, only came into play once there was a designated slum to clear away, according to Moses biographer Robert A. Caro. Moses' plans for other city districts encountered little more than nuisance resistance, but in the Village he ran into crippling opposition.

As a result of pressure from residents, the 1956 Washington Square Village turned out to be a compromise, a scaled-down development. Its towers are the sort of banal structures that can be seen in any American city.

A decade later, the less insensitive University Towers rose to the south of the earlier project, and their central plaza was soon graced by the Picasso work. It stands as a minor victory for taste in a sterile sea of architectural pablum.

Bust of Sylvette by Picasso, executed by Carl Nesjar. Set within University Village in 1970, it's about the only interesting thing to be found today on the site of Frenchtown.

7 THE EAST VILLAGE

Past and present, the Old World and the New, collide in the East Village.

Seated on a park bench in Tompkins Square Park, a wizened woman dressed in black munches thoughtfully on a bialy, her eyes measuring the present as her mind drifts through the past. Balanced on a red skateboard, a youth of about sixteen in artfully torn jeans glides past, his eyes hidden behind opaque shades, his mind toying with tomorrow while earphones blot out today. A first impression might cast Tompkins Square as the Washington Square of the East Village, with the contrast dial turned up. An easy comparison, but deceptive. It's unwise to define the East Village in terms of the rest of Greenwich Village. That's how some of the problems of the East Village began.

The term "East Village" barely thirty years old. It was coined by real-estate people who wanted to profit from the growing cachet of Greenwich Village during the 1950s. The new name was designed to make marketable the land and apartments in the

1 St. Mark's-in-the-Bowery
2 Site of Stuyvesant's Pear Tree
3 106 E. 13th St. (site of 13th St. reservoir)
4 Old Merchant's House
5 New York Marble Cemetery
6 New York City Marble Cemetery
7 McSorley's
8 Ottendorfer Branch of the New York Public Library
9 Community Synagogue (former German Lutheran Church)
10 *General Slocum* Memorial
11 Former Yiddish Art Theatre
12 Site of the Café Royal
13 Veselka Ukrainian Coffee Shop (former Café Monopole)

14 Variety Photo Plays
15 208 East 13th St. (former Emma Goldman residence)
16 Cooper Union
17 Cooper Square
18 Formerly Arlington Hall (and former Electric Circus)
19 La Mama E.T.C.
20 Former Loew's Commodore (and former Fillmore East and the Saint)
21 CBGB
22 Formerly the Ritz (originally Webster Hall)
23 Site of Manic Panic
24 P.S. 122
25 WOW Café

northern reaches of the Lower East Side. These blocks were home to overlapping communities of Italians, Germans, Russian Jews, Poles, Romanians, Greeks, and Czechs. For over a century, its residents were tied more closely to their homelands than to the new land in which they lived. Here weddings and funerals were held in just about every language but English.

Changes began after the Second World War. The overlapping ethnic communities east of Fourth Avenue started to shrink through attrition and assimilation. The low rents that resulted attracted such marginal wage earners as writers and artists, who inadvertently paved the way, as often happens, for speculators. Many had come here to reinvent themselves in the bohemian manner of their spiritual ancestors in the West Village. Speculators soon decided to reinvent the entire neighborhood while the residue of its predecessor lingered on. Changes that the West Village had a century to accommodate were fostered here overnight, and the result was an urban identity crisis. The Tompkins Square riot of August 1988 may have been sparked by a disputed local curfew, but it was fueled by fundamental questions over the sort of neighborhood this was to be.

The forced transformation of the Lower East Side into the "East Village" accounts for the high-voltage excitement that has been the area's hallmark in recent years. If the rest of Greenwich Village has invented much of "today," the volatile mix we call the East Village is now hard at work creating what will turn out to be "tomorrow."

Given its recently forged ties to Greenwich Village, it's a surprise to learn the East Village has common origins with its namesake to the west. And it's with those ties that our tour of the East Village begins.

STUYVESANT'S CHAPEL

St. Mark's-in-the-Bowery opened in 1799 and is now the second oldest house of worship in Manhattan. Over its two centuries, the church has seen many notables come and go, but it remains most closely linked to the fourth director of New Amsterdam, the peg-legged benevolent tyrant, Peter Stuyvesant.

Just as Astor Place today follows the route of the dirt path that ran west to the *bouwerie* of Wouter Van Twiller, so Stuyvesant Street follows the lane that led to the estate of Van Twiller's successor, Peter Stuyvesant. On taking office in 1647, Stuyvesant looked around for his own country property and in 1651 settled on a parcel of fertile land east of the Bouwerie Road (now Fourth Avenue). As an entrance to the property he created what is now Stuyvesant Street. It bisected his land and ran east past today's Second

St. Mark's-in-the-Bowery today. Its interior was rebuilt after a 1978 fire.

Avenue all the way to the bank of the East River, about a block north of Avenue A and Fourteenth Street. After his death in 1672, Stuyvesant was buried in a vault beneath the small chapel he built on his property.

He's still there, though the chapel was razed in 1793 by his great-grandson to make possible the construction of its replacement, St. Mark's-in-the-Bowery, on that same site. Buried near Stuyvesant in St. Mark's cemetery are many of his descendants, several British colonial governors, and even one early U.S. Vice-President, Daniel Tompkins, after whom Tompkins Square was named. No longer buried here is department store magnate A. T. Stewart, whose corpse was stolen in 1878 and held for $250,000 ransom. When it was returned to his widow after two frustrating years, she had the body interred in a new vault in Garden City, Long Island, which was outfitted with its own burglar alarm.

Never content merely to be situated in its neighborhood, St. Mark's has become part of it. Dr. William Guthrie back in the 1920s used American Indian chants and Greek dances to demonstrate to a diverse local population the essential unity among religions. More recently, in the 1960s, the church set out to rebuild its Second Avenue yard, employing the youth of the community in its reconstruction. St. Mark's has also actively fostered civil rights, promoted voter registration, supported prison reform, and opened the nation's first lesbian health care clinic.

But it's in the arts that St. Mark's made its biggest splash. Under Dr. Guthrie, such poets as William Carlos Williams, Kahlil Gibran, Amy Lowell, Edna St. Vincent Millay, and Carl Sandburg came here to read from their works. Isadora Duncan and Ruth St. Denis danced here, and Houdini performed his sleight-of-hand here as well. More recent readers and performers at St. Mark's include Allen Ginsberg, Merce Cunningham, and Andy Warhol, who raised a bit of a ruckus among the congregants by screening for them several of his early underground films.

Playwright Sam Shepard is the most celebrated alumnus of the theater company formed at St. Mark's in 1964. Shepard had come east only a year earlier and, while working as a waiter at the Village Gate over on Bleecker Street, heard about the company from its organizer, Ralph Cook, who at the time was the Gate's headwaiter. With the Theatre Genesis production of Shepard's *Cowboys* in October 1964, the playwright began his rise as the wonder boy of Off–Off Broadway. Fifteen of his plays were written and staged around the Village before the decade was out, but Theatre Genesis remained his emotional home base until Cook's departure in 1969.

That same year, Shepard chose St. Mark's as the setting for his wedding to actress O-Lan Johnson. Three years before this real ceremony, the church had been used for a fictional wedding filmed for *The Group,* the Hollywood version of Mary McCarthy's 1963 best-seller. But the interior seen in that film no longer exists. On July 27, 1978, as a three-year church renovation neared completion, an acetylene torch accidentally set fire to the east gallery of the church. In less than thirty minutes, the dry timbers of the 179-year-old peaked roof fell in flames into the sanctuary, nine stained-glass windows were shattered, and the 150-foot steeple stood on the verge of collapse. A community that had long been supported by the church formed the Citizens to Save St. Mark's. They embarked on a reconstruction of the gutted church, which was completed and dedicated in 1986.

Stuyvesant's Pear Tree in 1865. The building at left, 109 Third Avenue, still stands, but the corner building was replaced in 1910 with the present structure, rebuilt in 1987 as Pear Tree Place.

PEAR TREE CONDO

A seventeen-unit condominium building, which stands at the northeast corner of Third Avenue and Thirteenth Street, is called Pear Tree Place, although there's no pear tree in sight. But still, the name is quite fitting, considering this corner's history.

Soon after taking up residence on his *bouwerie* in 1651, Peter Stuyvesant planted a pear tree here, presumably one of several. This one was lucky. It was spared when both the street and the avenue were cut through, and it was close enough to the intersection to escape being trapped within a building plot. As the neighborhood developed, the tree's history became legend, and an iron fence was erected around it to offer some measure of protection. Standing only inches from the curb, it bore fruit for nearly two hundred years, until a carriage accident in 1867 left the tree fatally damaged and forced its removal.

BOWERY VILLAGE

Just as the West Village developed from a Dutch *bouwerie* into a country village, the East Village initially followed a similar pattern. In the last years before it was replaced by St. Mark's, the old Stuyvesant chapel became the centerpiece of a now-forgotten neighborhood known as Bowery Village. Early in the 1790s, a small market opened on the site of the present Cooper Square. A cistern there served the residents, along with a tavern used as a drop for mail headed for the city, which was then two miles to the south. At the present corner of Tenth Street and Third Avenue, Bowery Village even had its own windmill.

On that corner today, if you overlook the arrogant architecture

Stuyvesant Street, a remnant of the vanished Bowery Village, and its intrusive NYU neighbor.

of the 1987 NYU dormitory on Third Avenue—a difficult challenge—you can still see vestiges of the Bowery Village. At 21 Stuyvesant Street stands the 1803 house built by Stuyvesant's great-grandson as a wedding gift to his daughter Elizabeth on her marriage to Major Nicholas Fish, a wealthy old-line New Yorker. Their son Hamilton, born here in 1808, became the state governor and later secretary of state under President Grant. At nearby 44 Stuyvesant Street is what remains of the 1795 home of Elizabeth's brother, Nicholas Stuyvesant, now altered beyond period authenticity.

One landmark of Bowery Village was Elizabeth Stuyvesant's garden, laid out on the triangular property east of the Stuyvesant-Fish home. In 1861 son Hamilton sold the property to a developer who, it is believed, retained James Renwick to design the sixteen houses now standing on that property. The so-called Renwick Triangle houses were rescued from years of neglect with a renovation in the 1960s. They were landmarked in 1969 as the St. Mark's Historic District, which also includes the church itself and the two Stuyvesant family houses.

Similarly, the Bowery is now undergoing the early stages of a transformation that will end—who knows where? To be sure, the Bowery bums are still to be seen, particularly south of Houston Street, passed out on the sidewalk or panhandling around the cars that stop at traffic lights. Developers have begun moving in on the blocks lining this broad, potentially appealing boulevard, though not without some neighborhood disruption. Meanwhile, an impromptu market where tattered clothes and discarded magazines are sold now enlivens the sidewalks around Cooper Square, where the Bowery Village market flourished over two centuries ago.

30,000,000 OUNCES OF PREVENTION

New Yorkers assume that the first system to successfully meet the city's water needs was the Croton System, which opened in 1842. Though clearly the most extensive, it was not the first, an honor taken in 1829 by a site east of Fourth Avenue on the south side of Thirteenth Street.

Several municipal water systems of the eighteenth century failed, as did one private venture undertaken by the 1799 Manhattan Water Company formed by Aaron Burr. (Its banking interests, however, survived to become the Chase Manhattan Bank of today.) In the late 1820s the city tried once more. At what is now 106 East Thirteenth Street it built an octagonal tower with an iron tank capable of holding 233,000 gallons of water. A system of underground tunnels was dug below the water table for several hundred feet, and the tank was filled with the aid of pumps. From the tank, water was fed to the city through pipes running south under

The City Reservoir of 1829, today the site of a firehouse at 106 East Thirteenth Street.

Fourth Avenue and branching out under side streets. The 1829 reservoir proved successful enough to spur the city to undertake the Croton System, which is still in use. By the close of the century, the Thirteenth Street Reservoir had been replaced by a fire station, and that in turn was eventually replaced by the present firehouse, which was built in 1929. The labyrinthine tunnels that were built a century earlier no longer function but undoubtedly still exist.

VILLAGE LANDMARKS: THE OLD MERCHANT'S HOUSE

Virtually all of the homes of the wealthy on or near Bond Street vanished long ago, but one has survived—incredibly, with its original furnishings intact. Wealthy merchant Seabury Tredwell bought the house that stands at 29 East Fourth Street in 1835, when it was three years old. Nearly a century later, his daughter was still in residence there when she died at the age of ninety-three. In 1936, three years after her death, the Old Merchant's House opened as a museum, offering the public access to the only Greek Revival interior in New York City that retains its original appearance. The house was threatened with demolition in the mid-1960s, but it was saved by Joseph Roberto, who secured landmark designation for it and then had it fully restored in 1974.

The Old Merchant's House, a landmark at 29 East Fourth Street, awaiting construction of its new neighbors.

Until 1987, three adjoining homes—greatly altered—stood between the Tredwell house and 37 East Fourth, which was built in 1845 for Tredwell's cousin and which is now also a landmark. A new structure is to rise between the two old houses—one which the developer asserts will be "sensitive" to the landmarks it will join.

VILLAGE LANDMARKS: THE MARBLE CEMETERIES

When the city banned burials south of Canal Street in 1830, several businessmen opened the New York Marble Cemetery as a profit-making venture and the first nonsectarian cemetery in the city. On half an acre at the center of the block west of Second Avenue between Second and Third streets, they built 156 underground vaults and sold them to wealthy subscribers. Their venture was successful enough to warrant opening a second cemetery a year later one block to the east. Known as the New York City Marble Cemetery, it's the permanent residence

of publisher Charles Scribner, a few Roosevelts, and members of the Kip family, forever connected with the Kip's Bay district of Midtown East. President James Monroe was buried here for a few years, before being disinterred and reburied in his native Virginia. Similarly, John Ericsson, designer of the ironclad *Monitor*, was removed from his East Village grave and returned to his native Sweden.

The New York City Marble Cemetery, 52–74 East Second Street, since 1831 a business venture so successful that people were dying to get in.

Details may have changed slightly, but the spirit of McSorley's bar remains as it was when painted in oil in 1912 by John Sloan (1871–1951).

THE OLDEST ESTABLISHED

When the wealthy withdrew from Bond Street and vicinity, the first wave of immigrants arrived and began turning the former Bowery Village into the Lower East Side. Though most of the poor Irish who fled the potato famine of the 1840s settled near the East River docks, a few made it to the present East Village. One of them was John McSorley, who left County Tyrone and, in 1854, leased the ground floor of 15 East Seventh Street, where he opened an ale house.

It's still in operation there after more than a century, making it the oldest saloon in New York. McSorley's potbelly stove is still there, as are the gas lamps and the carved mahogany bar. The pressed-tin walls are littered with the ephemera collected by McSorley before his death in 1910, including a rare poster offering a reward for Abraham Lincoln's assassin.

John Sloan painted a famous view of the interior of McSorley's. The old ale house has been celebrated in the verse of E. E. Cummings and toasted by Brendan Behan, long a regular here. The sawdust on the floor was always changed daily, but until 1971 the place was closed to women. In that year, under court order, women were admitted—though the first to enter got a pitcher of ale poured over her head. Otherwise, life at McSorley's has been little changed by the arrival of women, who are now welcomed without the overhead libation.

GERMANTOWN

A relic of Germantown at 135 Second Avenue, now a branch of the New York Public Library.

By 1893, more Germans lived in New York than in any city but Berlin. Germans had arrived here in two waves, the first following the failed revolution of 1848, and the second in the wake of the anti-socialist legislation passed in Germany in 1878. Once here, they replaced the Irish on the blocks east of Fourth Avenue and re-created many of their social institutions on the side streets off Second Avenue.

Walk through the area today, and you'll see that many of the buildings here still speak German, even if their residents no longer do. In 1884, for example, the Freie Bibliothek und Lesehalle was built at 135 Second Avenue. Its name is boldly chiseled into the building facade and can be easily read after more than a century. The first free library building in Manhattan erected for that purpose, it was a gift to the community from Oswald Ottendorfer, a wealthy German philanthropist and editor of the *Staats-Zettung,* one of nearly a dozen German papers then printed in New York. The building became the German language branch of the Free Circulating Library, and it was ultimately absorbed by the New York Public Library as the Ottendorfer Branch.

Ottendorfer also built the German Dispensary building adjacent to his library as the new home for an East Side facility that had been founded thirty years earlier. When anti-German sentiment arose during World War I, its name was changed to the Stuyvesant Polyclinic, its present name, but the building facade retains its German appearance, which is enhanced by the inclusion on it of busts honoring the great men of medicine.

Across the face of 12 St. Mark's Place, letters still announce that the Deutsch-Amerikanische Scheutzen Gesellschaft—the German-American Shooting Club—was the organization that built this clubhouse in 1885. In 1987 its ground floor became the spacious new home of the St. Mark's Bookshop, which had long been the leading radical bookstore of the East Village, even before it left its original cramped quarters at 13 St. Mark's Place, just across the street.

Ghosts of German immigrants may haunt several other surviving structures. The Germantown branch of the YMCA still stands at 140 Second Avenue, just below Tenth Street, though it has shifted its allegiance and is now active as the Ukranian Community Center. A German athletic club opened its doors at 66 East Fourth Street in 1871, but today those doors lead to offices used by the La Mama Experimental Theatre Company. Their stages, however, are a few doors away at 72 East Fourth Street, a former concert hall that incorporates into its facade—in the German tradition—busts of Mozart, Beethoven, and Wagner. Another German concert hall, the one at 62 East Fourth, is undergoing renovation for use as a theater, but the ornamental fire escape built into this 1889 structure will remain.

THE GENERAL SLOCUM MEMORIAL

This is Arbor Day, 1904, in Tompkins Square. Six weeks later, many of the children seen here were likely among the dead in the *General Slocum* fire, a disaster that also led to the death of Germantown.

The center of the immigrant German community had long been the German Lutheran Church at 323 East Sixth Street, which was built in 1848. On June 15, 1904, the congregation held a picnic excursion for the wives and children of those men who worked that Wednesday. They had leased the *General Slocum,* a popular pleas-

ure steamer, for a sail up the East River to the scenic Bronx shore. As the ship passed through Hell Gate off Astoria, a flash fire broke out on board. In minutes, the wooden ship had burned to the waterline. Over a thousand people were killed, most of them the children of Germantown. Men came home from work to find that their entire families had been lost. Overwhelmed with grief, many men suffered mental breakdowns, and a few committed suicide.

The people of Germantown raised a monument to the lost children. It is still standing in Tompkins Square though long ago whitewashed into illegibility and forgotten. But even when new, the monument could not hold together a shattered community. The few remaining families moved away through the following year or so, and Germantown itself quickly died. The Lower East Side soon became home to the rising number of immigrant Jews from Eastern Europe. That shift is symbolized by the renaming of the United German Lutheran Church on Sixth Street, known today and through most of this century as the Community Synagogue.

The childhood home of George and Ira Gershwin at 91 Second Avenue, as it looks today.

AN AMERICAN IN SECOND AVENUE

Among the first Russian Jews to immigrate to America was Morris Gershovitz, who left a shoe factory in St. Petersburg in 1892 to live above a pawnshop at Hester and Eldridge streets. Prosperity followed, and Gershovitz moved to a succession of homes, among them the Brooklyn house where his son Jacob was born in 1898. Six weeks later, Morris moved his young family to the second floor of 91 Second Avenue, back in Manhattan.

This remained for several years the home of the Gershvin family (Morris had been tinkering with his surname), and in time, his son Jacob became the roller-skating champ of East Seventh Street. And it was through these windows—now above a discount pharmacy—that a piano was hoisted in 1910. The Gershvins had bought it for older son Israel (Ira), but to the family's surprise, it was twelve-year-old Jacob—whose friends had taken to calling him George—who sat down and promptly banged out a tune. Luckily nobody tried to get him away from the keyboard.

The former Yiddish Art Theatre, 189 Second Avenue, as it looked in 1988 when it was slated to be gutted and rebuilt as a multiplex cinema.

THE JEWISH RIALTO

The musical version of Chaim Potok's novel, *The Chosen*, clearly wasn't chosen. Its six official performances in January 1988 blew $2.6 million, making it the most costly flop in Off-Broadway history. Its demise also brought down the curtain on live theater for the jewel of the Jewish Rialto, the Yiddish Art Theatre.

Maurice Schwartz built his $1 million playhouse at 189 Second Avenue as the permanent home for his Yiddish Art Theatre troupe, founded by him in 1918. For the theater's 1926 opening Schwartz staged a musical version of Abraham Goldfaden's 1887 play, *The Tenth Commandment*. Seated beneath a vast dome that incorporated a plasterwork Star of David, the audience marveled at the elaborate setting for the show, which marked the professional debut of set designer Boris Aronson.

A unique blend of Jewish legends and traditions, Yiddish theater in America had its origins only a few blocks away. In the wake of the assassination of Czar Alexander II, poor Eastern European Jews began an exodus to the Lower East Side in 1882, and on August 12 of that year, an amateur Yiddish theater group gave a performance at the German athletic club at 66 East Fourth Street. In its cast was a sixteen-year-old Boris Thomashefsky, who was destined to become the great matinee idol of Yiddish theater—and the grandfather of conductor Michael Tilson Thomas. For decades, Thomashefsky's female fans swooned at the sight of his celebrated calves, an asset he managed to display no matter how melodramatic his role. In his later years, he had his own theater, a vast barn of a playhouse that stood at Second and Houston until the late 1950s.

Professional Yiddish theater in America began in 1887, after a ban by the new czar led Jewish actors to join the exodus to New York. Its first star was Abraham Goldfaden, whose debut here in that year proved unsuccessful but paved the way for the Yiddish stars to come. The most celebrated of them was Joseph Adler, a tragedian noted for his bold interpretation of Shylock and his Yiddish King Lear. Three of his children—Stella, Celia, and Luther—also achieved theatrical fame, though not until after Joseph Adler's 1926 death, which brought half a million grieving fans to Second Avenue. More recently, Paul Muni, Jacob Ben-Ami, Menasha Skulnick, Morris Carnovsky, Sam Levene, and Harold Clurman won fame that extended beyond Yiddish theater, as did actress Molly Picon, whose career was reputedly boosted in 1929 when her singing of a Yiddish ballad brought tears to Al Capone's eyes.

After the Yiddish Art Theatre company disbanded in 1950, its former home became the Phoenix Theatre and the scene for distinguished productions of theatrical classics. In addition, the Phoenix Company sponsored the creation of a few brand-new plays, principally the award-winning musical by Jerome Moross and John Latouche, *The Golden Apple* (1954). It transferred to Broadway, as did later independent productions that premiered here, including *Oh! Calcutta!* (1969), *Grease* (1972), and *The Best Little Whorehouse in Texas* (1978). The theater is presently slated to be rebuilt as a multiscreen movie theater, unless it wins a reprieve via the Landmarks Commission, which has twice before considered but left unresolved an official designation for it.

The cornerstone of the Yiddish Art Theatre, which was uncovered prior to renovation. *Sic transit gloria mundi.*

THE YIDDISH SARDI'S

Any number of dairy restaurants and coffee shops appeared along the Jewish Rialto over the years, but only at the southeast corner of Second Avenue and Twelfth Street could you arrive in search of a blintze and leave with a part in an upcoming play. The Café Royal opened there in 1920 and for over thirty years was informally known as the Yiddish Sardi's. The Royal was a mad whirl of out-of-work actors and impresarios on the make, where stars could (and did) turn tableclothes into signed contractual agreements. Agents and managers took to phoning the Café Royal when they were out of town, knowing that their casting problems could be solved by long-distance. Hopeful playwrights often gave out the pay phone number as their own, and they would conduct negotiations on the line while across the room the merits of their script were being hotly debated.

Each summer a row of box hedges appeared along Second

Avenue in front of the Café Royal, and the whole operation spilled out onto the sidewalk. Village writers like John Dos Passos and E. E. Cummings took to hanging out at the Royal to enjoy its frenetic atmosphere; other celebrities frequently seen here included Fannie Brice, Moss Hart, and Charles Chaplin. The Café Royal closed in the early 1950s; its site at this writing is now an empty store for lease. However, a decade before its demise, the Royal was fictionalized by Hy Kraft in his 1942 Broadway comedy, *Café Crown*. Despite good reviews, a nation distracted by war had little use for the play, which remained unrevived in New York until the acclaimed production at the Public Theater in October 1988.

THE FIRST OF THE LAST OF THE RED HOT MAMAS

After Louis Tuck abandoned his young bride, she was reduced to singing for her supper—literally. One day in 1906, she walked into the Café Monopole on the Lower East Side and struck just such a deal with its manager, who then asked the woman her name. Too embarrassed by her poverty to use either her maiden name or her married name, Sophie Abuza Tuck invented a name on the spot, one with which she made history.

Sophie Tucker became the first entertainer to break through the "Jewish barrier" that had limited many show business careers. She did this by inventing a character, presenting herself neither in the role of the virginal nor the fallen woman. Instead, Sophie Tucker created the "knowing woman," the woman who had been around and had found wisdom and a sense of humor after she "lost her virtue." With her rich, throaty voice and impeccable phrasing, she was also a damn good singer. And with her character and talent, the self-styled Last of the Red Hot Mamas became the first "ethnic" performer to find mainstream success without the use of self-parody. Barely two years after her debut at the Café Monopole, Sophie Tucker was a star.

The Monopole is long gone, but its shell still stands at 144 Second Avenue on the southeast corner on Ninth Street, and its street floor is now occupied by the Veselka, a Ukrainian coffee shop. Also gone are Ratner's Deli, which has been replaced at 111 Second Avenue by a supermarket, and Rapoport's, a dairy restaurant that operated for many years at 93 Second Avenue, one door north of the former Gershwin family apartment. A few traditional Jewish spots remain open, however, notably Moishe's Bake Shop at 115 Second Avenue (closed on Saturdays) and the Second Avenue Deli, which has kept the southeast corner of Eleventh Street kosher since 1954. This delicatessen honors Yiddish theater stars with plaques embedded in the sidewalk out front—a Yiddish version of the Hollywood Walk of Fame.

Veselka's, the Ukrainian restaurant at 144 Second Avenue at Ninth Street, where Sophie Tucker offered ethnic entertainment to a nonethnic audience.

Once an Off-Broadway house, Theatre 80 St. Mark's now shows screen classics. Two sidewalk signatures are visible below the pedestrian. If you ever wondered whether Joan Crawford really could plan ahead, the answer's in cement at 80 St. Mark's Place.

OFF-BROADWAY EAST

As Yiddish theater declined in the 1950s, the East Village welcomed the profitable rise of Off Broadway. The former Yiddish Art Theatre, with 1,100 seats, was an ideal setting for the classics of the Phoenix Theatre, but the cavernous Public Theatre at 66 Second Avenue proved far too large to adjust. Renamed the Phyllis Anderson Theatre, its 1,700 seats have been empty for most of the past thirty years, and not even a brief stint as a rock theater affiliated with CBGB could redirect its derelict and doubtful future.

Both the Cricket and the Gate were carved out of unused space in 162 Second Avenue and opened as Off-Broadway theaters. Other theaters sprang up along East Fourth Street, though the most successful East Village house was also the oldest. The Orpheum at 126 Second Avenue, just below St. Mark's Place, opened in 1905 as a concert garden. Movies were added to the bill in 1911, at which time the building was altered to incorporate the present entrance on Second Avenue. Films alternated with Yiddish variety shows at the Orpheum until 1958, when the theater went legit. Its most recent hit was the four-year run of *Little Shop of Horrors*.

Around the corner, Theatre 80 St. Mark's went from a legit policy to a film repertory, and so the theater that offered the 1967 hit, *You're a Good Man, Charlie Brown,* now mixes popular Hollywood fare with more obscure titles. Initially restricting itself to musicals, Theatre 80 St. Mark's later embraced the nostalgia craze of the early 1970s by instituting its own sidewalk version of Grauman's Chinese Theatre. The hand- and footprints of Ruby Keeler, Alexis Smith, Gloria Swanson, and others, preserved in cement, are seldom noticed by passing pedestrians.

The neon-embellished marquee dates from the 1930s, but Variety Photo Plays, at 110–112 Third Avenue, is some twenty years older. In fact, it opened in 1914 as a nickelodeon, which made it the oldest movie theater still operating in the city when it closed in February 1989. Considering the development being planned for the rest of this block, it's unlikely that Variety Photo Plays will survive without landmark protection.

VILLAGE PEOPLE: EMMA GOLDMAN

Born in Lithuania in 1869, Emma Goldman was one of thousands of Jews to flee Eastern Europe during the 1880s. After arriving on the Lower East Side in 1889 by way of Rochester, New York, Goldman found herself drawn into a community steeped in radical philosophy. Goldman became a regular at Justus Schwab's saloon at 51 First Avenue, the unofficial socialist clubhouse of the Lower East Side. There she heard discussions of women's rights, worker's rights, and women's right to have access to birth control information. Quickly moving from listener to speaker, Emma Goldman saw her moment in history and seized it. Her name became an epithet to many, while others saw her as a fiery champion of the disenfranchised, the embodiment of radical idealism.

At this time Union Square was becoming the focus point for protest rallies, a function it served through the depression of the 1930s. At one of the first rallies held there, a hunger demonstration during the financial collapse of 1893, Emma Goldman held thousands spellbound as she preached a kind of activism people were unaccustomed to hearing at the time. If you are hungry, she told them, go out and take whatever you need. Goldman was

Emma Goldman, the Hausfrau Anarchist, with her lover, anarchist Alexander Berkman—hardly the image of bomb-throwing radicals.

promptly arrested on charges of inciting a riot, but ten months in prison only steeled her resolve and enhanced her reputation. Unrepentant, she continued to preach her own brand of activist socialism, inspired by the philosophic anarchism that formed a basis for the growing labor movement. To her enemies she became "Red Emma," a threat made more unnerving by her considerable energy. To her friends, she was a tireless supporter, a source of chicken soup and bail money, the Hausfrau Anarchist.

During one lecture tour of Europe, she met and then imported anarchist Hippolyte Havel. After a few moves, the couple settled into the top floor apartment at 210 East Thirteenth Street, a tenement built in 1903. Soon thereafter, in response to the anti-anarchist legislation that she saw as an abridgment of free speech, Goldman turned her apartment into a publishing office and began work on the March 1906 debut issue of her own magazine, *Mother Earth*.

Goldman, who lived on Thirteenth Street until 1913, was convinced that the government's suppression of liberalism proved her charges that in America democracy was a fraud. She remained a Village fixture until 1920, when she was expelled from America with fellow anarchist Alexander Berkman in the wake of a "red scare" whipped up by the federal government. But by the time Goldman died in 1940, many of the causes for which she was pilloried had become the law of the land.

Goldman was played by no less than Maureen Stapleton in the 1981 film, *Reds*. Her apartment building was featured five years earlier in Martin Scorsese's *Taxi Driver*. However, the apartment as she knew it no longer exists; it was gutted by a fire that swept the upper floors of 210 East Thirteenth Street in January 1977. A year or so later the building's new owners changed its street number to 208 East Thirteenth—motivated, some East Villagers report, by their desire to distance the building from its notorious (or heroic) early tenant, Emma Goldman.

Anarchist Alexander Berkman addressing a May Day Rally in Union Square in 1908.

VILLAGE PEOPLE: PETER COOPER

At first glance, millionaire Peter Cooper might seem to be the sort Emma Goldman would have opposed. In fact, he was among the most respected New Yorkers to emerge from the Lower East Side, all but idolized by many among the poor on his death in 1883.

The son of a hat maker, Peter Cooper had no time for education. As a youth, he apprenticed himself first to his father, then in turn to a brewer, a coach maker, and a cabinetmaker. In 1816 the twenty-five-year-old Cooper moved to Bowery Village to run his own business, a grocery that stood on the north side of Stuyvesant Street. Three years later, he used his profits to buy a glue factory, which in turn funded his 1,830 purchase of an iron works. In that year Cooper won his first fame as designer and builder of Tom Thumb, the first American-built locomotive. Shortly after this, Cooper earned his first fortune when his foundry produced the iron rails required by the fast-spreading railroads. Cooper then made his second fortune by investing in Manhattan real estate. One of the parcels he bought was on Stuyvesant Street across from his 1816 grocery. It was on this lot that Cooper built his extraordinary thank-you gift to the city of New York—Cooper Union for the Advancement of Science and Art.

When Cooper Union opened in 1859, it was the nation's first free nonsectarian coeducational college. It still operates in its original building on Stuyvesant Street, its courses are still free to students who qualify, and it offers specializations in engineering, art, and architecture. Initially, its funding was derived from several

Cooper Union, on Fourth Avenue at East Seventh Street, with its cylindrical elevator shaft visible on the roof. This building's iron-beam construction makes it a progenitor of the modern skyscraper.

street-level shops and from printing presses located on its fifth floor, both of which are now long gone. However, its endowment continues and is now valued at over $35 million. This money derives from such Cooper-owned properties as the land on which the Chrysler Building stands in Midtown. That plot alone produced $8 million in fiscal 1987.

Though the school has since expanded into several neighboring buildings, the 1859 Cooper Union remains its center as well as the gateway to the East Village. It is a designated city landmark and is also on the National Register of Historic Places. The 1975 renovation revealed proof of what had long been known—that Cooper used modified railroad rails as structural crossbeams, making this the earliest extant iron-frame building in the nation. Though the rails are concealed under a brownstone skin, this weight-bearing frame makes Cooper Union a progenitor of the modern skyscraper.

Cooper had the foresight to include in his design a shaft to accommodate an elevator, even though that device was still in the developmental stages at the time. He envisioned the new elevator as cylindrical in shape, however, not rectangular as it is today. In 1975, after more than a century, renovation architect John Hejduk custom-designed a cyclindrical elevator to fit Cooper's original shaft. The top of the shaft is now clearly visible above the roof of Cooper Union.

Cooper Union alumni include Manhattan builder Irwin Chanin, theater architect Thomas Lamb, sculptor George Segal, and inventor Thomas Edison, although Edison never took his degree. Following Cooper's death, sculptor Augustus Saint-Gaudens designed the grand Cooper statue mounted in 1897 in Cooper Square on a base designed by Stanford White. Saint-Gaudens was just the man for this task: he was also a Cooper Union graduate.

The Great Hall

Abraham Lincoln cited two events that he believed won him the presidency. Both occurred in Greenwich Village on February 27, 1860.

That afternoon Lincoln had his photograph taken by Mathew Brady in his studio at 643 Broadway, just below Bleecker Street. Then he delivered his famous "Might Makes Right" speech in the vaulted Great Hall beneath Cooper Union. Both the photo and the speech were published nationwide, and for the first time voters were able to associate a candidate's words with his likeness. The Lincoln legend was formed in the public's mind, and Cooper Union's Great Hall became the nation's forum for over half a century.

Through Woodrow Wilson, every American President and many candidates for the presidency spoke here. Mark Twain began his career as a lecturer here, and in this auditorium Susan B. Anthony and Victoria Woodhull called for women's rights and suffrage as early as the 1870s. In 1871 the opponents of Boss Tweed gathered here to bring down both Tweed and the entire city administration. And if that's not enough, the Great Hall echoes with the voices of Emma Goldman, William Jennings Bryant, Orson Welles, Eleanor Roosevelt, Fiorello La Guardia, H. L. Mencken, Bertrand Russell, and Andrew Carnegie.

INVENTING THE EAST VILLAGE

In 1951 a struggling young writer named Allen Ginsberg rented a flat at 206 East Seventh Street. That apartment soon became the nerve center for Beat Generation writers such as Jack Kerouac, William Burroughs, and Gregory Corso. Not far away at 77 St. Mark's Place, poet W. H. Auden rented an apartment in 1953; he remained in residence there for some twenty years. The top floor of 39 First Avenue became home for Norman Mailer at about this same time. If you knew where to look in the early 1950s, you could see that the East Village was quietly on its way.

With the removal of the Third Avenue El in 1955, the psychological barrier that had marked the eastern boundary of Greenwich Village was gone. Blocks that once had no prestige were suddenly seen as intriguing, and apartments here were less costly than those in Greenwich Village. Inverting their usual rhetoric, rental agents for the blocks east of Third Avenue took ads announcing that apartments were available for "$40 a room, and down." And at the same time, the block between Broadway and Fourth Avenue, long the site of A. T. Stewart's and later Wanamaker's department store, was bringing forth the 1961 Stewart House, the area's first high-rent high-rise apartment building.

As artists and writers moved east, the blocks from St. Mark's Place to Tenth Street were the first to hint that the Lower East Side was being transformed. Realtors began marketing the area as "Village East," and by 1961 as the "East Village," a name that stuck. The declining ethnic population retained its organizations, but community-wide groups were non-existent. Into this power vacuum in 1959 came Robert Moses, that barracuda of city planning, who saw

Street vendors on St. Mark's Place, the main drag of the East Village.

this disjointed neighborhood in flux as ripe for "improvement." Though still smarting from his South Village defeats, he issued his staggering plan: the twelve city blocks between Second Avenue and the Bowery, from Ninth Street south to Delancey, were to vanish. Nearly three thousand low-rent tenants were to be evicted to make way for the construction of co-op housing, with Moses' agencies profiting.

It was war, and Moses' opponents did not stay unorganized for long. In March 1959 the Cooper Square Committee was formed to investigate Moses' plan and to examine his supporting documentation. Moses had claimed that displaced residents from this area could easily be absorbed into other neighborhoods. That turned out to be untrue. Moses had also come up with figures showing that only 10 percent of those residents spoke Spanish; committee surveys proved that the real figure was 30 percent. Further, Moses stated that most displaced residents would relocate into his new high-rise co-ops; the committee found that 93 percent of the neighborhood residents couldn't afford the rent Moses would charge.

As an alternative to the Moses plan, the committee came up with a new concept in municipal urban redevelopment. In 1961 they offered a gradual renovation of the existing neighborhood—a plan that promised no construction profits for Robert Moses. The city opposed this plan for nine years—even after the *Village Voice* in 1965 uncovered a greasy backstairs quid pro quo deal between Moses and City Assemblyman Louis DeSalvio.

The committee plan was finally accepted by the city in February 1970. Despite funding setbacks and various other delays, work has proceeded, concentrating initially on the blocks from Fourth Street south. As South Village activist Anthony Dapolito has observed, no one created more community activists than Robert Moses.

THE EAST VILLAGE OTHER

Had Robert Moses succeeded in wiping away the east side of Cooper Square, the cultural explosion in the East Village during the 1960s might not have occurred. The flophouse-bar that was its springboard would have been demolished before it had any effect.

As the fifties opened, there was little that distinguished the Five Spot from other seedy Bowery bars. But by mid-decade its regulars were joined by young artists who found the atmosphere to their liking. A new underground formed here, and painters, writers, and jazz musicians joined forces to stage an assault on the very definitions of art, music, theater, and literature. New images and words were suddenly everywhere; a can of Campbell's soup could be the subject of artwork, as could a frame of a comic strip.

By 1963 the Five Spot had evolved from springboard to nerve center after moving a few doors south to new quarters on the Bowery. Kerouac and de Kooning were here at 2 A.M., listening to the hip jazz of Ornette Coleman, Charles Mingus, and Thelonius Monk. Here the arts became democratized. In this neighborhood anyone could create, and everyone did. Commercial restrictions on tenancy were reduced to a minimum or eliminated completely and a new generation of galleries and clubs appeared near Tenth Street and Third Avenue. Gallery owner Mickey Ruskin traded in his Tenth Street Gallery and opened Les Deux Mégots, the café at 64 East Seventh Street that introduced poetry readings to the East Village. When this became Paradox, a macrobiotic restaurant, Ruskin moved his readings to Le Métro Café at 149 Second Avenue. A combined coffeehouse and antique shop, it proved so popular that by 1964 lines were forming along the avenue as people waited to get in. Such turn-away business fueled the creative burst at St. Mark's-in-the-Bowery half a block away, leading to the formation of Theatre Genesis later that year.

This new counterculture art clearly needed its own newspaper, and that need led to the founding of the *East Village Other* by Don and Allen Katzman. Radical in its politics as well as its art, the *Other* quickly built up a circulation of 100,000—and attracted the unwanted attention of the FBI. The Katzman brothers found themselves being harassed, in part because their offices on Second Avenue had served in 1967 as the birthplace of the Youth International Party (Yippies), formed by Abbie Hoffman and Jerry Rubin. As hippie activists, they felt a need for a radical political party, though they were soon directing their energy into protest rallies and demonstrations intended to end the Vietnam War.

The new guerrilla artists of the East Village assaulted the arts establishment as well as the political establishment. In music and literature, the battle often centered on obscenity, which some writers reveled in simply *because* it was unacceptable. In the early sixties, the basis for today's alternative rock was established at Stanley's, a bar on East Twelfth Street at Avenue B, when Tuli Kupferberg and Ed Sanders began singing their scatological songs. They called themselves the Fugs—a near-obscenity coined by Norman Mailer for his novel, *The Naked and the Dead*—and their songs ranged from the mindless ("Group Grope") to the savage ("Kill for Peace"). Sanders also dabbled in an early form of desktop publishing with his mimeographed *Fuck You, A Magazine of the Arts*. To no one's surprise, it was banned from the mail by postal officials, but that didn't deter Sanders. He sold copies at his Psychedelicatessen on Avenue A at Tenth Street, now acknowledged to have been the first head shop.

Once the home of the frenetic Electric Circus of the 1960s, today 23 St. Mark's Place is a community center attracting little publicity.

SATURDAY NIGHT FEVER

By 1966, the action in the East Village centered on the Electric Circus at 23 St. Mark's Place. This high citadel of hippiedom had opened in the 1890s as Arlington Hall as an auditorium used by the community for meetings and social functions of local trade organizations as well as for speeches and concerts. It later housed a catering business and then a Polish community center. The building began its hip new life in the early 1960s as the Dom, an effort by Stanley Tolkin to expand the arts scene beyond his bar on Avenue B. His home-grown group, the Fugs, played here around 1964, after which he rented the club to Andy Warhol. He transformed the place into the Exploding Plastic Inevitable, and it became the forerunner of the disco, though Warhol had intended the place less as a dance palace than as a free-form, unstructured "exhibit." Here Warhol presented the Velvet Underground—Lou Reed, John Cale, and Nico—a group he'd discovered during their unsuccessful engagement at the Café Bizarre in the South Village. Under Warhol, they introduced elements of the rock experimentation of the seventies and eighties, wearing weird makeup and early versions of glitter-rock and punk outfits.

After it became the Electric Circus, the club hosted such high-decibel groups as Sly and the Family Stone and the un-amplified Voices of East Harlem. Yet it remained a living experiment combining theater, rock music, dance, lighting—and even its own merry-go-round.

The club's sensational elements soon attracted outsiders, much as the East Village found itself under assault by thrill-seekers with no interest in either protest art or protest politics. Drugs were suddenly everywhere, and trouble wasn't long in arriving. In March 1970 a small bomb exploded on the dance floor, injuring seventeen people, and the Electric Circus never recovered from the adverse publicity that followed. It closed forever in August 1971, but the building finally emerged, after years of intermittent use, as a community center not unlike the original Arlington Hall of a century earlier.

UNDERGROUND HIT

 quarter-century after its founding, an underground theater from the first wave of East Village arts is still in operation. Its funding is now more secure than ever, but despite years of success the La Mama Theatre remains resolutely underground, still a testament to its indomitable, dynamic founder.

Ellen Stewart backed into her role as the mother of the East Village theater scene. Born of Cajun ancestry in Louisiana, Stewart had run through several careers before landing in the East Village, middle-aged and out of work. She decided to open her own boutique-theater and used an unemployment check for $54 to rent the basement of 321 East Ninth Street. Her first dramatic offering was a July 1962 version of Tennessee Williams's story, *One Arm*. Encouraged by its one-week run, Stewart produced other plays and in time drew around her a loyal band of actors and playwrights who were like a family. To them, Stewart was Mother Earth—or, in her lilting dialect, La Mama. In no time, the name was applied to the theater as well as its founder.

City agencies, local utilities, and landlords made life anything but easy for the struggling theater family, but La Mama persisted. The communal dinners she prepared for her casts became legend, as did her appeal to the powerful Actors Equity for relief from its salary requirements. Her actors joined in and supported her appeal, and eventually she won. When her new quarters at 82 Second Avenue proved too small for her expanding operations, she persuaded her closing-night audience members to take a table or chair and move La Mama's furniture to 122 Second Avenue.

By 1969, the La Mama Experimental Theatre Club had won broad audience and critical support as well as corporate and public funding. Stewart leased and renovated an old German concert hall at 74 East Fourth Street where she continues to bring each audience to order by ringing an old cowbell. Many of the 1,500 plays she has produced were the early work of playwrights who later achieved prominence. They include Leonard Melfi, Megan Terry, Lanford Wilson, Tom Eyen, Sam Shepard, Murray Schisgal, Israel Horo-

Ellen Stewart: La Mama herself.

vitz, Ed Bullins, Jean-Claude van Italie, and Charles Ludlam. Her original theater on Ninth Street was the setting in June 1963 for the first American production of any work by Harold Pinter, while her Fourth Street playhouse offered separate premieres of the three plays that form Harvey Fierstein's award-winning play, *Torch Song Trilogy*.

Through these portals . . . The entrance to the Saint, at 105 Second Avenue, a few days after its 1988 closing.

"MORE STARS THAN THERE ARE IN HEAVEN"

It opened late in the 1920s as an ornate movie palace and may be rebuilt in the early 1990s as a bland six-plex cinema. But there were glory days at 105 Second Avenue, days that are now passing into legend.

As Loew's Commodore, the 1928 theater was affiliated with MGM and showed films that promised—in that studio's phrase—"more stars than there are in heaven." However, a declining ethnic population and an abundance of hippies in the neighborhood caused the house to pass in the 1960s into the hands of rock promoter Bill Graham. He renamed it the Fillmore East after his club in San Francisco and presented live stars like Elton John, Grace Slick, and Janis Joplin where the images of MGM stars like Gable and Garbo once flickered. And here in November 1969 audiences saw the first stage performance of *Tommy*, the rock opera created by the Who. However, a rising tide of drugs and violence swamped the operation, and the Fillmore East presented its last concert in June 1971.

After a decade of fitful operation as a concert hall called the Village East, the frayed old theater was turned into the Saint, the most spectacular dance club New York had ever seen and the most expensive gay business venture ever attempted. In the words of managing director Bruce Mailman, "We wanted to create a class operation, a magical environment that could provide gay men with a sense of security, a safe alternative. I think it was the best of what it was, though it had cost us $4.6 million by our opening day."

Mailman's idea had been to open a dance club within a custom-designed and fully functional planetarium. Gutting the Commodore to its shell, Mailman installed a 5,000-square-foot circular dance floor under a dome larger than the one at New York's Hayden Planetarium. At its center, a planetarium star projector ten times brighter than usual outshone some 1,500 disco lights to permit dancing under the stars of the northern hemisphere shining fifty feet overhead.

Soon after opening as a membership club on September 20, 1980, the Saint became the hottest disco in town. Its rotating projector created the illusion that the entire floor was revolving as people danced. A twenty-foot wall section of the dome might retract unexpectedly, revealing a stage on which Grace Jones, Natalie Cole, or Tina Turner would appear to belt out her latest hit to the best-looking crowd in New York. On such nights the place was once again filled with more stars than there were in heaven.

As the AIDS epidemic began its relentless decimation of the gay community, the Saint made its facilities available for benefits for organizations intent on providing help that the government would not offer. "The Saint reflected what was happening to the gay community," Mailman recalled. "Here's a group that had no established social consciousness, and it organized itself instantly to deal with a nightmare. Like that community, the Saint began with one purpose, but shifted to another. I thought it had to be done." Though large amounts of money were raised, attendance began to decline. In October 1985 the club opened to nonmembers, and about a year later to its first non-gay crowd. "In the end, we stopped because I was just burned out," Mailman commented, "and there was no one else to do it."

News of the Saint's impending closing went through the gay community like word of a death in the family. Appreciative articles appeared in the gay press prior to a final fifty-hour party. Songwriter Paul Jabara came to say good-bye and to sing his hit tune, "Last Dance." Disco diva Thelma Houston came by as well to belt out her torchy hit, "Don't Leave Me This Way." But they did leave, and in the early morning of May 2, 1988, the Saint closed its doors. Within days, those doors were spray-painted with words of memory, words of hope for a dark night: "Hold on to my love—J. Ruffin."

Fitting that a disco lyric should become the epitaph of an era. And sad that so many of the stars that once danced in this place have moved on.

An overflow crowd for Hardcore, the Sunday afternoon concert at CBGB, 315 The Bowery, an East Village institution of the 1980s.

VILLAGE LANDMARKS: CBGB

Hilly's, a raucous rock club, was banished in the early 1970s from its sedate West Thirteenth Street neighborhood. Owner Hilly Kristal moved to 315 The Bowery, reasoning that no matter how wild his place became, in that decrepit neighborhood it could only be a step up.

CBGB-OMFUG, its new name, was an acronym for a music policy that failed: country, blue grass, blues, and other music for uplifting gourmandizers. When the Broadway Central collapsed in August 1973, taking the Mercer Arts Center with it, the new direction for CBGB became clear. An otherwise forsaken stretch of The Bowery became the stomping ground for underground rock bands, and CBGB became the birthplace of the punk look.

It began with Richard Hell, the bass player for Television, the first psychosexual rock group booked into CBGB. "The glitter look turned into the street kid look," recalled Kristal, as quoted by Roman Kozak in his CBGB history, *This Ain't No Disco.* "Maybe they took the torn T-shirt look from us in London, and added razor blades and funny colored things in their hair, but the torn T-shirts started here."

The Ramones were the first group fashioned for the CBGB crowd; they were also the first megahit group to emerge from the place, but hardly the last. CBGB drew crowds to hear Patti Smith, Debbie Harry and Blondie, Stiv Bators and the Dead Boys, David

Byrne and Talking Heads, and the Shirts. The tone shifted from punk to new wave and beyond, and CBGB sailed from simple irreverence to excess. Stiv Bators took a fancy to hanging himself from the stage rafters with his mike cord around his neck. Reversing the tradition in which fans scrambled onto the stage, performers began throwing themselves from it onto their tightly packed audience—slam dancing was born. Another barrier of some sort was cleared by the Plasmatics, when lead singer Wendy O. Williams brought a chain saw onstage; in seconds, a guitar was reduced to splinters as quadraphonic amplification ensured that the buzz would be loud enough.

But enough wasn't enough for some, particularly the crowd too young to gain legal admittance to what was still essentially a bar. For them CBGB instituted Hardcore in 1981. During the wild Hardcore performances on Sunday afternoons, no alcohol is served. The tables and chairs are cleared away so that the extravagantly costumed kids can safely slam-dance to their hearts' content.

And tomorrow? It's hard to know what's coming down next. Wendy Williams now stars in big-budget films, and such bizarre CBGB favorites as the Sic F*cks and the Butthole Surfers have recordings on the market. Doubtless a clue to the future can be found in the Missing Foundation, a self-styled anarchist rock group that views recent East Village strife as a sort of Preview of National Coming Attractions. Their slogan, "Devalue Property," makes them sound like Emma Goldman with a backbeat, but their tactics are angry and in earnest. One recent show at CBGB had them dousing their drums with kerosene and setting them ablaze, causing damage to the club itself. Whatever else may be said of the Missing Foundation, they aren't lacking in commitment.

THE MANY LIVES OF WEBSTER HALL

The Ritz opened in May 1980 at 119 East Eleventh Street, bringing new life to an eighty-five-year-old building that had long been known as Webster Hall. As polished as CBGB was raw, the Ritz offered a rock venue five times the size of the older club. This permitted the Ritz to draw more established performers, including Madonna, Prince, Eric Clapton, Tina Turner, Sting, Kiss, and B. B. King. Its premises were also used for fashion shows, media presentations, award ceremonies, and even the shooting of a sequence for the 1988 Tom Hanks film, *Big*. The Ritz was also the first club designed with a video component, setting a style that was later borrowed by other clubs nationwide. Its video system was the only component of the Ritz that was taken along when the club moved uptown to the former Studio 54 in April 1989. Its exit made Webster Hall available for the opening of a new disco on

Eleventh Street, but new lives are nothing new to this old structure.

Before the Ritz opened, this was Webster Hall Studios, the major East Coast recording facility for RCA Records. From pop albums to symphonies, everything was recorded here—but Webster Hall became most closely associated with RCA's Broadway cast recordings. Here such hits as *Hello, Dolly!* and *Fiddler on the Roof* were taped for release, and here Julie Andrews made her American recording debut as a cast member of *The Boy Friend*.

Built in 1895, Webster Hall had still another life before becoming a studio. Although it was first used as a community center and lecture room, Webster Hall soon became notorious as the setting of the legendary Village Balls. These mad affairs followed a tradition begun in 1913 with a single fund-raiser for the *Masses,* the liberal magazine. To gain admittance to that affair for half-price, guests arrived in costume as the advertisements had requested, though the costume in some instances was merely a sheet passed off as a Roman toga. Later that year the Liberal Club sponsored its first Pagan Rout, and with this ball, nudity became something of a trend. Soon every Village organization was giving a costume ball at

Webster Hall, and these events were often planned around a theme of some sort. Guests managed to attend semi-clothed, whatever the theme, though some sort of record for undress was established in the late 1920s by Aimee Cortez, a free-spirited flapper renowned for claiming to have the most beautiful body in Greenwich Village. Cortez arrived at one Webster Hall blowout in full gorilla costume. Having created a sensation with it, she gradually removed it while performing a simian *danse exotique*—at the end of which she was nude but for a single strategically placed leaf, which she later dispatched in her Tribute to Autumn.

HOLLYWOOD ON THE HUDSON, EAST

The 1978 film *Hester Street* wasn't shot on Hester Street, which the producers felt no longer looked enough like the Lower East Side circa 1900. Instead they "dressed" a block of Morton Street in the West Village and shot the movie there.

Since then, however, Hollywood has discovered the East Village and has begun using it for location work. Actual locations were used in *Crossing Delancey,* the 1988 romance in which Amy Irving's character finds love with a young pickle vendor on the Lower East Side. Director Martin Scorsese turned an East Village warehouse into an artist's loft for his segment of the 1989 omnibus feature, *New York Stories*. East Fourth Street, not far away, was an ideal setting in which to re-create a hippie commune of the 1960s for *Rude Awakening,* a 1989 comedy that starred Eric Roberts and Cheech Marin.

Filmmakers in the East Village can even supplement their exterior locations with studio work without leaving the neighborhood. Mothers Film Stages operates three sound stages at 210 East Fifth Street. The building is a converted banquet and wedding hall built over a century ago as the Beethoven Mænnerchor, the home of a local German music society. Converted to studios in 1955, it was according to manager Nicholas Smith the scene of early experiments in videotape work conducted by Ampex. During recent years thousands of television commercials and public service spots have been shot here, including some that featured such stars as Joan Rivers, Anne Meara and Jerry Stiller, Beverly Sills, Rita Moreno, and Woody Allen. Those stylish coffee commercials starring Miss Greenwich Village of 1942 (Lauren Bacall) were also filmed in this studio. And increasingly, music videos have been shot here, featuring Tracy Chapman, Duran Duran, Whitney Houston, and Cyndi Lauper, who did "Girls Just Wanna Have Fun" here.

The most elaborate East Village film work was the location shoot for *Batteries Not Included,* a 1987 science-fiction fantasy produced by Steven Spielberg and starring Jessica Tandy and Hume

Cronyn. Its designers spent $3 million dressing a deserted block of East Eighth Street, creating a crumbling tenement so realistic that guards were needed to keep city sanitation men away from the prop garbage cans each morning. Though a number of local residents were hired as extras for $50 a day, the production company felt uneasy about using a real blighted neighborhood to portray a fictional blighted neighborhood. Accordingly, *Batteries Not Included* set aside several thousand dollars of its budget to be used as donations to community organizations. When word of this spread, grateful neighborhood residents began referring to the film's Eighth Street locations as "Batteries Park."

Andy Warhol and Jean Michel Basquiat in 1985, with some of their graffiti-style artworks, which sell for $50,000 to $80,000.

BOHEMIA REBORN?

At twenty he was penniless and homeless, sleeping on the sofas of his friends. At twenty-two he was internationally known, creating in a week artworks that sold for $25,000 to Paul Simon or Richard Gere, to the collections of the Whitney or the Museum of Modern Art. And on August 12, 1988, at twenty-seven, Jean Michel Basquiat was dead.

A mourning art world attributed the loss to career pressures and drugs, suggesting Basquiat was the victim of his success. As gallery owner Mary Boone commented, "He was unable to keep his own center." But as with many creative artists, the forces that drove Basquiat's destructive rage also fueled his talent. The two were as inseparable for Basquiat as they had been for the first bohemians a century before him. In recent times artists have moved from social outcasts to superstars, and yet a middle class that is appreciative of their work remains unable to deal with the way they live their lives.

Like so many bohemians of earlier generations, Basquiat dropped out of a middle-class home, in his case in Brooklyn, and into a marginal life in Greenwich Village. When he was barely fifteen, he spent a year indulging in street drugs. Eventually, though, he was able to escape from drugs through art. With his friend Al Diaz he invented SAMO, a graffiti artist whose Magic-Marker drawings and catchphrases began appearing around the East Village, signed and—significantly—copyrighted. For a year no SoHo gallery could open its latest show without patrons noticing that SAMO had gotten there the night before. Just as SAMO was discovered to be two street kids, Basquiat had a falling out with Diaz and publicly killed his alter ego with new graffiti: "SAMO is dead."

By 1980, graffiti art was "in," prompting art consultant Jeffrey Deitch to seek out SAMO's creator in his East Village apartment. He found an artist who was too poor to purchase supplies and who turned salvaged street junk into angry works of art. As Basquiat's star quickly rose, he could suddenly afford the paints and canvases he needed to create his masked primitive figures lost in an urban wilderness of skyscrapers and arrows, of rockets and words. Most sold as fast as they were created, in some cases with the paint barely dry. He became a familiar figure on The Bowery, passing out hundred dollar bills to fellow blacks less lucky than himself, yet his dreadlocks often made it impossible for him to get a taxi even when he had $10,000 in his pocket.

Basquiat became known as temperamental, though stories circulated about him were often left incomplete. When he destroyed ten unfinished canvases in 1982, his vandalism only made him more of a star, but his actions were assumed to be a "star trip" rather than artistic choice or a justifiable rage. Another famous story had Basquiat spilling fruit and nuts out the window onto the head of a departing art dealer. Dropped from this story was the dealer's calculated effort to profit by manipulating the artist; knowing his fondness for health foods, she had brought the jar of fruit and nuts along to soften him up, then lied to him that her black chauffeur was more an artistic adviser than her driver.

In 1984, as his star faded somewhat, Basquiat formed a professional friendship with Andy Warhol, exemplar of the artist-as-artwork school of thought and long Basquiat's idol. In addition to collaborating with Basquiat on several works, Warhol was able to keep the youth's drug habit in check—until his own untimely death in February 1987. Basquiat's critical acclaim began a rebound, but so did his heroin use. He died alone in a studio rented from the Warhol estate. In his wardrobe were the paint-splattered $800 suits Basquiat often wore while working.

Private realities side by side on the benches of Tompkins Square, 1988.

"THERE'S A RIOT GOIN' ON"

Tompkins Square has long been the front yard of the Lower East Side. In recent years it has been caught up in a three-way tug-of-war among upwardly mobile newcomers, low-rent residents who like the ethnic mix as it is, and the homeless, drug dealers, and nonresident counterculture radicals for whom the area is the last refuge from conformity. This volatile mix has led to a game of Whose Neighborhood Is It, Anyway? that had simmered in an uneasy peace for years. But when the tense tranquillity was shattered in August 1988, ironically by the forces of "law and order," it was hardly the first time Tompkins Square had been the scene of violence.

The ten acres of Tompkins Square were laid out in 1834 and named for the New York governor who sponsored the legislation that abolished slavery in the state. Sadly, Daniel Tompkins didn't live to see the full results of that legislation. While governor, Tompkins also personally funded local defense efforts during the War of 1812 after government treasury notes proved worthless. Among his efforts were the earthwork fortifications built in the marsh that was later transformed into Tompkins Square. His pop-

A pamphleteer on Second Avenue at St. Mark's Place, 1988.

ularity later won him the U.S. vice-presidency under James Monroe, but he made powerful political enemies who swore to ruin him. His opponents issued scurrilous charges against Tompkins when he tried to win reimbursement for his generosity during the war. His spirit and sanity broken, Tompkins died in 1825 at the age of fifty-one and now rests in his vault at St. Mark's-in-the-Bowery off Tenth Street.

The former battleground was given Tompkins's name and proved popular with the German immigrants who moved into the neighborhood in the 1850s. People constructed vast snow houses here each winter and enjoyed more mundane pleasures like sledding and snowball fights. The economic collapse of 1857 produced the first of many protest rallies here, the so-called Hunger Riot—an unfortunate name that gives an inaccurate impression of the event. This was a simple rally protesting the conditions that were causing the panic, and it aroused the sympathy of a generous local baker who decided to do something to help. When he arrived in the square with trays of fresh bread, protesters jumped him for reasons that remain obscure—and spent the rest of the afternoon pelting one another and the baker with his loaves of bread.

An 1874 rally also turned into a riot, though with more serious ramifications. Another financial panic had hit the neighborhood hard, but the permit for a January 13 rally was withdrawn at the last minute. When they assembled in the square, immigrant families found themselves being charged by mounted policemen. The terrifying scene left a vivid impression on the young Samuel Gompers, who was present. It steeled his determination to work in behalf of working-class citizens and directly led to his founding the American Federation of Labor in 1886. Gompers became the AFL's first president and was reelected some forty times. He remained a major force in America's rising labor movement well into the 1920s.

Though Tompkins Square has seen numerous rallies and protests over the years, the August 1988 police riot here has raised serious questions on a number of issues, not the least of which is the neighborhood's split personality. These days even the name of the area varies depending on whom you ask. Some people prefer the name that was invented in the 1950s—the East Village. But others, even some of the younger residents, are likely to bristle defensively and say, "This *isn't* the East Village. This is the Lower East Side."

Spurred by requests from some newcomers to the area, the city imposed a curfew on the square during the summer of 1988. Other factions opposed the curfew. During a rally held in the square on August 6 the crowd was unexpectedly attacked by many of the 440 police officers who were on the scene to keep order. Some 121 civilian charges of police assault or misconduct were lodged; they are amply supported by a four-hour videotape of the riot, shot from a fire escape. It showed officers clubbing and arresting protesters and even bystanders while charging through the streets in groups and on horseback with their badge numbers taped over or with the badges removed—a violation of policy and a clear indication to many that the police violence was both unprovoked and planned.

Unfortunately, the riot shifted public attention away from the simmering rifts within the neighborhood. Valerio Orselli, who at the time was director of the Cooper Square Committee, put it succinctly: "The police managed to link a small group of crazies to the legitimate sentiments of those opposed to gentrification. The issue has suddenly become police brutality, not housing and neighborhood concerns, and it's set everyone back."

These issues still festered in the spring of 1989 when the Civilian Complaint Board of NYPD issued its response to the charges of police brutality: fewer than twenty officers were to be brought up on charges of misconduct. Neighborhood anger could be seen as clearly as the writing on the wall, where as graffiti it freely surfaced. Some slogans have been associated with fans of Missing Foundation, the anarchist rock group. On one wall: "1988 = 1933," a reference to the overthrow of the Weimar Republic by Hitler and his police state. On another wall: an overturned martini glass, symbolically announcing that the party's over. One wonders whether the role of the East Village is the invention of tomorrow or the prevention of its invention by others.

A sidewalk café of the East Village in the turbulent summer of 1988.

ADAPTIVE REUSE

The community recycling fostered by the Cooper Square Committee has become the basis for a new approach to interior design. "Adaptive reuse, that's what we call it," says Steve Corwin, co-owner of the Great American Salvage Company on Cooper Square. Neatly squirreled away on the second floor of the store is an entire Stanford White house, disassembled. "It's all there, from the windows and doors to the staircases; rather than simply destroy the place, its owners turned it over to us. All a buyer would need is a new wood frame."

The variety of items found here occasionally brings the owners of the Salvage Company into contact with Hollywood; they supplied the antique bathroom fixtures used in the climax of the 1987 thriller, *Fatal Attraction*. And even the building housing the Salvage Company has itself been recycled. It was the original American home of Hartz Mountain, the pet food company.

Need a wooden phone booth for your apartment? An elevator cab? An entire wrought-iron department store facade complete with revolving doors? The Great American Salvage Company at 34 Cooper Square is your kind of store.

East Village originals Snooky and Tish Bellomo in their punk rock shop, Manic Panic, a few weeks before its 1989 closing.

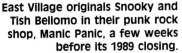

HOW TO LOOK LIKE AN EAST VILLAGER

America's first punk rock shop began as an extension of Tish and Snooky Bellomo's closet. "Everybody was always copying our style," Snooky recalled, "so we wondered if we could sell it." The result was Manic Panic, which was a fixture at 33 St. Mark's Place from its June 1977 opening until it closed early in 1989.

"You wouldn't believe this neighborhood back then," said Tish. "The East Village had bottomed out, and most of the storefronts on St. Mark's Place were empty. We took this place for $250 a month, which seemed like a lot."

Snooky admitted that they knew little about operating a business when they opened the shop. "We started with a few go-go boots and two racks of clothes brought from home in the Bronx. But people were afraid to come into this neighborhood at first. Some days we'd make fifty cents when somebody bought a button from us. But then we started getting good press and things began to change."

Expanding beyond the basic stock of motorcycle jackets and Doc Martin boots, Manic Panic stocked such glitter-punk accessories as turquoise hair dye, metallic gold corsets, wigs, glitter eyeliner, stage blood, liquid latex, and spike-heeled shoes. "You couldn't order spike heels back then," Tish said. "You had to find them. We'd go into old shoe stores and ask if they had any old stock, and they'd say, 'Yes, but nothing you girls would want, just old spike heels.' And they wouldn't believe it when we'd buy them out, maybe a hundred pairs in their original boxes. We'd bring them back here and display them on the walls, put them in the windows, just the greatest stuff. Like that place down on Reade Street, remember, Snooky? The place Debbie Harry found?"

Debbie Harry was more than an early celebrity customer—Tish and Snooky were backup singers with the punk group Blondie in its early dates at CBGB. "Before they got signed," Tish added, with no trace of regret.

"So we got together a group called the Drop-Outs," said Snooky, "and then in 1977 our friend Russell Wolinsky came by the shop and put us in this new band he was starting for one show at CBGB's. He called the group the Sic F*cks, spelled with an asterisk because 'All We Need is U!' Anyway, we packed the place 'cause everybody wanted to see what kind of crazy band would call itself the Sic F*cks. Then Lester Bangs gave us this terrific writeup, so we kept doing it, made a record, and still do about one concert a year."

News of the shop began to circulate, and Manic Panic attracted a healthy mix of local customers and celebrities. "The Ramones and the Dictators shopped here a lot," Tish began, referring to the CBGB favorites.

"But when we first opened, so did Caroline Kennedy," Snooky added. "And Bill Murray, he's shopped here for years. Cher bought a Sic F*cks nightshirt from me, but she'd never heard of the group. 'I just like the shirt,' she said in that voice of hers."

"Bruce Springsteen bought shoes here," Tish recalled, "and Sid Vicious bought one of our torn T-Shirts. Cyndi Lauper used to shop here, too, before she made it. She doesn't come around anymore, but she deserved to make it; she's a good soul. But we're not doing as much of our original design work anymore. Uptown designers used to send scouts down here to see what we were doing. Then they'd knock the design off and make a fortune at it. We got tired of that, so we stopped. Let *them* think for a change."

Of course, East Village fashions change, and the dyed spiked hair of the early 1980s has given way to tight pants and straggly hair that recall the hippies of the 1960s. But even this may not be the latest East Village look. "You wanna look like you belong here?" Tish snapped. "Dress like a Yuppie. They've taken over here, behaving like we're the outsiders. They have as much to do with the East Village as the Gap," she said, referring to the clothing chain, which had recently opened a conventional-clothing store around the corner on Second Avenue. "Well, a Steve's Ice Cream store failed because nobody from the neighborhood would shop there. Maybe these people will get the same treatment."

Through the 1980s, the success of Manic Panic inspired numerous imitators along St. Mark's Place, though Snooky Bellomo thought the serious attitude such imitators had about business kept them from becoming direct competition. But rents along the street have risen sharply, and by 1988 the storefront they took for $250 was up to $3,000 a month. "We're not into homesteading again," Tish mused, "so we're thinking of closing and just doing wholesale."

"On the other hand," Snooky said, "we had this blowout going-out-of-business sale about three years ago, which got this big writeup in *New York* magazine. Everybody came down for one last shopping spree, and then we were still here! I'd hate to do that again. It was so embarrassing."

VILLAGE VOICES: MARK RUSSELL

I think theater backed away from experimentation," reflected Mark Russell, "and that baton passed to the dance community. Young dancers began to amplify movement with language and personal experience, to abandon the rigid definition of what dance was." Experimentation today thrives at P.S. 122, the performance arts space on First Avenue at Ninth Street, of which Russell is executive director.

"MGM rented this old school to film *Fame* here in 1979. A number of neighborhood groups had been using it in the three years since the city closed it, to prevent its being overrun with vandals." On returning, these groups were joined by young experimental artists in need of a place to try their artistic wings. The building continued as a combined neighborhood center and experimental arts incubator. Among those who work here are Eric Bogosian, Paul Zaloom, Ann Carlson, and Reno, along with artists who have yet to achieve national prominence.

"Our audiences are ready to risk something, ready to take a chance. Our calendar often tells them very little about a particular event, but they come and deal with performers and take the ride. The performer here who doesn't push enough is the performer who belongs in a more traditional club, like the Duplex. And some of the work being done here may never be suitable for a large audience; some things may be best when they are staged for only two hundred people. But if I think an artist's sensibility is at work, I'll book them and we'll see. Maybe they come and just talk, maybe they dance their butt off and we're supposed to get it, or maybe it's film or an opera? *I'm* ready. *I'll* show up."

WOMEN'S RITES

In its programs and its structure, WOW is an unusual theater even by East Village standards. Run as a collective, with no administrative board, it's a performance space by and for women. Men are welcome on stage and in the audience, but only as guests.

Tucked neatly into a loft at 59 East Fourth Street, WOW grew out of the Women's One World festival of a decade ago, an event that was organized principally by Peggy Shaw and Lois Weaver.

Though the festival was an international gathering, it revealed an abundance of local women with talent—among them Holly Hughes, Susan Young, and Alice Forrester—all eager for a performance space they could call their own. WOW Café was the result, though a 1985 move from its original storefront on Eleventh Street to Fourth Street signaled a shift from coffeehouse to theatrical emphasis.

"Collective members attend annual retreats to evaluate the previous season and plan the next," explained Quinn, a young playwright-director of WOW's second generation. "We gather in a circle, and anyone who's been active at WOW can request time for a project she'd like to work on. The house manager of one show might be the author of the next, though increasingly people at WOW are specializing, becoming sharper, expecting more of themselves.

"WOW shows are often outlandish, zany, trying new approaches to storytelling, which shows a strong influence of the New East Village. You may not see people from WOW or other East Village clubs turn up tomorrow on the Carson show, but they will have an impact on those who do.

"WOW audiences are very supportive and nurturing," Quinn observed, "and mindful that even when a show's content isn't overtly political, the fact that women have created it is itself a statement. And WOW is not exclusively a lesbian organization, though it tends to be primarily lesbian. But I don't see WOW as insular, or even wanting to be. Though the lack of mainstream attention has allowed us to try new things, WOW increasingly wants to be open to and respected by all audiences while retaining its status as a women's space. These days lesbian characters and women's issues turn up on prime-time television, and mainstream audiences are dealing with it. So I think maybe they're ready for us and we're ready for them."

Downtown Beirut at 158 First Avenue, a bar typical of the East Village clubs that relish their seediness.

THE EAST VILLAGE TODAY —AND TOMORROW

Even as East Village rents skyrocket, enough funky operations survive to sustain the excitement of the area and prevent it from becoming one large Burger King franchise.

Located on First Avenue, Downtown Beirut looks scuzzy enough to cultivate almost anything, but the talents of tomorrow may have sprouted here last night. A block east on Avenue A is King Tut's Wah Wah Hut, whose performing artists often move on to better-known showcases such as P.S. 122 after surfacing here. In time, the Wah Wah Hut may become as firmly established as the Pyramid Club, the Avenue A nightspot that has remained at the pinnacle of punk rock for years. Passing farther east to Avenue B, new music and poetry readings are on the menu at the Gas Station, a club fashioned from an old . . . guess what. The term "café theater" seems inadequate to describe the free-form events staged at Dixon Place on East First Street, though its chairs are certainly as uncomfortable as the mini-stools at the old Caffe Cino of the 1950s. And around the corner on Second Street is the World, a multiple-choice bar billed as an all-purpose alternative club for everyone.

Despite changes in style and economics, Bohemia is a hardy flower. Once it takes root in an area, it is persistent and all but impossible to eradicate. But it's pointless to try—there will always be brush to be cleared on the outskirts of acceptability, and the first flower to take root there will be the Bohemia of tomorrow. And the most wonderful thing about this perennial is that no one ever knows what its next blossoms will look like.

This Beaux Arts gem at 44 Great Jones Street, the present home of Engine Company 33, was built in 1898 as the headquarters of New York's Fire Department.

As Anthony Springer shows, local artists still find inspiration in Washington Square.

AFTERWORD

Apocryphal or true, one Greenwich Village tale has been told since the 1920s: Two giggling uptown flappers seated themselves at Polly's Restaurant and made the mistake of asking the waiter if the place was within the boundaries of Greenwich Village. Unfortunately for them, their waiter was Hippolyte Havel, anarchist and professional curmudgeon. "What are you talking about?" he snarled in reply. "Greenwich Village *has* no boundaries. It's a state of mind!"

There is a Village mentality. It existed long before Hippolyte Havel arrived in 1905, and it was probably part of the reason he stayed. It was here in 1818, when Villagers fought off the city plan for the street grid. It may always have been here, and it's still here despite changing patterns, new influences, rising rents. It's that resistance to authority, that acceptance of diversity and individuality, that willingness to join forces when threatened. It resists the American obsession with "development," preferring to preserve the old settings and structures. It tends to create new ways of living and new forms of expression. It can discover humanity in a bar filled with bums, or turn street junk into a visionary work of art.

But there are old houses and twisting streets forming districts in other American cities: Beacon Hill in Boston, Georgetown in Washington, D.C., the Vieux Carre in New Orleans. New ideas, creations, and life-styles have surfaced elsewhere. Old buildings alone can't explain the persistence of the Village mentality, generation after generation. What is it about this place that has fixed it in the modern mind as the place to come to write? to paint? to reinvent yourself, to build a life that is unique, individual, and true?

Why does Greenwich Village persist?

One answer is suggested by Kent Barwick, director of the Municipal Art Society and long a Village resident. He wonders if "Village mentality" is a term we use for the union of continuity and diversity. "The Village population has a better sense of its continuity than any community I've seen. Yet it's a series of separate, intertwined communities, which leave the neighborhood itself beyond the control of any single group. There's always been a tension here, between the Italians and the bohemians and the stockbrokers and the gays and the lawyers and the dockworkers. No one is in

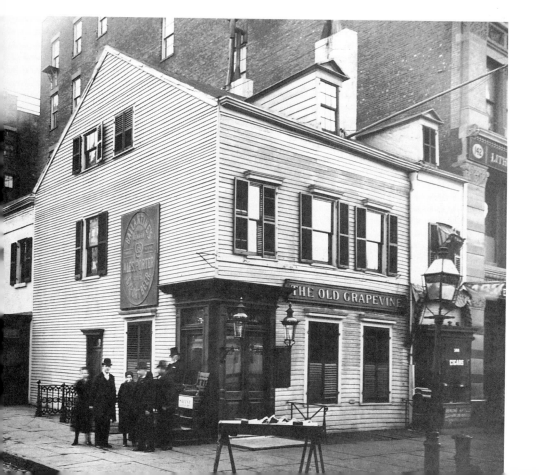

charge here, no one ever has been. Therefore it's not a neighborhood that can be easily handled, easily controlled by outsiders. And
because that diversity runs across different generations, that diversity recycles itself, persists. A community not held by one group
is one where everyone can be what they need to be. We call that
the Village mentality, but it's the unique community tension that
permits creativity, accepts difference, and ultimately creates
harmony."

Or the answer may be more mysterious: an underground renewal of America persisting much as Minetta Brook does, flowing
beneath the streets of Greenwich Village. Its nourishing influence
may at times seem murky, its impact quirky and unexpected. But
then, Minetta Brook is a name derived from the Indian word "manatus"—"devil water."

Village poet William Carlos Williams observed a type of out-
sider, doomed to what others call failure, who is essential to the
ongoing creation of America. He observed a quality that may be, in
the words of one of his titles, in the American grain, a quality
common to those souls who go before others, who clear the trail
where others will later prosper even though they themselves may
not. If Williams is right, the American frontier is a state of mind,
not merely the terrain waiting to be explored.

If Williams is right, Greenwich Village is the ultimate frontier
village—in its perennial self-invention the most American of places.

Chess in Washington Square, a
Village institution and a great
way to meet people and
immediately beat them at their
own game.

ACKNOWLEDGMENTS

I am grateful to those who, in various capacities, have made this book possible: Dino Alatsas (Tiffany's Restaurant), Jim Bennett and Deacon Maccubbin (Lambda Rising Bookstore), Gary Bernstein (The Big Kahuna), John Bitici (Minetta Tavern), Terry Boggis (The New School), Richard Buck (The New York Public Library), Freddie Caldwell, Faith Coleman, Quentin Crisp, Tish Dace, Jack Damlos (Macy's), Pryor Dodge, Anita Duguette (The Whitney Museum), The Federation to Preserve the Greenwich Village Waterfront & Great Port, Inc. (Bob Oliver, Ben Green), Maja Felaco (Prints & Photographs, The Library of Congress), Richard Fitzgerald, Phil Gerard, Mark Trent Goldberg, Gloria Goldblatt, Ben Guber (The Mayor's Office of Film & Broadcasting), Laurie Hanson (Consolidated Edison), Stephen Hoffius (South Carolina Historical Society),

Robert Jackson (Librarian, the New York Fire Department), Carl Kaiserman, Arnold I. Kisch, Barbara Kump, Thomas Lardeo (One Fifth Restaurant), Tony Lazzarra, Craig Lowder (Reader's Digest), Theodore Mann, Donna Manning, Jonathan McCrary, Keith McErlean, Mario Mercado, Jan Miller (City & Country School), Serge Mogliat (The Public Theater), Cammie Naylor and Dale Neighbors (The New-York Historical Society), Caroline Oyama (The New York Public Library), Doris Pettijohn (La Mama Theatre), Everett Quinton (The Ridiculous Theatrical Company), Louis Rachow (The Players), Jackie Raynal-Sarré (The Bleecker Street Cinema), Don Reynolds, Gary Rich (56 Bleecker Gallery), Irvyne and Roger Richards (The Rare Book Room), John D. Robiloto, Vito Russo, Judith Schwartz and Joan Nestle (The Lesbian Herstory Archives), H. Joseph Smith (Modernage Labs), Tom Spicuzza (The Village Nursing Home), English Strunsky, Michael Strunsky, Swen Swenson, Sarah Weiner (Art Properties, Columbia University), Marie Weiss (The Little Red Schoolhouse), Richard White (Music Collection, The Library of Congress), Richard Wilcox, Lili Wright (The Villager), Winifred Wuesthoff, and Janet Zapata (Tiffany & Co.).

I would also like to thank those whose generosity of participation deserve additional gratitude: the Research Staff of Bell Laboratories, New Jersey (Betsy Harrod, Sheldon Hochheiser, Norma McCormick, and Elizabeth Roach), Cheryl Finley (Commerce Graphics, Inc.), the staff of the Jefferson Market Branch of the New York Public Library (and especially Adele Bellinger and Tom Sharkey), Carol Pesner (Kraushaar Galleries), and Kay Young (The Detroit Institute of Art). I'd also like to acknowledge the many visual artists whose works enliven these pages, notably photographers Jessie Tarbox Beals, Arthur D. Chapman, James D. Gossage, Susan Kuklin, and most notably, Berenice Abbott. And no book on Greenwich Village could be written without the pioneering research of author Albert Parry.

My thanks as well to my interview subjects, who so generously shared their thoughts, feelings, and lives with me: Kent Barwick, Carmi Bee, Snooky Bellomo, Tish Bellomo, Bill Bigelow, Steve Corwin, Anthony Dapolito, Terry Fugate-Wilcox, Griffin Gold, Robin Hirsch, Barney Josephson, Bruce Mailman, Florent Morellet, Gene Norman, Valerio Orselli, Emily Strunsky Paley, Quinn, Renata Rizzo-Harvi, Mark Russell, Valerie Shakespeare, Steve Shlopak, Verna Small, Nicholas Smith, Ermanno Stingo, Dr. Henriette Stoner, Jan Wallman, Palmer Williams, and Ruth Wittenberg.

For their special involvement and support in this project, I gratefully acknowledge the Museum of the City of New York and its staff: Terry Ariano, Dr. Rick Beard, Patrick Hoffman, Kathy Magee, and particularly, Dr. Jan Ramirez.

At Crown Publishers, thanks to Betty A. Prashker, Michelle

ACKNOWLEDGMENTS

Sidrane, and Phyllis Fleiss for their support of this project; to June
Marie Bennett, whose jaunty design for this book so well captures
the Village spirit; to Mark McCauslin, my production editor; Bill
Peabody, my production supervisor; and to my editor, David Groff,
and his associates, Wilson Henley and Carol Taylor.

On a personal note, I'm most grateful to those whose support
kept me going during the several years this project has been in
preparation: Bob Acito, Wendy Adams, James Braun, David Carson, Laurie Farr, Richard Forstmann, Peter Friedman, Steve Grant,
Parks Hill, Barry Hoff, Annik LaFarge, Peter Loffredo, Richard
Northcutt, and Raymond Simon. Additional thanks to my parents,
Sally and Merle Miller, whose belief in me has never wavered, and
to my sister, Debby Burke, who more than once kept the wolf from
the door when circumstances made the "starving author" cliché all
too real. And if, at times, this project seemed a daunting affair, I've
been lucky to have the company of Edward L. Robinson along on
my journey, and that has made all the difference.

Finally, I'd like to acknowledge those Villagers whose lives
and deeds have made this community so special. Their names may
not appear in these pages, and in many cases may be lost in the folds
of history, but they are no less valued for their role in this story. It is
to them that this book is respectfully dedicated.

One of the stylish doors of the Village, 59 Morton Street.

SELECTED BIBLIOGRAPHY

BOOKS

Alleman, Richard. *The Movie Lover's Guide to New York*. New York: Harper & Row, Perennial, 1988.

[Barrett, Bowser, et al.]. *The New Guide to Greenwich Village*. New York: Corinth Books, 1959.

Bergreen, Laurence. *James Agee, A Life*. New York: Dutton, 1984.

Brady, Kathleen. *Ida Tarbell: Portrait of a Muckraker*. New York: Putnam, Seaview, 1984.

Brown, Henry Collins. *In the Golden 90s*. Hastings-on-Hudson, N.Y.: Valentine's Manual, 1928.

Brown, Milton W. *The Story of the Armory Art Show*. New York: Abbeville, 1988.

Brown, T. Allston. *A History of the New York Stage, 1732–1901*. New York: Dodd, Mead, 1903.

Burton, T. J. *Greenwich Village and Landmarks in Its Vicinity*. New York: n.p., 1894.

Bussing, Ann Van Nest. *Reminiscences of the Van Nest Mansion*. New York: Private printing, 1897.

Cantor, Mindy, ed. *Around the Square, 1830–1890*. New York: New York University Press, 1982.

Caro, Robert A. *The Power Broker: Robert Moses and the Fall of New York*. New York: Knopf, 1974.

Carruth, Gorton, ed. *The Encyclopedia of American Facts & Dates*. New York: Crowell, 1956.

Chapin, Anna Alice. *Greenwich Village*. New York: Dodd, Mead, 1917.

Churchill, Allen. *The Improper Bohemians*. New York: Dutton, 1959.

Clayton, Bruce. *Forgotten Prophet: The Life of Randolph Bourne*. Baton Rouge: Louisiana State University Press, 1984.

Coleman, Ray. *Lennon*. New York: McGraw-Hill, 1984.

Condict, Carl W. *The Port of New York*. Chicago: University of Chicago Press, 1980.

Considine, Shaun. *Barbra Streisand*. New York: Delacorte, 1985.

Costello, Augustine E. *Our Firemen: A History of the N.Y. Fire Dept*. New York: A. E. Costello, 1887.

Cowley, Malcolm. *Exile's Return: A Literary Odyssey of the 1920s*. New York: Viking, 1956.

Cudahy, Brian J. *Rails Under the Mighty Hudson*. Brattleboro, Vt.: Stephen Greene Press, 1975.

Davidson, Jo. *Between Sittings*. New York: Dial Press, 1951.

Delaney, Edmund T. *New York's Greenwich Village*. Barre, Mass.: Barre Publishers, 1968.

Delaney, Edmund T., and Charles Lockwood. *Greenwich Village: A Photographic Guide*. Rev. ed. New York: Dover, 1984.

Dell, Floyd. *Homecoming*. Port Washington, N.Y.: Kennikat Press, 1969.

D'Emilio, John. *Sexual Politics, Sexual Communities*. Chicago: University of Chicago Press, 1983.

Diamonstein, Barbaralee. *The Landmarks of New York*. New York: Abrams, 1988.

Du Maurier, George. *Trilby*. New York: Harper, 1895.

Dunshee, Kenneth H. *As You Pass By*. New York: Hastings House, 1952.

Eastman, Max. *Love and Revolution*. New York: Random House, 1964.

Edel, Leon. *Henry James: A Life*. New York: Harper & Row, 1985.

Edmiston, Susan, and Linda D. Cirino. *Literary New York*. Boston: Houghton Mifflin, 1976.

Ellman, Richard. *Oscar Wilde*. New York: Knopf, 1988.

Erenberg, Lewis A. *Steppin' Out: New York Nightlife and the Transformation of American Culture,*

1890–1930. Chicago: University of Chicago Press, 1984.

Falk, Candace. *Love, Anarchy, and Emma Goldman*. New York: Holt, Rinehart & Winston, 1984.

Fawkes, Richard. *Dion Boucicault*. London: Quartet Books, 1979.

Field, Andrew. *Djuna: The Life and Times of Djuna Barnes*. New York: Putnam, 1983.

Fischler, Stan. *Uptown, Downtown*. New York: Hawthorn Books, 1976.

Frick, John W. *New York's First Theatrical Center: The Rialto at Union Square*. Ann Arbor, Mich.: UMI Research Press, 1985.

Friedman, B. H. *Gertrude Vanderbilt Whitney*. Garden City, New York: Doubleday, 1978.

Gayle, Margot, and Edmund V. Gillon, Jr. *Cast-Iron Architecture in New York*. New York: Dover, 1974.

Gaylord, R. Bruce. *The Picture Book of Greenwich Village*. New York: Gaylord's Guides, 1985.

Gelb, Arthur, and Barbara Gelb. *O'Neill*. New York: Harper & Row, 1962.

Gilbert, Douglas. *American Vaudeville*. New York: Dover, 1963.

Gilmer, Walker. *Horace Liveright, Publisher of the Twenties*. New York: David Lewis, 1970.

Glackens, Ira. *William Glackens and the Ashcan Group*. New York: Crown, 1957.

Gody, Lou, ed. *The WPA Guide to New York City*. New York: Pantheon Books, 1982.

Goldstone, Harmon H., and Martha Dalrymple. *History Preserved: A Guide to New York City Landmarks and Historic Districts*. New York: Simon & Schuster, 1974.

Gordon, Max. *Live at the Village Vanguard*. New York: Da Capo Press, 1982.

Grandpierre, Charles. *The History of Fourth Street*. New York: Greenwich Village Weekly News, n.d.

Grandpierre, Charles. *Rambling Through Greenwich Village*. New York: Greenwich Village Weekly News, 1935.

Green, Martin. *New York 1913*. New York: Scribner's, 1988.

Harlow, Alvin F. *Old Bowery Days*. New York: Appleton, 1931.

Harris, Charles T. *Memories of Manhattan in the Sixties & Seventies*. New York: Derrydale Press, 1928.

Hemp, William H. *New York Enclaves*. New York: Clarkson N. Potter, 1975.

Henderson, Mary. *The City and the Theatre*. Clifton, N.J.: James T. White, 1973.

Herschkowitz, Leo. *Tweed's New York*. Garden City, N.Y.: Doubleday, Anchor Press, 1977.

Hicks, Granville. *John Reed: The Making of a Revolutionary*. New York: Macmillan, 1936.

Horne, Lena, and Richard Schickel. *Lena*. Garden City, N.Y.: Doubleday, 1965.

Hughes, Glenn. *A History of the American Theatre*. New York: Samuel French, 1951.

Jablonski, Edward. *Gershwin*. Garden City, N.Y.: Doubleday, 1987.

Jones, Theodore F., ed. *New York University, 1832–1932*. New York: New York University Press, 1933.

Kane, Joseph N. *Famous First Facts*. New York: Wilson, 1964.

Kaplan, Justin. *Mr. Clemens and Mark Twain*. New York: Simon & Schuster, 1966.

Katz, Jonathan N. *Gay American History*. New York: Crowell, 1976.

Katz, Jonathan N. *Gay/Lesbian Almanac*. New York: Harper & Row, 1983.

Kaytor, Marilyn. *"21"—The Life & Times of N.Y.'s Favorite Club*. New York: Viking, 1975.

Kelley, Frank B. *Excursion Planned for the City History Club: Greenwich Village & Lispenard's Meadow*. New York: City History Club of New York, 1902.

King, Moses. *King's Handbook of New York*. 1893. Reprint. New York: Blom, 1972.

Kisch, Arnold I. *The Romantic Ghost of Greenwich Village, Guido Bruno*. Frankfurt: Peter Lang, 1976.

Kouwenhoven, John A. *The Columbia Historical Portrait of New York*. Garden City, N.Y.: Doubleday, 1953.

Kozak, Roman. *This Ain't No Disco*. Winchester, Mass.: Faber & Faber, 1988.

[Kreuger, Miles]. *The 50th Anniversary of Vitaphone*. New York: Institute of the American Musical, 1976.

[Landmarks Preservation Commission]. *Greenwich Village Historic District Designation Report*. City of New York, 1969.

[Landmarks Preservation Commission]. *A Guide to New York City Landmarks*. City of New York, 1979.

Langner, Lawrence. *The Magic Curtain*. New York: Dutton, 1951.

Lawliss, Chuck. *New York Theatre Guide*. New York: Rutledge Press, 1981.

Lewis, Richard A. *Poor Richard's Guide to Non-Tourist Greenwich Village*. New York: Cricket Press, 1959.

Leyda, Jay. *The Melville Log*. New York: Gordian Press, 1969.

Limpus, Lowell M. *History of the N.Y. Fire Department*. New York: Dutton, 1940.

Lingeman, Richard. *Theodore Dreiser: At the Gates of the City, 1871–1907*. New York: Putnam, 1986.

Lockwood, Charles. *Bricks & Brownstone: The New York Row House 1783–1929*. New York: McGraw-Hill, 1972.

Lockwood, Charles. *Manhattan Moves Uptown*. Boston: Houghton Mifflin, 1976.

Ludington, Townsend. *John Dos Passos, a 20th Century Odyssey*. New York: Dutton, 1980.

Marcuse, Maxwell F. *This Was New York*. New York: LIM Press, 1969.

Marotta, Toby. *The Politics of Homosexuality*. Boston: Houghton Mifflin, 1981.

Mayer, Grace M. *Once upon a City: New York from 1890 to 1910*. New York: Macmillan, 1958.

McAuliffe, Kevin Michael. *The Great American Newspaper: The Rise and Fall of the "Village Voice."* New York: Scribner's, 1978.

McCabe, James D., Jr. *Lights & Shadows of New York Life*. Philadelphia: National, 1872.

McCausland, Elizabeth, and Berenice Abbott. *Changing New York*. New York: Dutton, 1939.

McDarrah, Fred. *Greenwich Village*. New York: Citadel Press, 1963.

Miller, Richard. *Bohemia: The Protoculture Then and Now*. Chicago: Nelson-Hall, 1977.

[Moore, Clement Clarke]. *A Plain Statement Addressed to the Proprietors of Real Estate in the City and County of New York*. New York: Eastburn, 1818.

Morris, Lloyd. *Incredible New York*. New York: Random House, 1951.

Munson, Gorham. *The Awakening Twenties*. Baton Rouge, La.: Louisiana State University Press, 1985.

Nelson, Raymond. *Van Wyck Brooks: A Writer's Life*. New York: Dutton, 1981

Nicosia, Gerald. *Memory Babe: Jack Kerouac*. New York: Grove Press, 1983.

Norman, Charles. *The Magic-Maker: E. E. Cummings*. New York: Macmillan, 1958.

Parry, Albert. *Garrets and Pretenders: A History of Bohemianism in America*. New York: Covici-Friede, 1933.

Petronius [pseud.]. *New York Unexpurgated*. New York: Matrix House, 1966.

Poland, Albert, and Bruce Mailman, eds. *The Off–Off Broadway Book*. Indianapolis: Bobbs-Merrill, 1972.

Ratkoff, Peter, and William Scott. *The New School*. New York: Macmillan, 1986.

Reitz, Rosetta, and Joan Geisler. *Where to Go in Greenwich Village*. New York: Paperback Gallery, 1961.

Rich, Frank, and Lisa Aronson. *The Theatre Art of Boris Aronson*. New York: Knopf, 1987.

Rider, Fremont, ed. *Rider's N.Y.C. Guidebook for Travelers*. New York: Macmillan, 1924.

Rivers, Joan, and Richard Meryman. *Enter Talking*. New York: Delacorte Press, 1986.

Robertson, Patrick. *The Book of Firsts*. New York: Bramhall House, 1974.

Robinson, Phyllis C. *Willa: The Life of Willa Cather*. Garden City, N.Y.: Doubleday. 1983.

Rosenstone, Robert A. *Romantic Revolutionary: A Biography of John Reed*. New York: Knopf, 1975.

Rudnick, Lois Palkin. *Mabel Dodge Luhan: New Woman, New Worlds*. Albuquerque: University of New Mexico Press, 1984.

Sanders, Ronald. *The Lower East Side*. New York: Dover, 1979.

Schwartz, Judith. *Radical Feminists of Heterodoxy: Greenwich Village, 1912–1940*. Norwich, Vt.: New Victoria Press, 1986.

Shapiro, Mary J. *Greenwich Village*. New York: Dover, 1985.

Shewey, Don. *Sam Shepard*. New York: Dell, 1985.

Silver, Nathan. *Lost New York*. Boston: Houghton Mifflin, 1967.

Simon, Kate. *Fifth Avenue*. New York: Harcourt Brace Jovanovich, 1978.

Sloan, John. *John Sloan's New York Scene, 1906–1913*. New York: Harper & Row, 1965.

Sochen, June. *The New Woman: Feminism in Greenwich Village, 1910–1920*. New York: Quadrangle Books, 1972.

Stallman, R. W. *Stephen Crane*. New York: Braziller, 1968.

Stern, Robert A. M., Gregory Gilmartin, and John Massengale. *New York 1900*. New York: Rizzoli, 1983.

Stern, Robert A. M., Gregory Gilmartin, and Thomas Mellins. *New York 1930*. New York: Rizzoli, 1987.

Stine, Whitney, and Bette Davis. *Mother Goddam*. New York: Hawthorn Books, 1974.

Stokes, I. N. Phelps. *The Iconography of Manhattan Island, 1498–1909*. New York: Robert H. Dodd, 1915–1928.

Stone, William L. *History of New York City*. New York: Virtue & Yorston, 1872.

Sukenick, Ronald. *Down and In: Life in the Underground.* New York: Morrow, Beech Tree, 1987.

Swanberg, W. A. *Dreiser.* New York: Scribner's, 1965.

Teal, Donn. *The Gay Militants.* New York: Stein & Day, 1971.

Tobin, Kay, and Randy Wicker. *The Gay Crusaders.* New York: Paperback Library, 1972.

Twombly, Robert. *Louis Sullivan, His Life and Works.* New York: Viking, 1986.

Ulmann, Albert. *A Landmark History of New York.* New York: Appleton-Century, 1939.

Unterecker, John Eugene. *Voyager, A Life of Hart Crane.* New York: Farrar, Straus & Giroux, 1969.

Ware, Caroline F. *Greenwich Village, 1920–1930.* Boston: Houghton Mifflin, 1935.

Watson, Edward B. *New York, Then and Now.* New York: Dover, 1976.

Wertheim, Arthur Frank. *The New York Little Renaissance, 1908–1917.* New York: New York University Press, 1976.

Wexler, Alice. *Emma Goldman, An Intimate Life.* New York: Pantheon Books, 1984.

White, Norval, and Elliot Willensky. *AIA Guide to New York City.* New York: Macmillan, 1968. Rev. ed., 1978.

Whitehouse, Roger. *New York, Sunshine & Shadow.* New York: Harper & Row, 1974.

Wilson, Rufus R., and E. Otile. *New York in Literature.* Elmira, N.Y.: Primavera Press, 1947.

Wolfe, Gerard R. *New York: A Guide to the Metropolis.* New York: New York University Press, 1975.

Young, William C. *Documents of American Theatre History, 1716–1971;* Chicago: American Library Association, 1973.

Zaleski, Jeffrey P. *The Greenwich Village Waterfront: An Historical Study.* New York: Greenwich Village Society for Historic Preservation, 1986.

Zurier, Rebecca. *Art for "The Masses"—A Radical Magazine and Its Graphics, 1911–1917.* Philadelphia: Temple University Press, 1988.

OTHER SOURCES

Archives, AT&T–Bell Laboratories
Archives, the Museum of the City of New York
Files, the Landmarks Preservation Commission, New York
Files, the Lesbian Herstory Archives
Long Island Connection
The Manhattan City Register
New York Dramatic Mirror
New York magazine
New York Native
New York Sun
New York Times
Villager
Village Voice

The roof of Washington Square Arch, looking west. The skylights provide light for the open chamber under the roof, while the metal dome on the roof tops the stairwell built within the arch's west pier.

PHOTOGRAPH CREDITS

Metropolitan Museum of Art: [2 (top), artwork by John Hill, *View from My Work Room Window in Hammond Street, New York City,* 1825, pen and black ink, gray and blue wash on paper. 54.90.283], [15 (right), artist unknown, *State Prison, on the Bank of the North River, New York,* circa 1797, engraving. 54.90.965], [154, artwork by Endicott & Sweet, *Baptizing Scene near the White Fort, Hudson River, New York,* 1834, lithograph. 54.90.656]. These three photographs are from the Museum of the City of New York, bequest of Edward W. C. Arnold, The Edward W. C. Arnold Collection of New York Prints, Maps, and Pictures, 1954. All rights reserved, The Metropolitan Museum of Art.

Museum of the City of New York: [8 (top), artwork by Esther Goetz], [9 (left), artwork by Mary Bussing], 16 (bottom), [19, 128, 179, photographs by Arthur D. Chapman], 21 (top), 39 (top), 40, 49, 62 (bottom), [71 (top), artwork by Josephine Barry], 73, 79, [83, artwork by Currier & Ives], [87, photograph by Irving Underhill], 93, 94, 95, 97, [109, 110, 117, 131 (bottom), 134 (top), 136, 146, 199, 233, photographs by Berenice Abbott], 114, [115 (top), photograph by Byron Studio], 116, 132, [139, artwork by William Zorach], 197, [198, artwork by Glenn O. Coleman], 199 (top and bottom), 200, [222, photograph by Jessie Tarbox Beals], 247, 255

Theatre Collection, Museum of the City of New York: 32, 45, 91 (right), 104, 105, 218

AT&T Archives: 8 (bottom), 169 (top and bottom), 170, 171 (top and bottom), 172, 173 (top)

Library of Congress: 24 (bottom), 90

Prints and Photographs Division, Library of Congress: [129, photograph by J. E. Purdy]

New-York Historical Society, New York: 24 (top), [39 (bottom), 68 (bottom), 108, 281 (top), photographs by Jessie Tarbox Beals], 43, 88, 89, [100, artwork by C. W. Jefferys], [135, 282, photographs by Robert Louis Bracklow], 155, [156, 207, photographs by George P. Hall], 161, 167, 211, 215, 241, 243

UPI/Bettmann Newsphotos: 29

Susan Kuklin: 34

Ridiculous Theatrical Company: [36 (top), photograph by Anita and Steve Shevett]

Kraushaar Galleries: [59, 217, artwork by John Sloan, photographed by Geoffrey Clements]

Commerce Graphics Ltd., Inc.: [60, photograph by Berenice Abbott]

Emily Strunsky Paley: [62, photograph by De Tartas]

Arnold I. Kisch: 67, 68 (top), 69

Brown Brothers: 72 (top and bottom)

Chandler Chemical Museum Collection, Columbia University: [74 (bottom), artotype after John W. Draper's daguerreotype of 1840]

Rare Book and Manuscript Library, Columbia University: 126

Harvard Theatre Collection: 91 (left), 286

Consolidated Edison: 103

Film Stills Archive, Museum of Modern Art: 106

Yale Collection of American Literature, Beinecke Rare Book and Manuscript Library, Yale University: 120, 121, 177, 223

Walter Kuhn Papers, Archives of American Art, Smithsonian Institution: 122

Tamiment Institute Library, New York University: 123

Whitney Museum of Art: [125, artwork by Robert Henri, *Gertrude Vanderbilt Whitney,* 1916, oil on canvas, 50″ × 72″. Collection of Whitney Museum of American Art. Gift of Flora Whitney Miller. 86.70.3], [212, artwork by John Sloan, *Sixth Avenue Elevated at Third Avenue,* 1928, oil on canvas, 30″ × 40″. Collection of Whitney Museum of American Art. Purchase. 36.154]

Wide World Photos: 137 (top), 185, 227, 269, 285 (top)

Verna Small: 140

R. H. Macy's & Co.: 149

James D. Gossage: 209, 210

The Reader's Digest Association, Inc.: 226 (left and right). Used by permission. Copyright © 1922 The Reader's Digest Association, Inc. All rights reserved. *Reader's Digest* is a registered trademark.

Detroit Institute of Arts (Founders Society Purchase): [245 (bottom), artwork by John Sloan, American, 1871–1951, *McSorley's Bar,* 1912, oil on canvas, 26″ × 32″, 24.2]

National Archives: 254

La Mama E.T.C.: 262

INDEX

Abingdon Square, 154
Academy of Music, 103–104
adaptive reuse, 3–4, 10, 274
Agee, James, 184, 234
Alamo, 84
alleys, 3, 57–58, 133–134, 136, 184–185, 198
Amos, Richard, 180–181
Arlington Hall, 262
art, *see specific areas*
Astor, John Jacob, 80, 81, 85, 197
Astor Library, 78, 81–82
Astor Place, 82–85
Astor Place Opera House riot, 82–84
Astor Place Theatre, 80–81
Atrium, 230
Automatic Vaudeville, 105

Bank Street, 174–175
Bank Street School, 175
Barnes, Djuna, 134, 219
bars, 7
    on Broadway, 89–92, 94, 104
    in East Village, 245–246, 259–260, 279
    in North Village, 112–113, 117–118, 135, 146
    in Sheridan Square, 28–30, 37–38, 41–42
    in South Village, 198–199, 203–205, 214, 215–218, 225–226, 234
    in West Village, 161–163, 186–187
    see also clubs
Barwick, Kent, 191, 192, 282–283
Basquiat, Jean Michel, 269–270
Bayard-Condict Building, 92–93
William Bayard's house, 164
Beadleston & Woerz brewery, 16
Beatnik Country, 227–230
Bedford Street, 200–206
Bell Laboratories, 167–172
Bellomo, Tish and Snooky, 275–276
Benedick, 71
Berkman, Alexander, 254–255
Biograph Studios, 105–106
Bitter End, 230
black clubs, 198–199
Bleecker Street, 23, 24, 107, 195–196, 230, 231–232, 234
Bleecker Street Cinema, 234
Bodenheim, Maxwell, 230–231
Bohemia, bohemianism, 28, 63, 88–92, 108, 238, 269–270, 279
Bond Street, 96
Boni Brothers, 119–120, 219

Bon Soir, 126–127
Bookazine, 16
bookstores, 100, 119–120, 219, 247
Bourne, Randolph, 125–126, 143
Bowery, 78–79, 109–110, 242, 259–260, 265–266
Bowery Village, 241–242, 245
Brady, Mathew, 74, 257
Brevoort, Hendrick, 78–79, 98, 114
Brevoort, Henry, 98, 114, 137
Brevoort Hotel, 114–116
Broadway, 76–111
    art near, 84–85
    bars on, 89–92, 94, 104
    bend in, 100–101
    bookstores on, 100
    brothels near, 95–96
    cast-iron facades and buildings on, 96, 97–98, 100, 110
    churches on, 94, 98–99
    dance halls and concert saloons near, 94, 95, 104
    map of, 77
    movies and, 105–107, 111
    restaurants near, 107–109
    shopping on, 80, 97–98, 100, 110
    theaters near, 80–84, 86, 88, 92, 102–107, 110, 111
    at Third Street, 86–88
Broadway Central Hotel, 86–88
brothels, 95–96
Brown, Isaac Hull, 99, 103
Bruno, Guido, 67–70
Buchignani's, 107–108
Burgess, Gelett, 70
Bust of Sylvette, 235

Café Bizarre, 229, 261
Cafe Feenjon, 126
Café Monopole, 251
Café Royal, 250–251
Cafe Society, 34–35
café theater, 229–230, 278–279
Caffe Borgia, 229
Caffe Cino, 208–210, 229
Caffe Reggio, 229
Carmines, Al, 64
cast-iron facades and buildings, 96, 97–98, 100, 110
Castle Garage, 164
Cather, Willa, 70, 174, 175
CBGB, 252, 265–266
Cedar Street Tavern, 117–118
cemeteries, 51, 52–54, 135, 207–208, 239–240, 244–245

Charles Lane, 3, 184–185
Charles Street, 178, 181, 182–183
Charlton-King-Vandam Historic District, 197
Charlton Street, 196, 197
Chemical Bank, 161
Cherry Lane Theatre, 200–201
Christopher's End, 161–162
Christopher Street, 9, 12–25, 55
    map of, 13
    markets near, 15, 16, 17, 46
    movies and, 20, 23, 25
    naming of, 133, 154, 181
    row houses near, 17–18, 19, 20, 22–23
    school near, 19
    state prison near, 15–16, 46, 151, 184
    and waterfront, 14
Chumley's, 203–205
churches, 3, 17–18, 64–67, 94, 98–99, 118, 198, 199, 207, 238–240, 247–248
Church of the Ascension, 118
Cino, Joe, 208–210
Circle in the Square, 31, 218
Circle Repertory Company, 29
City Theatre, 105–107
Clairmont, Robert, 224–225
Clare, Ada, 91–92
clubs, 28–29, 30, 34, 36, 128, 161–163, 186–187, 198–199, 261–267, 278–279
Cobble Court, 182–183
Cocks, Samuel, 19–20
coffeehouses, 195–196, 208–210, 227–229
Collier's Building, 160
Colonnade Row, 79–81
Commerce Street, 196, 200–202
Community Synagogue, 248
concert saloons, 94, 104
Congress Street, 211
Cooper, Peter, 255, 256–257
Cooper Square, 241, 242, 259, 274
Cooper Square Committee, 259, 273, 274
Cooper Union, 255–257
Cornelia Street, 208–210
Cornelia Street Café, 210
Cottage Row, 146–147
Crisp, Quentin, 1
Cummings, E. E., 23, 134, 160, 184, 221, 246
Cut, the, 26–27, 37, 181

dance clubs and bars, 36, 234, 263–264
dance halls, 94, 95

Davis, Bette, 219
Delamater Iron Works, 160–161, 162
Dell, Floyd, 221
Delmonico's, 148
Dial, 143–144, 145
Dodge, Mabel, 120–124
Dom, 261
Draper, John W., 74–75
Dreiser, Theodore, 100, 136, 141, 184,
    206–207
Drick, Gertrude, 59
Duplex, 126–127, 277

East Village, 236–279
    art in, 240, 258, 259–260, 269–270
    bars in, 245–246, 259–269, 279
    cemeteries in, 239–240, 244–245
    churches in, 238–240, 247–248
    clubs in, 261–267, 278–279
    ethnic communities in, 238, 245, 246–
        247, 248, 258–259
    inventing of, 258–259
    map of, 237
    movies and, 240, 252–253, 254, 263,
        266, 268–269, 274, 277
    naming of, 237–238, 258
    park in, 236–237, 239, 247–248,
        271–273
    present and future of, 238, 273, 278–
        279
    theaters in, 240, 249–250, 252, 262–
        263, 277–279
Edison, Charles, 69
Eighth Street, 116, 124–128
Eighth Street Playhouse, 113, 127–128
Electric Circus, 261–262
Electric Lady Sound Studios, 128
elevated freight service, 157–158
Eleventh Street, 113–114, 135–137, 180
Ell, Christine, 221, 224
ensemble rows, 79–81, 136
Epitome, 230
ethnic communities, 196, 198–200, 238,
    245, 246–247, 248, 258–259
Exploding Plastic Inevitable, 261

Fantasticks, The, 232–233
Federal Archive Building, 15
Federal houses, 22–23, 44, 197, 201,
    202, 205, 213–214
Fifth Avenue, 55, 56–57, 60, 112–124
Fillmore East, 263
Film Guild Cinema, 113, 127
Fisk, Jim, 86, 104
Fitzgerald, Richard, 231–232
Five Spot, 259–260
Fleischmann's Model Vienna Bakery, 99–
    100
flophouse-bars, 259–260
Forbes Gallery, 119
Forbidden Planet, 100
Fort Gansevoort, 151, 154–155
Fourteenth Street, 148–149

Fourth Street, 9, 40–41, 180, 223–225
Frenchtown, 95–96, 199
Fugate-Wilcox, Terry, 181–182

Gansevoort Meat Center, 155
Garden Row, 136
Gaslight Café, 227–228
gay bars, 161–163
Gay Street, 44–46
General Slocum Memorial, 247–248
German Lutheran Church, 247–248
Germantown, 246–248
Gershwin, George and Ira, 61–62, 248
Glackens, William, 60, 65, 130
Gold, Griffin, 190–191
Golden Eagle Press, 184
Golden Swan (Hell-Hole), 215–218
Goldman, Emma, 176, 216, 253–254
"goofy" clubs, 28–29, 34, 128
Gould, Joe, 225–226
Grace Church, 98–99
Grand Ticino Restaurant, 234
Grapevine, 135
Great American Salvage Company, 274
Greenberg, Clement, 118
Greenwich Avenue, 175–180
Greenwich House, 200
Greenwich Market, 15, 16, 17, 46
Greenwich Village:
    adaptive reuse in, 3–4, 10, 274
    historical layers in, 9–10, 126–127
    history of, 1–2
    mentality of, 281–283
    naming of, 152
    present and future of, 7–10, 282–283
    street grids in, 23–24, 46, 178, 180
Greenwich Village Inn, 29–31
Greenwich Village Theatre, 31–33
Grove Court, 19–20
Grove Street, 18–21
guerrilla art, 260

Halloween Parade, 188–189
Hancock Street, 212–213
hanging tree, 54
Harry Hill's Dance Hall, 94
Havel, Hippolyte, 176, 216, 254, 281
Irad Hawley House, 118
HB Studio, 175
Hell-Hole, 215–218
Hentoff, Nat, 187
Hirsch, Robin, 210
Holiday, Billie, 35
Polly Holladay's restaurants, 216, 219,
    222–223, 281
Holley Monument, 69
homesteaders, 140–141
Hotel Gonfarone, 127
House of Bachelors, 71
House of Genius, 70–71
Houston Street, 93–94
Howells, William Dean, 130
Hudson Park, 207
Hyde House, 20–21

Iggie, 112–113, 146
Indian paths, 55–56, 78
International Stud, 163
Irving, Washington, 118–119, 202
Irwin, Elisabeth, 231–232
Isaacs-Hendricks House, 202

Jackson Square Library, 142–143
James, Henry, 1, 52, 60
Jane Street, 164, 180
jazz, 34–35, 186–187, 259, 260
Jefferson Market, 16, 46–49
Jefferson Market Courthouse, 4, 46–49,
    178–179, 191
Jewish Rialto, 249–250
Johnson, Alvin, 138, 139
Johnston, John Taylor, 73, 116–117,
    131–132
Johnston's White House, 116–117
Josephson, Barney, 34–35
Judson Memorial Church, 64–65, 75
Julius', 186
Jumble Shop, 58

Katzman, Don and Allen, 260
kiosks, 85
Kristal, Hilly, 265

Ladies' Mile, 97–98, 100
Lafayette Place, 80, 109
La Mama Experimental Theatre Company,
    247, 262–263
Lamb, Thomas, 105–107, 111
landmarking, 191–193
Landmarks Preservation Commission, 17,
    81, 82, 85, 182, 191, 192, 205–206,
    214, 250
Latin Quarter, 95–96, 199
legends, 4, 22, 61, 67, 70, 79, 140, 174,
    181, 200–202, 241, 267
LeRoy Place, 80
Leroy Street, 208
Liberal Club, 196, 219, 221–222, 267
Lincoln, Abraham, 246, 257
Little Africa, 198–199
Little Harlem, 44–45
Little Italy, 7, 194–195, 196, 199–200
Little Red Schoolhouse, 231–232
Loew's Commodore, 263, 264
Lone Star Café, 112–113, 146
Lower East Side, *see* East Village
Lüchow's, 108–109
Ludlam, Charles, 36–37

McCreery's, 100, 101
MacDougal Alley, 58, 124
MacDougal Street, 6, 32–33, 56, 126–
    127, 218–222, 225–229
McKenney, Eileen, 45–46
McKenney, Ruth, 45–46, 128
Macready, Charles, 82–84
McSorley's, 245–246
R. H. Macy's, 148–149
Mad Hatter, 223–224

Mailman, Bruce, 264
Mandeville, Yellis, 152
Manhattan Refrigerating Company, 158
Manic Panic, 275–277
Marie's Crisis, 37–38
markets, 15, 16, 17, 46, 155, 159
Masses, 175–178, 267
Megie shack, 54–55, 67, 68
Melville, Herman, 155–156
Memphis Downtown, 183
Menken, Adah Isaacs, 91, 92
Mercantile Library, 84
Mercer Arts Center, 88, 265
Metropolitan Museum of Art, 114, 116–117, 124
Millay, Edna St. Vincent, 139, 202, 219
Miller Elevated West Side Highway, 157–158
Milligan Place, 133
Mills House, 230
Mineshaft, 162–163
Minetta Brook, 54, 55, 202, 283
Minetta Brook fountain, 55, 116
Minetta Lane, 198–199
Minetta Street, 198
Minetta Tavern, 225–226
Moore, Clement Clarke, 18
Morellet, Florent, 159–160
Mori's, 234
Morse, Samuel F. B., 74
Moses, Robert, 51–52, 102, 235, 258–259
Mothers Film Stages, 268
Mousetrap, 28–29
movies, moviemaking, 7
    Broadway and, 105–107, 111
    Christopher Street and, 20, 23, 25
    East Village and, 240, 252–253, 254, 263, 266, 268–269, 274, 277
    North Village and, 127–128, 130
    South Village and, 202, 208, 228, 234
    West Village and, 151, 171, 173–174, 180, 187

National Historic Landmarks, 93, 98, 256
National Maritime Union Building, 146–147
New School, 113–114, 138–139
New York Marble Cemetery, 244–245
New York University, 52, 61, 65, 70, 72, 73–75, 133, 221, 229, 233, 242
Niblo's Garden, 103
Nick's, 186
Ninth Avenue El, 167
Ninth Street, 129–131
Noortwyck, 1, 152, 153
Norman, Gene, 191
Northern Dispensary, 42–43
North Village, 112–149
    alleys in, 133–134, 136
    art in, 114–125, 131–133
    bars in, 112–113, 117–118, 135, 146
    cemetery in, 135
    churches in, 118

homesteaders in, 140
hospital in, 139, 146–147
map of, 113
movies and, 127–128, 130
notable people of, 130–131
restaurants in, 145–146, 148
row houses in, 124, 125, 133–134
schools in, 136, 138–139, 141–142
shopping in, 148–149
Nucciarone Funeral Home, 234
Nut Club, 29

Off Broadway, 31, 64, 80, 102, 196, 230, 249, 252
Off-Off Broadway, 163, 171, 208–210, 240
Old Merchant's House, 243–244
One Bank Street, 175
One Bond Street, 96
One Fifth Avenue, 56–57
O'Neill, Eugene, 33, 110, 124, 133–134, 216–218, 219–221
One Sheridan Square, 34–37
One Sheridan Square Theatre, 35–37
Orpheum, 252
Orteig, Raymond, 115–116
Ottendorfer Branch, New York Public Library, 246

Paley, Emily Strunsky, 62, 63
Palladium, 111
parks, 4–6, 28, 50–75, 111, 207–208, 236–237, 239, 247–248, 271–273
Patchin Place, 133–134, 223
Patterson Grocery, 23, 24–25
Pear Tree Place, 241
Pepper Pot, 223
Pfaff's, 89–92
piano bars, 37–38
Pirate's Den, 28–29
Poe, Edgar Allan, 44, 66, 89, 207, 233, 234
Poe House, 207, 233–234
prisons, state, 15–16, 46, 151, 184
Provincetown Players, 33, 124, 133–134, 180, 218–221
Provincetown Playhouse, 180, 203, 218–221
Public School (P.S.) sites, 19, 136, 141–142, 178, 277
Public Theater (Astor Place), 78, 81–82
Public Theatre (Second Avenue), 252
publishing, 67–68, 70, 80, 89, 90, 101–102, 119–120, 143–145, 175–178, 198, 226, 260
punk rock shops, 275–276
PureOil Gas Station, 205

Rainey, William, 201–202
Reader's Digest, 226
Red Head, 214
Reed, John, 63, 124, 134, 176–178, 223
Reno Sweeney, 145–146
Renwick, James, Jr., 98, 119, 136, 242

Renwick Triangle houses, 242
Restaurant Florent, 159–160
restaurants, 56, 62, 107–109, 145–146, 148, 159–160, 208–210, 216, 219, 222–223, 234
Rhinelander Gardens, 136
Richmond Hill, 196–197
Rienzi, 227
Ritz, 266–267
rock clubs, 261–267, 278
Rodman, Henrietta, 221–222
row houses, 3, 7, 44, 174
    near Christopher Street, 17–18, 19, 20, 22–23
    in North Village, 124, 125, 133–134
    in South Village, 197, 201, 202, 205, 206–207, 213–214, 223
    in Washington Square, 57–58, 60, 73
rows, ensemble, 79–81, 136
Russell, Mark, 277

Saint, 263–264
St. Denis Hotel, 101
St. Luke's-in-the-Field Chapel, 17–18
St. Luke's Place, 206–208
St. Luke's Place cemetery, 207–208
St. Mark's Bookshop, 247
St. Mark's Historic District, 242
St. Mark's-in-the-Bowery, 238–240, 260
St. Mark's Place, 246–247, 252, 258, 261–262, 275–277
St. Thomas' Episcopal Church, 94
St. Vincent's Hospital, 139, 146–147, 180
Samovar, 223, 224
San Remo, 227, 228, 231
Sapokanican, 1, 55, 56, 152
schools, 19, 136, 138–139, 141–142, 153, 175, 178, 231–232, 277
Second Avenue, 246–252, 263–264
Seeger, Alan, 70
Seventh Avenue, 26–27, 37, 181–182
Shearith Israel Cemetery, 135
Shepard, Sam, 240
Sheridan Square, 14, 25–49
    bars in, 28–30, 37–38, 41–42
    clubs of, 28–29, 30, 34, 36
    jazz in, 34–35
    map of, 13
    park in, 28
    during Prohibition, 28–30, 32, 38–41
    tearooms in, 38–41
    theaters in, 29, 31–33, 35–37
Shlopak, Steve, 203
shopping, 80, 97–98, 100, 110, 148–149, 275–276
Sixth Avenue, 7, 140–141, 196, 211–218
Sloan, John, 59, 60, 216, 246
Small, Verna, 140–141, 193
Sonia the Cigarette Girl, 40–41, 214
South Village, 194–235
    alley in, 198
    bars in, 198–199, 203–205, 214, 215–218, 225–226, 234

cemetery in, 207–208
churches in, 198, 199, 207
coffeehouses in, 195–196, 208–210, 227–229
ethnic communities in, 196, 198–200
legends in, 200–202
map of, 195
movies, TV and, 202, 207, 208, 228, 234
parks in, 207–208
restaurants in, 216, 219, 222–223, 234
row houses in, 197, 201, 202, 205, 206–207, 213–214, 223
school in, 231–232
tearooms in, 223–224
theaters in, 196, 198, 208–210, 218–221, 229–230, 232–233
Stewart, Alexander T., 97, 239–240
A. T. Stewart's Village store, 97–98, 258
Stewart, Ellen, 262–263
Stewart House apartments, 97, 258
Stingo, Ermanno, 212–213
Stoner, Henriette, 61, 62
Stonewall Inn, 41–42
Strand Book Store, 100
street grids, 23–24, 46, 178, 180
Strunsky, Albert "Papa," 61–63, 75
Stuyvesant, Peter, 238–239, 241, 242
Sullivan Street Playhouse, 232–233

Tammany Hall, 104
Tanner, Marion, 185
Tarbell, Ida, 129
tearooms, 38–41, 223–224
television technology, 7, 150–151, 172
Tenth Street, 130–134, 180, 181
Tenth Street Studio, 113, 131–133
theaters, 163
near Broadway, 80–84, 86, 88, 92, 102–107, 110, 111
in East Village, 240, 249–250, 252, 262–263, 277–279
in Sheridan Square, 29, 31–33, 35–37
in South Village, 196, 198, 208–210, 218–221, 229–230, 232–233
near Washington Square, 64, 66–67, 69–70
Theatre De Lys, 31
Theatre 80 St. Mark's, 252
Thimble Theatre, 69–70
Thirteenth Street, 113, 139–147, 241, 242–243, 254
Thirteenth Street Reservoir, 242–243
Three Steps Down, 62
Tile Club, 133
Toby Club, 28
toll broadcasting, 168–170
Tompkins, Daniel, 239, 271–272
Tompkins Square, 236–237, 239, 247–248, 271–273
Tredwell house, 244
Triangle Shirtwaist Fire, 72
Trilling, Lionel, 184
Tucker, Sophie, 251

Twain, Mark, 119, 130, 257
Tweed, "Boss," 86, 104, 257
Twelfth Street, 138–139, 164
Twin Peaks, 21–22

Union Square, 79, 102, 105–111, 253–254
Union Square Theatre, 105, 110–111
University Towers and Village, 235
Urban, Joseph, 114, 138

Van Nest Mansion, 154, 181
Van Twiller, Wouter, 18, 55–56, 127, 196, 202, 238
Variety Photo Plays, 253
vaudeville, 104–107, 111
Veselka Ukrainian Coffee Shop, 251
Village Balls, 267–268
Village Barn, 128
Village Cigars & Hess Estate street mosaic, 37
Village Gate, 230
Village Historic District, 33, 182, 191–193, 205
Village Presbyterian Church, 3
Village Vanguard, 186–187
Village Voice, 101–102, 118, 259
"Village Volcano," 151, 164

Wagenfeld, Sandra and Robert, 205–206
James J. Walker Park, 207–208
Wallack's Theatre, 105
Wanamaker's, 80, 97–98, 258
Warhol, Andy, 261, 270
Warren estate, 7, 133, 153–154, 180–181
Peter Warren's mansions, 153, 154
Washington Court, 214–215
Washington Mews, 57
Washington Square, 4–6, 50–75, 102
alleys near, 57–58
art in, 58, 60, 114, 115
cemetery in, 51, 52–54
churches in, 64–67
hanging tree in, 54
map of, 51
notable people of, 55–56, 65–66
Republic of, 6, 59
restaurants near, 56, 62
row houses in, 57–58, 60, 73
theaters near, 64, 66–67, 69–70
university in, 52, 61, 65, 70, 72, 73–75, 133, 221, 229, 233, 242
Washington Square Arch, 4–6, 52–54, 56, 59
Washington Square Bookshop, 119, 219
Washington Square Church, 66–67
Washington Square East, 66, 71, 73–75
Washington Square North, 9, 52, 60, 73
Washington Square Outdoor Art Exhibit, 114, 115
Washington Square South, 54–55, 61–70, 75
Washington Square Village, 235

waterfront, 14, 160–161, 165, 192–193
Waverly Place, 43–44, 154
Weathering Cement Triangle, 181–182
Webster Hall, 266–268
Weehawken Street, 16
Wells, James N., 17, 19
Westbeth, 167–173
West Coast Apartments, 158
West Side Highway, 165–166
West Street, 167–173
West Village, 150–193
alley in, 184–185
art in, 158, 181–182
bars in, 161–163, 186–187
freight trains in, 157–158
gardens in, 179–180
Halloween Parade in, 188–189
housing in, 151–152
jazz in, 186–187
landmarking of, 191–193
map of, 151
markets in, 15, 16, 17, 46, 155, 159
movies in, 151, 171, 173–174, 180, 187
naming of streets in, 180–181
notable writers of, 184–185
restaurants in, 159–160
row houses in, 174
schools in, 153, 175, 178
state prison in, 15–16, 46, 151, 184
technology in, 167–172
waterfront in, 14, 160–161, 165, 192–193
see also Christopher Street; Sheridan Square
White Horse Tavern, 7
Whitman, Walt, 89–90
Whitney, Gertrude Vanderbilt, 58, 124, 125
Whitney Museum of American Art, 58, 114, 124–125, 223
Whitney Studio, 58, 124
Whittemore, Samuel, 22, 34, 44
Whittemore Mansion, 22–23
Wilde, Oscar, 131
Williams, Palmer, 30
Williams, William Carlos, 283
Wilson, Doric, 163, 208–209
Wilson, Lanford, 209, 210
Winter Garden Theatre, 86
Wolfe, Thomas, 184
Worrell Sisters' Theatre, 104
WOW Café, 277–278

Yiddish Art Theatre, 249–250, 252
Yiddish theater, 249–250, 251, 252

Zinno, 145–146
Zoo, 162–163

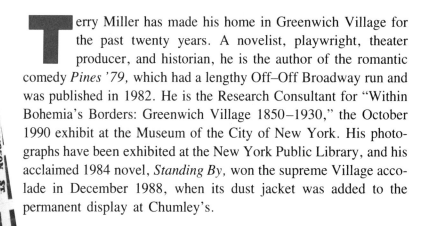

DAVID L. CARSON

Terry Miller has made his home in Greenwich Village for the past twenty years. A novelist, playwright, theater producer, and historian, he is the author of the romantic comedy *Pines '79,* which had a lengthy Off–Off Broadway run and was published in 1982. He is the Research Consultant for "Within Bohemia's Borders: Greenwich Village 1850–1930," the October 1990 exhibit at the Museum of the City of New York. His photographs have been exhibited at the New York Public Library, and his acclaimed 1984 novel, *Standing By,* won the supreme Village accolade in December 1988, when its dust jacket was added to the permanent display at Chumley's.